Integrated Chinese

CHENG & TSUI PUBLICATIONS OF RELATED INTEREST

Making Connections: Enhance Your Listening Comprehension in Chinese
(Text & Audio CD Set)
Madeline K. Spring

▲ Includes lessons for *Integrated Chinese* users.

Simplified Characters	0-88727-366-1
Traditional Characters	0-88727-365-3

Chinese BuilderCards: The Lightning Path to Mastering Vocabulary
Song Jiang and Haidan Wang

▲ Includes vocabulary from *Integrated Chinese*.

Simplified Characters	0-88727-434-X
Traditional Characters	0-88727-426-9

Cheng & Tsui Chinese-Pinyin-English Dictionary for Learners
Wang Huan, Editor-in-Chief

Paperback	0-88727-316-5

Cheng & Tsui Chinese Character Dictionary
Wang Huidi, Editor-in-Chief

Paperback	0-88727-314-9

Crossing Paths: Living and Learning in China, An Intermediate Chinese
Course
Hong Gang Jin and De Bao Xu, with Der-lin Chao, Yea-fen Chen, and Min Chen

Paperback & Audio CD Set	0-88727-370-X

Shifting Tides: Culture in Contemporary China, An Intermediate Chinese
Course
Hong Gang Jin and De Bao Xu, with Songren Cui, Yea-fen Chen, and Yin Zhang

Paperback & Audio CD Set	0-88727-372-6

Please visit www.cheng-tsui.com for more information on these and many other language-learning resources, and for information on web-based and downloadable products.

Integrated Chinese

中文聽說讀寫

Traditional Character Edition

TEXTBOOK

2nd Edition

Tao-chung Yao and Yuehua Liu

**Liangyan Ge, Yea-fen Chen, Nyan-Ping Bi,
Xiaojun Wang and Yaohua Shi**

CHENG & TSUI COMPANY ▲ BOSTON

Second Edition

10 09 08 07 06   10 9 8 7 6 5 4 3 2

Published by
Cheng & Tsui Company, Inc.
25 West Street
Boston, MA 02111-1213 USA
Fax (617) 426-3669
www.cheng-tsui.com
"Bringing Asia to the World"™

Library of Congress Cataloging-in-Publication Data

Integrated Chinese = [Zhong wen ting shuo du xie].
Traditional character edition. Level 1, part 1 / Tao-chung Yao ... [et al.].— 2nd ed.
      p. cm. — (C&T Asian language series)
Chinese and English.
Includes index.
ISBN 0-88727-459-5 (Traditional ed. : pbk.) — ISBN 0-88727-460-9 (Simplified ed. : pbk.)
ISBN-13 978-0-88727-459-6   — ISBN-13 978-0-88727-460-2
1. Chinese language—Textbooks for foreign speakers—English. I. Title: Zhong wen ting shuo du xie. II. Yao, Daozhong. III. Series: C&T Asian languages series.
PL1129.E5I683 2004b
495.1'82421—dc22
                                                                2005047085

The *Integrated Chinese* series includes books, workbooks, character workbooks, audio products, multimedia products, teacher's resources, and more. Visit www.cheng-tsui.com for more information on the other components of *Integrated Chinese*.

Printed in the United States of America

THE INTEGRATED CHINESE SERIES

The *Integrated Chinese* series is a two-year course that includes textbooks, workbooks, character workbooks, audio CDs, CD-ROMs, DVDs and teacher's resources.

Textbooks introduce Chinese language and culture through a series of dialogues and narratives, with culture notes, language use and grammar explanations, and exercises.

Workbooks follow the format of the textbooks and contain a wide range of integrated activities that teach the four language skills of listening, speaking, reading and writing.

Character Workbooks help students learn Chinese characters in their correct stroke order. Special emphasis is placed on the radicals that are frequently used to compose Chinese characters.

Audio CDs include the narratives, dialogues and vocabulary presented in the textbooks, as well as pronunciation and listening exercises that correspond to the workbooks.

Teacher's Resources contain helpful guidance and additional activities online.

Multimedia CD-ROMs are divided into sections of listening, speaking, reading and writing, and feature a variety of supplemental interactive games and activities for students to test their skills and get instant feedback.

Workbook DVD shows listening comprehension dialogues from the Level 1 Part 1 Workbook, presented in contemporary settings in color video format.

PUBLISHER'S NOTE

When *Integrated Chinese* was first published in 1997, it set a new standard with its focus on the development and integration of the four language skills (listening, speaking, reading and writing). Today, to further enrich the learning experience of the many users of *Integrated Chinese* worldwide, the Cheng & Tsui Company is pleased to offer the revised, updated and expanded second edition of *Integrated Chinese*. We would like to thank the many teachers and students who, by offering their valuable insights and suggestions, have helped *Integrated Chinese* evolve and keep pace with the many positive changes in the field of Chinese language instruction. *Integrated Chinese* continues to offer comprehensive language instruction, with many new features.

The Cheng & Tsui Asian Language Series is designed to publish and widely distribute quality language learning materials created by leading instructors from around the world. We welcome readers' comments and suggestions concerning the publications in this series. Please send feedback to our Editorial Department (e-mail: editor@cheng-tsui.com), or contact the following members of our Editorial Board.

CONTENTS

Lesson 1: Greetings   29

Lesson 2: Family   51

Lesson 3: Dates and Time   72

Lesson 4: Hobbies   97

▼ ▼

▼▼

PREFACE

The *Integrated Chinese* series is an acclaimed, best-selling introductory course in Mandarin Chinese. With its holistic, integrated focus on the four language skills of listening, speaking, reading, and writing, it teaches all the basics beginning and intermediate students need to function in Chinese. *Integrated Chinese* helps students understand how the Chinese language works grammatically, and how to use Chinese in real life.

The Chinese title of *Integrated Chinese*, which is simply 中文聽說讀寫 (*Zhōngwén Tīng Shuō Dú Xiě*), reflects our belief that a healthy language program should be a well-balanced one. To ensure that students will be strong in all skills, and because we believe that each of the four skills needs special training, the exercises in the *Integrated Chinese* Workbooks are divided into four sections of listening, speaking, reading, and writing. Within each section, there are two types of exercises, namely, traditional exercises (such as fill-in-the-blank, sentence completion, translation, etc.) to help students build a solid foundation, and communication-oriented exercises to prepare students to face the real world.

How *Integrated Chinese* Has Evolved

Integrated Chinese (IC) began, in 1993, as a set of course materials for beginning and intermediate Chinese courses taught at the East Asian Summer Language Institute's Chinese School, at Indiana University. Since that time, it has become a widely used series of Chinese language textbooks in the United States and beyond. Teachers and students appreciate the fact that IC, with its focus on practical, everyday topics and its numerous and varied exercises, helps learners build a solid foundation in the Chinese language.

What's New in the Second Edition

Thanks to all those who have used *Integrated Chinese* and given us the benefit of their suggestions and comments, we have been able to produce a second edition that includes the following improvements:

▲ Typographical errors present in the first edition have been corrected, and the content has been carefully edited to ensure accuracy and minimize errors.

▲ The design has been revised and improved for easier use, and the Textbooks feature two colors.

▲ **Revised illustrations** and **new photos** provide the reader with visual images and relevant cultural information.

▲ Many **new culture notes** and examples of **functional expressions** have been added.

▲ **Grammar and phonetics explanations** have been rewritten in more student-friendly language.

▲ **Workbook listening and reading sections** have been revised.

▲ **A new flexibility for the teaching of characters** is offered. While we believe that students should learn to read all of the characters introduced in the lessons, we are aware that different Chinese programs have different needs. Some teachers may wish to limit the number of characters for which students have responsibility, especially in regards to writing requirements. To help such teachers, we have identified a number of lower-frequency Chinese characters and marked them with a pound sign (#) in the vocabulary lists. Teachers might choose to accept *pinyin* in place of these characters in homework and tests. The new edition adds flexibility in this regard.

▲ **The Level 1 Workbooks** have been reorganized. The Workbook exercises have been divided into two parts, with each part corresponding to one of the dialogues in each lesson. This arrangement will allow teachers to more easily teach the dialogues separately. They may wish to use the first two or three days of each lesson to focus on the first dialogue, and have students complete the exercises for the first dialogue. Then, they can proceed with the second dialogue, and have students complete the exercises for the second dialogue. Teachers may also wish to give separate quizzes on the vocabulary associated with each dialogue, thus reducing the number of new words students need to memorize at any one time.

▲ **Level 2 offers full text in simplified and traditional characters.** The original Level 2 Textbook and Workbook, which were intended to be used by both traditional- and simplified-character learners, contained sections in which only the traditional characters were given. This was of course problematic for students who were principally interested in learning simplified characters. This difficulty has been resolved in the new edition, as we now provide both traditional and simplified characters for every Chinese sentence in both the Textbook and the Workbook.

Basic Organizational Principles

In recent years, a very important fact has been recognized by the field of language teaching: the ultimate goal of learning a language is to communicate in that language.

Integrated Chinese is a set of materials that gives students grammatical tools and also prepares them to function in a Chinese language environment. The materials cover two years of instruction, with smooth transitions from one level to the next. They first cover everyday life topics and gradually move to more abstract subject matter. The materials are not limited to one method or one approach, but instead they blend several teaching approaches that can produce good results. Here are some of the features of *Integrated Chinese* which make it different from other Chinese language textbooks:

Integrating Pedagogical and Authentic Materials

All of the materials are graded in *Integrated Chinese*. We believe that students can grasp the materials better if they learn simple and easy to control language items before the more difficult or complicated ones. We also believe that students should be taught some authentic materials even in the first year of language instruction. Therefore, most of the pedagogical materials are actually simulated authentic materials. Real authentic materials (written by native Chinese speakers for native Chinese speakers) are incorporated in the lessons when appropriate.

Integrating Written Style and Spoken Style

One way to measure a person's Chinese proficiency is to see if s/he can handle the "written style" (書面語, shūmiànyǔ) with ease. The "written style" language is more formal and literal than the "spoken style" (口語, kǒuyǔ); however, it is also widely used in news broadcasts and formal speeches. In addition to "spoken style" Chinese, basic "written style" expressions are gradually introduced in *Integrated Chinese*.

Integrating Traditional and Simplified Characters

We believe that students should learn to handle Chinese language materials in both the traditional and the simplified forms. However, we also realize that it could be rather confusing and overwhelming to teach students both the traditional and the simplified forms from day one. A reasonable solution to this problem is for the student to concentrate on one form, either traditional or simplified, at the first level, and to acquire the other form during the second level. Therefore, for Level 1, *Integrated Chinese* offers two editions of the Textbooks and the Workbooks, one using traditional characters and one using simplified characters, to meet different needs.

We believe that by the second year of studying Chinese, all students should be taught to read both traditional and simplified characters. Therefore, the text of each lesson in Level 2 is shown in both forms, and the vocabulary list in each lesson also contains both forms. Considering that students in a second-year Chinese language class might come from different backgrounds and that some of them may have learned the traditional form and others the simplified form, students should be allowed to write in either traditional or simplified form. It is important that the learner write in one form only, and not a hybrid of both forms.

Integrating Teaching Approaches

Realizing that there is no one single teaching method which is adequate in training a student to be proficient in all four language skills, we employ a variety of teaching methods and approaches in *Integrated Chinese* to maximize the teaching results. In addition to the communicative approach, we also use traditional methods such as grammar-translation and direct method.

Online Supplements to Integrated Chinese

Integrated Chinese is not a set of course materials that employs printed volumes only. It is, rather, a network of teaching materials that exist in many forms. Teacher keys, software, and more are posted for *Integrated Chinese* users at www.webtech.cheng-tsui.com, Cheng & Tsui Company's online site for downloadable and web-based resources. Please visit this site often for new offerings.

Other materials are available at the IC website, http://eall.hawaii.edu/yao/icusers/, which was set up by Ted Yao, one of the principal *Integrated Chinese* authors, when the original edition of *Integrated Chinese* was published. Thanks to the generosity of teachers and students who are willing to share their materials with other *Integrated Chinese* users, this website is constantly growing, and has many useful links and resources. The following are some of the materials created by the community of *Integrated Chinese* users that are available at the *Integrated Chinese* website.

▲ Links to resources that show how to write Chinese characters, provide vocabulary practice, and more.

▲ *Pinyin* supplements for all *Integrated Chinese* books. Especially useful for Chinese programs that do not teach Chinese characters.

▲ Preliminary activities for an activity book for *Integrated Chinese* Level 1 (in progress), by Yea-fen Chen, Ted Yao and Jeffrey Hayden. (http://eall.hawaii.edu/yao/AB/default.htm)

▲ Teacher's resources.

About the Format

Considering that many teachers might want to teach their students how to speak the language before teaching them how to read Chinese characters, we decided to place the *pinyin* text before the Chinese-character text in each of the eleven lessons of the Level 1 Part 1 Textbook.

Since *pinyin* is only a vehicle to help students learn the pronunciation of the Chinese language and is not a replacement for the Chinese writing system, it is important that students can read out loud in Chinese by looking at the Chinese text and not just the *pinyin* text. To train students to deal with the Chinese text directly without relying on *pinyin*, we moved the *pinyin* text to the end of each lesson in the Level 1 Part 2 Textbook. Students can refer to the *pinyin* text to verify a sound when necessary.

We are fully aware of the fact that no two Chinese language programs are identical and that each program has its own requirements. Some schools will cover a lot of material in one year while some others will cover considerably less. Trying to meet the needs of as many schools as possible, we decided to cover a wide range of material, both in terms of vocabulary and grammar, in *Integrated Chinese*. To facilitate oral practice and to allow students to communicate in real-life situations, many supplementary vocabulary items are added to each lesson. However, the characters in the supplementary vocabulary sections are not included in the Character Workbooks. In the Character Workbooks, each of the characters is given a frequency indicator based on the *Hànyǔ Pínlù Dà Cídiǎn* (漢語頻率大辭典). Teachers can decide for themselves which characters must be learned.

Acknowledgments

Since publication of the first edition of *Integrated Chinese,* in 1997, many teachers and students have given us helpful comments and suggestions. We cannot list all of these individuals here, but we would like to reiterate our genuine appreciation for their help. We do wish to recognize the following individuals who have made recent contributions to the *Integrated Chinese* revision. We are indebted to Tim Richardson, Jeffrey Hayden, Ying Wang and Xianmin Liu for field-testing the new edition and sending us their comments and corrections. We would also like to thank Chengzhi Chu for letting us try out his "Chinese TA," a computer program designed for Chinese teachers to create and edit teaching materials. This software saved us many hours of work during the revision. Last, but not least, we want to thank Jim Dew for his superb professional editorial job, which enhanced both the content and the style of the new edition.

As much as we would like to eradicate all errors in the new edition, some will undoubtedly remain, so please continue to send your comments and corrections to editor@cheng-tsui.com, and accept our sincere thanks for your help.

ABBREVIATIONS FOR GRAMMAR TERMS

abbr	*Abbreviation*
adj	*Adjective*
adv	*Adverb*
av	*Auxiliary verb*
ce	*Common expression*
coll	*Colloquialism*
conj	*Conjunction*
exc	*Exclamation*
interj	*Interjection*
m	*Measure word*
n	*Noun*
np	*Noun phrase*
nu	*Numeral*
p	*Particle*
pn	*Proper noun*
pr	*Pronoun*
prefix	*Prefix*
prep	*Preposition*
ono	*Onomatopoeic*
qp	*Question particle*
qpr	*Question pronoun*
qw	*Question word*
t	*Time word*
v	*Verb*
vc	*Verb plus complement*
vo	*Verb plus object*

ABOUT NOTE REFERENCES

Different types of notes provide explanations for selected expressions in the text. In the dialogues, expressions followed by a superscript numeral are explained in notes directly below the text; expressions followed by a superscript "G" plus a numeral are explained in grammar notes in the grammar section of the lesson. "F" refers to "Functional Expressions" explained in the pages that follow the dialogues.

Introduction

I. Chinese Pronunciation

A Chinese syllable is composed of an initial and a final. Initials consist of consonants or semi-vowels; finals consist of vowels or vowels plus one of the two nasal sounds -[n] or -[ng]. In addition to an initial and a final, each Chinese syllable has a tone.

A. SIMPLE FINALS

There are six simple finals: **a**, **o**, **e**, **i**, **u**, **ü**

- ▲ When it is pronounced by itself, **a** is a central vowel. The tongue remains in a natural, relaxed position.

- ▲ **o** is a rounded semi-high back vowel. The lips are round when pronouncing **o**.

- ▲ **e** is an unrounded semi-high back vowel. To produce this vowel, first pronounce **o**, and then change the shape of the mouth from rounded to unrounded. At the same time spread the lips apart, as if you were smiling. This vowel is different from "e" in English, which is pronounced with the tongue raised slightly forward.

- ▲ **i** is an unrounded high front vowel. The tongue is raised higher than it would be to pronounce its counterpart in English.

- ▲ **u** is a rounded high back vowel. The tongue is raised higher than it would be to pronounce its counterpart in English.

- ▲ **ü** is a rounded high front vowel. To produce this vowel, first pronounce **i**, then modify the shape of the mouth from unrounded to rounded.

In the *pinyin* system **i** also represents two additional special vowels. One is a front apical vowel, the other a back apical vowel. Both of these vowels are homorganic with the very limited sets of initials with which they can co-occur (see below, **z**, **c**, **s** and **zh**, **ch**, **sh**, **r**). In our discussion of phonetics, we sometimes write these special vowels with an italicized *i* to distinguish it from the ordinary high front vowel **i**.

Note

In this book, Chinese sounds are represented by *pinyin*. The *pinyin* system uses twenty-five of the twenty-six letters of the Roman alphabet. Although *pinyin* symbols are thus the same as English letters, the actual sounds they represent can be very different from their English counterparts. Be careful to distinguish them.

B. INITIALS

There are twenty-one initial consonants in Chinese:

1.	**b**	**p**	**m**	**f**
2.	**d**	**t**	**n**	**l**
3.	**g**	**k**	**h**	
4.	**j**	**q**	**x**	
5.	**z**	**c**	**s**	
6.	**zh**	**ch**	**sh**	**r**

In addition, the semi-vowels **y** and **w** also function as initials.

B.1: b, p, m, f

b is a bilabial unaspirated plosive. Note that the Chinese **b** is different from its English counterpart; it is not voiced. There are no voiced plosives in Chinese.

p is a bilabial aspirated voiceless plosive. In other words, there is a strong puff of breath when the consonant is pronounced. When pronouncing **b** and **p**, the lips are closed lightly between the front teeth and lower teeth.

m is a bilabial nasal sound, produced in the same manner as an English **m**.

f is a labio-dental fricative. To produce this sound, press the upper teeth against the lower lip, and let the breath flow out with friction, just as in pronouncing an English **f**.

Notes

Only the simple finals **a**, **o**, **i**, and **u** and the compound finals that start with **a**, **o**, **i**, or **u** can be combined with **b**, **p**, and **m**; only the simple finals **a**, **o**, and **u** and the compound finals that start with **a**, **o**, or **u** can be combined with **f**. When these initials are combined with **o**, there is actually a short **u** sound in between. For instance, the syllable **bo (bᵘo)** actually includes a very short **u** sound between **b** and **o**.

PRACTICE

B.1.a

ba	bi	bu	bo
pa	pi	pu	po
ma	mi	mu	mo
fa	fu	fo	

B.1.b b vs. p

ba	pa	bu	pu
po	bo	pi	bi

B.1.c m vs. f

ma	fa	mu	fu

B.1.d b, p, m, f

bo	po	mo	fo
fu	mu	pu	bu

B.2: d, t, n, l

When producing **d**, **t**, **n**, the tip of the tongue touches the upper teeth ridge. The tongue is raised more to the front than it would be to pronounce their English counterparts.

> **d** is a tongue tip alveolar unaspirated plosive. It is voiceless.

> **t** is a tongue tip alveolar aspirated stop. It is voiceless.

n is a tongue tip alveolar nasal. It is produced by placing the tip of the tongue against the ridge behind the upper teeth.

l is a tongue tip alveolar lateral. It is different from the English "**l**." To produce the Chinese **l** the tip of the tongue should touch the alveolar ridge, which is the ridge located at the back of the upper teeth.

Note

Only the simple finals **a**, **i**, **e**, and **u** and the compound finals that start with **a**, **i**, **e**, or **u** can be combined with **d**, **t**, **n**, and **l**; **n** and **l** can also be combined with **ü** and the compound finals that start with **ü**.

PRACTICE

B.2.a

da	di	du	de	
ta	ti	tu	te	
na	ni	nu	ne	nü
la	li	lu	le	lü

B.2.b d vs. t

da	ta	di	ti
du	tu	de	te

B.2.c l vs. n

lu	lü	nu	nü
lu	nu	lü	nü

B.2.d d, t, n, l

le	ne	te	de
du	tu	lu	nu

B.3: g, k, h

g is an unaspirated voiceless velar stop. **k** is an aspirated voiceless velar stop. When producing **g** and **k**, the back of the tongue is raised against the soft palate.

h is a voiceless velar fricative. When producing **h**, the back of the tongue is raised towards the soft palate. The friction is noticeable. With its English counterpart, however, the friction is not noticeable.

Note

Only the simple finals **a**, **e**, and **u** and the compound finals that start with **a**, **e**, or **u** can be combined with **g**, **k**, and **h**.

PRACTICE

B.3.a

gu	ge	ga
ku	ke	ka
hu	he	ha

B.3.b g vs. k

gu	ku	ge	ke

B.3.c g vs. h

gu	hu	ge	he

B.3.d k vs. h

ke	he	ku	hu

B.3.e g, k, h

gu	ku	hu
he	ke	ge

B.4: j, q, x

j is an unaspirated voiceless palatal affricate. To produce this sound, first raise the front of the tongue to the hard palate and press the tip of the tongue against the back of the lower teeth, and then loosen the tongue and let the air squeeze out through the channel thus made. It is unaspirated and the vocal cords do not vibrate. Note that the Chinese **j** is similar to English **j** but unvoiced and articulated, with the tip of the tongue resting behind the lower incisors.

q is an aspirated voiceless palatal affricate. It is produced in the same manner as **j**, but it is aspirated. Note that the Chinese **q** is similar to English **ch** except that it is articulated with the tip of the tongue resting behind the lower incisors.

x is a voiceless palatal fricative. To produce it, first raise the front of the tongue toward (but not touching) the hard palate and then let the air squeeze out. The vocal cords do not vibrate. Note that the Chinese **x** is similar to English **sh** except that it is articulated with the tip of the tongue resting behind the lower incisors.

Note

The finals that can be combined with **j**, **q** and **x** are limited to **i** and **ü** and the compound finals that start with **i** or **ü**. When **j**, **q** and **x** are combined with **ü** or a compound final starting with **ü**, the umlaut is omitted and the **ü** appears as **u**.

PRACTICE

B.4.a

ji	ju
qi	qu
xi	xu

B.4.b j vs. q

ji	qi	ju	qu

B.4.c q vs. x

qi	xi	qu	xu

B.4.d j vs. x

ji	xi	ju	xu

B.4.e j, q, x

ji	qi	xi
ju	qu	xu

B.5: z, c, s

z is an unaspirated voiceless apical affricate.

c is an aspirated voiceless apical affricate. The aspiration is strong. Note that **z** is like the **ts** sound in "that's odd," while **c** is like the **ts** sound in "it's hot."

s is a voiceless apical fricative. It is the same as English **s**.

The above group of sounds is pronounced with the tongue touching the back of the upper teeth.

Note

The simple finals that can be combined with **z**, **c**, **s** are **a**, **e**, **u** and the front apical vowel *i* (*not* the regular palatal high front vowel **i**).

In pronouncing the syllables *zi*, *ci* and *si* the tongue is held in the same position throughout the syllable except that it is slightly relaxed as the articulation moves from the voiceless initial consonant to the voiced vowel.

PRACTICE

B.5.a

za	zu	ze	zi
ca	cu	ce	ci
sa	su	se	si

B.5.b   s vs. z

sa	za	su	zu
se	ze	si	zi

B.5.c   z vs. c

za	ca	zi	ci
ze	ce	zu	cu

B.5.d   s vs. c

sa	ca	si	ci
su	cu	se	ce

B.5.e   z, c, s

sa	za	ca
su	zu	cu
se	ze	ce
si	zi	ci
za	cu	se

ci	sa	zu
su	zi	ce

B.6: zh, ch, sh, r

zh is an unaspirated voiceless blade-palatal affricate. To produce it, first turn up the tip of the tongue against the hard palate, then loosen it and let the air squeeze out the channel thus made. It is unaspirated and the vocal cords do not vibrate. Note that **zh** is similar to English **j** but unvoiced and with the tip of the tongue raised against the back of the gum ridge or front part of the hard palate.

   ch is an aspirated voiceless blade-palatal affricate. This sound is produced in the same manner as **zh**, but it is aspirated. Note that **ch** is similar to English **ch** except that it is produced with the tip of the tongue raised against the back of the gum ridge or front part of the hard palate.

sh is a voiceless blade-palatal fricative. To produce this sound, turn up the tip of the tongue toward (but not touching) the hard palate and then let the air squeeze out. The vocal cords do not vibrate. Note that **sh** is similar to English **sh** except that it is produced with the tip of the tongue raised against the back of the gum ridge or front part of the hard palate.

r is a voiced blade-palatal fricative. It is produced in the same manner as **sh**, but it is voiced. The vocal cords vibrate. It is very different from the English "r."

Note

The finals that can be combined with **zh**, **ch**, **sh**, **r** are **a**, **e**, **u** and the back apical vowel *i*, as well as the compound finals that start with **a**, **e**, or **u**. In pronouncing the syllables **zhi**, **chi**, **shi** and **ri** the tongue is held in the same position throughout the syllable except that it is slightly relaxed as the articulation moves from the initial consonant to the vowel.

PRACTICE

B.6.a

zha	zhu	zhe	zhi
chi	chu	che	chi
sha	shu	she	shi
ru	re	ri	

B.6.b zh vs. sh

| sha | zha | shu | zhu |

B.6.c zh vs. ch

| zha | cha | zhu | chu |

B.6.d ch vs. sh

| chu | shu | sha | cha |

B.6.e zh, ch, sh

shi	zhi	chi	shi
she	zhe	che	she

B.6.f sh vs. r

shu	ru	shi	ri

B.6.g r vs. l

lu	ru	li	ri

B.6.h sh, r, l

she	re	le	re

B.6.i zh, ch, r

zhe	re	che	re

B.6.j zh, ch, sh, r

sha	cha	zha	
shu	zhu	chu	ru
zhi	chi	shi	ri
che	zhe	she	re

A REFERENCE CHART FOR INITIALS

	UNASPIRATED STOPS	ASPIRATED STOPS	NASALS	FRICATIVES	VOICED CONTINUANTS
Labials	b	p	m	f	w*
Alveolars	d	t	n		l
Dental sibilants	z	c		s	
Retroflexes	zh	ch		sh	r
Palatals	j	q		x	y*
Velars	g	k		h	

*See explanations of **w** and **y** in the "Spelling Rules" section below.

C. COMPOUND FINALS

1. **ai**	**ei**	**ao**	**ou**				
2. **an**	**en**	**ang**	**eng**	**ong**			
3. **ia**	**iao**	**ie**	**iu***	**ian**	**in**	**iang**	**ing**	**iong**
4. **ua**	**uo**	**uai**	**ui***	**uan**	**un***	**uang**	**ueng**
5. **üe**	**üan**	**ün**					
6. **er**							

*The main vowel **o** is omitted in the spelling of the final **iu** (**iu** = **iou**). Therefore **iu** represents the sound **iou**. The **o** sound is especially conspicuous in third and fourth tone syllables.
The main vowel **e is omitted in the final **ui** (**ui** = **uei**). Like **iu** above, the **e** sound within **ui** is quite conspicuous in third and fourth tone syllables.
***The main vowel **e** is omitted in **un** (**un** = **uen**).

In Chinese, compound finals are comprised of a main vowel and one or two secondary vowels, or a main vowel and one or two vowels followed by one of the nasal endings **-n** or **-ng**. When the initial vowels are **a**, **e** and **o**, they are stressed. The vowels following are soft and brief. When the initial vowels are **i**, **u** and **ü**, the main vowels come after them. **i**, **u** and **ü** are transitional sounds. If there are vowels or nasal consonants after the main vowels, they should be unstressed as well. In a compound final, the main vowel can be affected by the phonemes before and after it. For instance, the **a** in **ian** is pronounced with a lower degree of aperture and a higher position of the tongue than the **a** in **ma**; and to pronounce the **a** in **ang** the tongue has to be positioned more to the back of the mouth than the **a** elsewhere.

As noted above, in *pinyin* orthography some vowels are omitted for the sake of economy, e.g., **i(o)u**, **u(e)i**. However, when pronouncing those sounds, the vowels must not be omitted.

Spelling Rules

▲1▲ If there is no initial consonant before **i**, **i** is written as a semi-vowel, **y**. Thus **ia**, **ie**, **iao**, **iu**, **ian**, **iang** become **ya**, **ye**, **yao**, you (note that the **o** cannot be omitted here), **yan**, **yang**. Before **in**, **ing**, and **o**, add **y**, e.g., **yin**, **ying**, **yo**.

▲2▲ If there is no initial consonant before **ü**, add a **y** and drop the umlaut: **yu**, **yuan**, **yue**, **yun**.

▲3▲ **u** becomes **w** if not preceded by an initial, e.g., **wa, wai, wan, wang, wei, wen, weng, wo. u** by itself becomes **wu**.

▲4▲ **ueng** is written as **ong**, if preceded by an initial, e.g., **tong, dong, nong, long**. Without an initial, it is **weng**.

▲5▲ In order to avoid confusion, an apostrophe is used to separate two syllables with connecting vowels, e.g., **shí'èr** (twelve) and the city **Xī'ān** (**shí** and **èr, xī** and **ān** are separate syllables).

PRACTICE

C.1:   ai   ei   ao   ou

| pai | lei | dao | gou |
| cai | mei | sao | shou |

C.2:   an   en   ang   eng   ong

C.2.a an vs. ang

| tan | tang | chan | chang |
| zan | zhang | gan | gang |

C.2.b en vs. eng

| sen | seng | shen | sheng |
| zhen | zheng | fen | feng |

C.2.c eng vs. ong

| cheng | chong | deng | dong |
| zheng | zhong | keng | kong |

C.3:   ia   iao   ie   iu   ian   in   iang   ing   iong

C.3.a ia vs. ie

| jia | jie | qia | qie |
| xia | xie | ya | ye |

C.3.b ian vs. iang

xian	**xiang**	**qian**	**qiang**
jian	**jiang**	**yan**	**yang**

C.3.c in vs. ing

bin	**bing**	**pin**	**ping**
jin	**jing**	**yin**	**ying**

C.3.d iu vs. iong

xiu	**xiong**	**you**	**yong**

C.3.e ao vs. iao

zhao	**jiao**	**shao**	**xiao**
chao	**qiao**	**ao**	**yao**

C.3.f an vs. ian

chan	**qian**	**shan**	**xian**
zhan	**jian**	**an**	**yan**

C.3.g ang vs. iang

zhang	**jiang**	**shang**	**xiang**
chang	**qiang**	**ang**	**yang**

C.4:   ua   uo   uai   ui   uan   un   uang

C.4.a ua vs. uai

shua	**shuai**	**wa**	**wai**

C.4.b uan vs. uang

shuan	**shuang**	**chuan**	**chuang**
zhuan	**zhuang**	**wan**	**wang**

C.4.c   un vs. uan

dun	duan	kun	kuan
zhun	zhuan	wen	wan

C.4.d   uo vs. ou

duo	dou	zhuo	zhou
suo	sou	wo	ou

C.4.e   ui vs. un

tui	tun	zhui	zhun
dui	dun	wei	wen

C.5:   üe   üan   ün

C.5.a   ün vs. un

jun	zhun	yun	wen

C.5.b   üan vs. uan

xuan	shuan	juan	zhuan
quan	chuan	yuan	wan

C.5.c   üe

yue	que	jue

C.6:   er

ger*

---

*Due to the lack of words with first tone **er** in them, the word "**ger**" (**ge** with **r** ending) is here to give the reader a feel for it. See **D.1 Practice III** below (p. 18) for more examples.

▼▼▼▼▼▼▼▼▼▼▼▼▼▼▼▼▼▼▼▼▼▼▼▼▼▼▼▼▼▼▼▼▼▼▼▼▼▼▼

D. TONES

Every Chinese syllable has a tone.

D.1: Four tones

There are four tones in Mandarin Chinese (i.e., 普通話 pǔtōnghuà, "common language" in mainland China; 國語 guóyǔ, "national language" in Taiwan; 華語 Huáyǔ, "the Chinese language" in Singapore and some other places): the first tone (陰平 yīnpíng), the second tone (陽平 yángpíng), the third tone (上聲 shǎngshēng), the fourth tone (去聲 qùshēng).

The first tone is a high level tone with a pitch value of 55 (see chart below); its tone mark is " ˉ ."

The second tone is a rising tone with a pitch value of 35; its tone mark is " ˊ ."

The citation form of the third tone has a pitch value of 214. However, in normal speech it almost always occurs as a "half third tone" with a pitch value of 21 or (in front of another third tone) transformed into a second tone with the pitch value of 35. Its tone mark is " ˇ ."

The fourth tone is a falling tone with a pitch value of 51; its tone mark is " ˋ ."

In addition to the four tones, there is also a neutral tone (輕聲 qīngshēng) in Mandarin Chinese. Neutral tone words include those that do not have fundamental tones (e.g., the question particle **ma**), and those that do have tones when pronounced individually, but are not stressed in certain compounds (e.g., the second **ba** in "**bàba**" or "father"). There are no tone marks for neutral tone syllables. A neutral tone syllable is pronounced briefly and softly, and its pitch value is determined by the stressed syllable immediately before it. A neutral tone following a first tone syllable, as in **māma** 媽媽, carries a pitch tone of 2. When it follows a second tone syllable, a third tone syllable, or a fourth tone syllable, its pitch value will be 3, 4, and 1 respectively.

Tones are very important in Chinese. The same syllable with different tones can have different meanings. For instance, **mā** 媽 is mother, **má** 麻 is hemp, **mǎ** 馬 is horse, **mà** 罵 is to scold, and **ma** 嗎 is an interrogative particle. The four tones can be diagrammed as follows:

	First Tone	Second Tone	Third Tone	Fourth Tone

(tone contour diagram with levels 5, 4, 3, 2, 1)

Tone marks are written above the main vowel of a syllable. The main vowel can be identified according to the following sequence: **a-o-e-i-u-ü.** For instance, in **ao** the main vowel is **a**. In **ei** the main vowel is **e**. There is one exception: when **i** and **u** are combined into a syllable, the tone mark is written on the second vowel: **iù, uì**.

D.1 PRACTICE I: MONOSYLLABIC WORDS

1.a   Four Tones

bī	bí	bǐ	bì
pū	pú	pǔ	pù
dà	dǎ	dá	dā
shè	shě	shé	shē
tí	tī	tǐ	tì
kè	kě	kē	ké
jǐ	jí	jì	jī
gú	gù	gū	gǔ

1.b   1st vs. 2nd

zā	zá
chū	chú
hē	hé
shī	shí

1.c   1st vs. 3rd

tū	tǔ
mō	mǒ
xī	xǐ
shā	shǎ

▼▼▼

1.d 1st vs. 4th		1.e 2nd vs. 1st	
fā	fà	hú	hū
dī	dì	xí	xī
qū	qù	zhé	zhē
kē	kè	pó	pō

1.f 2nd vs. 3rd		1.g 2nd vs. 4th	
gé	gě	lú	lù
tí	tǐ	mó	mò
jú	jǔ	cí	cì
rú	rǔ	zhé	zhè

1.h 3rd vs. 1st		1.i 3rd vs. 2nd	
tǎ	tā	chǔ	chú
mǐ	mī	kě	ké
gǔ	gū	xǐ	xí
chě	chē	qǔ	qú

1.j 3rd vs. 4th		1.k 4th vs. 1st	
bǒ	bò	jì	jī
nǐ	nì	là	lā
chǔ	chù	sù	sū
rě	rè	hè	hē

1.l 4th vs. 2nd		1.m 4th vs. 3rd	
nà	ná	sà	sǎ
zè	zé	zì	zǐ
jù	jú	kù	kǔ
lǜ	lǘ	zhè	zhě

D.1 PRACTICE II: BISYLLABIC WORDS

2.a   1st 1st

chūzū	tūchū	chūfā

2.b   1st 2nd

chātú	xīqí	chūxí

2.c   1st 3rd

shēchǐ	gēqǔ	chūbǎn

2.d   1st 4th

chūsè	hūshì	jīlù

2.e   2nd 1st

shíshī	qíjī	shíchā

2.f   2nd 2nd

jíhé	shépí	pígé

2.g   2nd 3rd

jítǐ	bóqǔ	zhélǐ

2.h   2nd 4th

qítè	fúlì	chíxù

2.i   3rd 1st

zǔzhī	zhǔjī	lǐkē

2.j   3rd 2nd

pǔjí	zhǔxí	chǔfá

2.k   3rd 4th

lǚkè	gǔlì	tǐzhì

2.l   4th 1st

zìsī	qìchē	lǜshī

2.m   4th 2nd

fùzá	dìtú	shìshí

2.n   4th 3rd

zìjǐ	bìhǔ	dìzhǐ

2.o   4th 4th

mùdì	xùmù	dàdì

D.1 PRACTICE III: WORDS WITH "ER" SOUND

3.a

érzi	érqiě

3.b

ěrduo	mù'ěr

3.c

shí'èr	èrshí

D.2: Tone sandhi

If two third tone syllables are spoken in succession, the first third tone becomes second tone. This tone change is known as "tone sandhi" in linguistics.

For instance,

xǐlǐ	→	**xílǐ**	(baptism)
chǐrǔ	→	**chírǔ**	(shame)
qǔshě	→	**qúshě**	(accept or reject)

Note

Following standard *pinyin* practice, we do not change the tone marks from third to second tone. Initially you might have to consciously remember that the first syllable actually is pronounced as a second tone syllable, but through pronunciation drills and hearing the language spoken, you will soon be making the sandhi change automatically and unconsciously.

D.2 PRACTICE

chǔlǐ	→	**chúlǐ**	**gǔpǔ**	→	**gúpǔ**
bǐnǐ	→	**bínǐ**	**jǔzhǐ**	→	**júzhǐ**
zǐnǚ	→	**zínǚ**	**zhǐshǐ**	→	**zhíshǐ**

D.3: Neutral tone

The neutral tone occurs in unstressed syllables. It is unmarked. For instance,

chēzi (car)	**māma** (mother, mom)	**chúzi** (cook)
shūshu (uncle)	**lǐzi** (plum)	**shìzi** (persimmon)

The pitch of the neutral tone is determined by the preceding syllable.

D.3 PRACTICE

1.	**māma**	**gēge**	**shīfu**	**chūqu**
2.	**dízi**	**bóbo**	**bízi**	**chúle**
3.	**lǐzi**	**qīzi**	**dǐzi**	**fǔshang**
4.	**bàba**	**dìdi**	**kèqi**	**kùzi**

E. COMBINATION EXERCISES

I.

shān	**xiān**	**sān**
cháng	**qiáng**	**cáng**
zhǐ	**jǐ**	**zǐ**
lüè	**nüè**	**yuè**
kè	**lè**	**rè**

II.

Zhōngguó	**xīngqī**	**lǜshī**	**zhàopiàn**
zàijiàn	**tóngxué**	**xǐhuan**	**diànshì**
yīnyuè	**kělè**	**yǎnlèi**	**shàngwǔ**
cèsuǒ	**chūntiān**	**xiàwǔ**	**bànyè**
gōngkè	**kāishǐ**	**rìjì**	**cāntīng**
zuìjìn	**xīwàng**	**yīsheng**	**chūzū**
zhōumò	**guānxi**	**dòufu**	**jiéhūn**
liúxué	**nü'ér**	**shénme**	**suīrán**
wǎngqiú	**xǐzǎo**	**niánjí**	**yóuyǒng**

II. Chinese Writing System

A. THE FORMATION OF CHINESE CHARACTERS

Unlike English, which is an alphabetic language, Chinese writing is represented by "characters," each of which represents a meaningful syllable. Characters are traditionally divided into the following six categories:

1. 象形 xiàngxíng pictographs, pictographic characters

Examples:

人  rén man

山  shān mountain

日  rì sun

月  yuè moon

木 朩　　　　　　　　mù　　　　tree

2. 指事 zhǐshì self-explanatory characters

Examples:

上 ⌐　　　　　　　　shàng　　　above

下 ⌐　　　　　　　　xià　　　　below

3. 會意 huìyì　associative compounds

Examples:

明 ☽　　　　　　　　míng　　　bright

休 ⺅木　　　　　　　xiū　　　　rest

4. 形聲 xíngshēng　pictophonetic characters (with one element indicating meaning and the other sound)

Examples:　　江，河，飯，姑

5. 轉注 zhuǎnzhù　mutually explanatory characters

Examples:　　老，考

6. 假借 jiǎjiè　phonetic loan characters

Examples:　　來，我

A popular myth is that Chinese writing is pictographic, and that each Chinese character represents a picture. It is true that some Chinese characters have evolved from pictures, but these comprise only a small proportion of the characters. The vast majority of Chinese characters are pictophonetic characters consisting of a radical and a phonetic element. The radical often suggests the meaning of a character, and the phonetic element indicates its original pronunciation, which may or may not represent its modern pronunciation.

B. BASIC CHINESE RADICALS

 Although there are more than fifty thousand Chinese characters in existence, one only needs to know two or three thousand of them to be considered literate. Mastering two or three thousand characters is, of course, a rather formidable task. However, the learning process will be more effective and easier if one knows well the basic components of Chinese characters. Traditionally, Chinese characters are grouped together according to their common components known as "radicals" (部首, bùshǒu). The 214 "Kangxi radicals" have been the standard set of radicals since the publication of the great *Kangxi Dictionary* (康熙字典 *Kāngxī Zìdiǎn*) in 1716, although some contemporary dictionaries, which treat simplified characters as primary forms, have reduced that number to 189. By knowing the radicals and other basic components well, you will find recognizing, remembering and reproducing characters much easier. Knowing the radicals is also a must when using dictionaries, which arrange characters according to their radicals. The following is a selection of forty radicals that everybody should know well when starting to learn characters.

	Chinese radical	Pinyin	English	Examples
1.	人 (亻)	rén	man	你，他
2.	刀 (刂)	dāo	knife	分，到
3.	力	lì	power	加，助
4.	又	yòu	right hand; again	友，取
5.	口	kǒu	mouth	叫，可
6.	囗**	wéi	enclose	回，因
7.	土	tǔ	earth	在，坐
8.	夕	xī	sunset	外，多
9.	大	dà	big	天，太

**used as radical only, not as a character by itself

10.	女	nǚ	woman	好，	媽
11.	子	zǐ	son	字，	學
12.	寸	cùn	inch	對，	付
13.	小	xiǎo	small	少，	尖
14.	工	gōng	labor; work	左，	差
15.	幺	yāo	tiny; small	幻，	幼
16.	弓	gōng	bow	張，	弟
17.	心 (忄)	xīn	heart	忙，	快
18.	戈	gē	dagger-axe	我，	或
19.	手 (扌)	shǒu	hand	打，	找
20.	日	rì	sun	早，	明
21.	月	yuè	moon	有，	明
22.	木	mù	wood	李，	杯
23.	水 (氵)	shuǐ	water	沒，	洗
24.	火 (灬)	huǒ	fire	燒，	熱
25.	田	tián	field	男，	留
26.	目	mù	eye	看，	睡
27.	示 (礻)	shì	show	社，	票
28.	糸 (糹)	mì	fine silk	紅，	素
29.	耳	ěr	ear	取，	聊
30.	衣 (衤)	yī	clothing	衫，	初
31.	言	yán	speech	說，	認
32.	貝	bèi	cowry shell	貴，	買

33.	走	zǒu	walk	趣，起
34.	足	zú	foot	跳，跑
35.	金	jīn	gold	錢，銀
36.	門	mén	door	問，間
37.	隹	zhuī	short-tailed bird	雖，難
38.	雨	yǔ	rain	電，雲
39.	食(飠)	shí	eat	飯，館
40.	馬	mǎ	horse	騎，驚

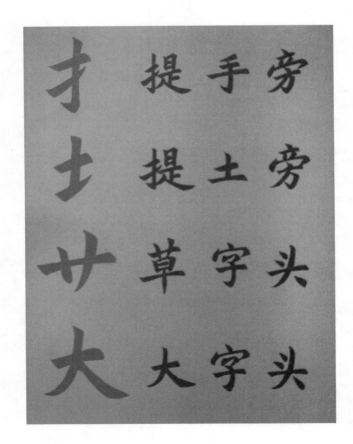

A Chinese radical chart.

C. BASIC STROKES

The following is a list of basic strokes:

	Basic stroke	Chinese	Pinyin	English	Examples
1.	" 丶 "	點	diǎn	dot	小，六
2.	" 一 "	橫	héng	horizontal	一，六
3.	" 丨 "	豎	shù	vertical	十，中
4.	" 丿 "	撇	piě	downward left	人，大
5.	" 乀 "	捺	nà	downward right	八，人
6.	" ㇀ "	提	tí	upward	我，江
7.	" ㇖ "	橫鈎	hénggōu	horizontal hook	你，字
8.	" 亅 "	豎鈎	shùgōu	vertical hook	小，你
9.	" 乀 "	斜鈎	xiégōu	slanted hook	戈，我
10.	" ㇆ "	橫折	héngzhé	horizontal bend	五，口
11.	" ㇄ "	豎折	shùzhé	vertical bend	七，亡

Note

With the exception of the "tí" stroke (which moves upward to the right) and the "piě" stroke (which moves downward to the left), all Chinese strokes move from top to bottom, and from left to right.

D. STROKE ORDER

Following is a list of rules of stroke order. When writing a Chinese character, it is important that you follow the rules. Following the rules will make it easier for you to accurately count the number of strokes in a character. Knowing the exact number of strokes in a character will help you find the character in a radical-based dictionary. Also, your Chinese characters will look better if you write them in the correct stroke order!

1. From left to right   (川，人)

2. From top to bottom   (三)

3. Horizontal before vertical (十)

4. From outside to inside   (月)

5. Middle before two sides   (小)

6. Inside before closing   (日，回)

Note: Learn the correct stroke order of the characters introduced in this book by using the *Integrated Chinese Level 1 Character Workbook*.

III. Useful Expressions

A. CLASSROOM EXPRESSIONS

The following is a list of classroom expressions that you will hear every day in your Chinese class.

1. Nǐ hǎo!	How are you? How do you do?
2. Lǎoshī hǎo!	How are you, teacher?
3. Shàng kè.	Let's begin the class.
4. Xià kè.	The class is over.
5. Dǎkāi shū.	Open the book.
6. Wǒ shuō, nǐmen tīng.	I'll speak, you listen.
7. Kàn hēibǎn.	Look at the blackboard.
8. Duì bu duì?	Is it right?
9. Duì!	Right! Correct!
10. Hěn hǎo!	Very good!
11. Qǐng gēn wǒ shuō.	Please repeat after me.
12. Zài shuō yí cì.	Say it again.
13. Dǒng bu dǒng?	Do you understand?
14. Dǒng le.	Yes, I/we understand.

▼▼

15. Zàijiàn!		Good-bye!
16. Qǐng yòng _____ zàojù!		Please make a sentence using _____!

B. SURVIVAL EXPRESSIONS

The following is a list of important expressions that will help you survive in a Chinese language environment. A good language student is constantly learning new words by asking questions. Learn the following expressions well and start to acquire Chinese on your own!

1. Duìbuqǐ!	Sorry!
2. Qǐng wèn...	Excuse me...; May I ask...
3. Xièxie!	Thanks!
4. Zhè shi shénme?	What is this?
5. Wǒ bù dǒng.	I don't understand.
6. Qǐng zài shuō yí biàn.	Please say it one more time.
7. "..." Zhōngguóhuà zěnme shuō?	How do you say "..." in Chinese?
8. "..." shì shénme yìsi?	What does "..." mean?
9. Qǐng nǐ gěi wǒ....	Please give me....
10. Qǐng nǐ gàosu wǒ....	Please tell me....
11. Duìbuqǐ, nín shi shuō...?	Sorry, do you mean...?

C. NUMERALS

Having good control of the Chinese numerals will facilitate your dealing with real life situations such as shopping, asking for time and dates, etc. You can get a head start by memorizing 1 to 10 well now.

1. yī	one	一	6. liù	six	六
2. èr	two	二	7. qī	seven	七
3. sān	three	三	8. bā	eight	八
4. sì	four	四	9. jiǔ	nine	九
5. wǔ	five	五	10. shí	ten	十

Do you know the names of the strokes below? Can you write them properly?

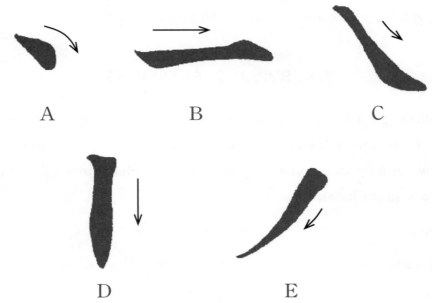

LESSON 1 ▲ Greetings
第一課 ▲ 問好
Dì yí kè ▲ *Wèn hǎo*

你好!
Nǐ hǎo!

Dialogue I: Exchanging Greetings

VOCABULARY

1.	先生	xiānsheng	n	Mr.; husband; teacher
2.	你好	nǐ hǎo	ce	How do you do? Hello!
	你	nǐ	pr	you
	好	hǎo	adj	fine; good; nice; O.K.
3.	小姐	xiǎojie	n	Miss; young lady
4.	請問	qǐng wèn	ce	May I ask...

	請	qǐng	v	please (a polite form of request)
	問	wèn	v	to ask (a question)
5.	您	nín	pr	you (singular; polite)
6.	#貴姓	guì xìng	ce	What is your honorable surname?
	貴	guì	adj	honorable
	姓	xìng	v/n	(one's) surname is...; to be surnamed; surname
7.	我	wǒ	pr	I; me
8.	呢	ne	qp	(an interrogative particle)
9.	叫	jiào	v	to be called; to call
10.	什麼	shénme	qpr	what
11.	名字	míngzi	n	name

Proper Nouns

12.	王朋	Wáng Péng	pn	(a personal name)
	王	wáng	n	(a surname); king
13.	李友	Lǐ Yǒu	pn	(a personal name)
	李	lǐ	n	(a surname); plum

DIALOGUE I

Wáng Xiānsheng[1] :	Nǐ hǎo[2]!
Lǐ Xiǎojie:	Nǐ hǎo!
Wáng Xiānsheng:	Qǐng wèn, nín guì xìng[3]?
Lǐ Xiǎojie:	Wǒ <u>xìng</u>[G1] Lǐ. Nǐ <u>ne</u>[G2]?
Wáng Xiānsheng:	Wǒ xìng Wáng, <u>jiào</u>[G3] Wáng Péng[4]. Nǐ jiào shénme míngzi[5]?
Lǐ Xiǎojie:	Wǒ jiào Lǐ Yǒu.

DIALOGUE I

王先生(1)：   你好(2)！

李小姐：   你好！

王先生：   請問，您貴姓(3)？

李小姐：   我姓(G1)李。你呢(G2)？

王先生：   我姓王，叫(G3)王朋(4)。你叫
            什麼名字(5)？

李小姐：   我叫李友。

A Note on the Notes

▲**1**▲ The # symbol preceding a character in the vocabulary section suggests that it's a low frequency one. The teacher might want to allow the student to use *pinyin* instead of writing the character when doing homework.

▲**2**▲ The numbering system for notes in this textbook works as follows:

    a. For numbers without any letter in front of them, see the Notes section.

    b. For numbers preceded with a "G," see the Grammar section.

    c. For the letter "F," see Functional Expressions.

Notes

▲**1**▲ Most Chinese family names or surnames (姓 xìng) are monosyllabic. There are, however, a few disyllabic family names, written with two characters. The number of Chinese family names is fairly limited. According to the most recent census, the most common family names are Li 李 (Lǐ), Wang 王 (Wáng), Zhang 張 (Zhāng), Liu 劉 (Liú), and Chen 陳 (Chén). Family names also precede official titles or other forms of address: 王先生 (Wáng Xiānsheng, lit. Wang Mister), 李老師 (Lǐ Lǎoshī, lit. Li Teacher), etc. When addressing someone without knowing his or her family name, it is proper to call him 先生 (xiānsheng, Mister) or her 小姐 (xiǎojie, Miss) if she is relatively young.

▲2▲ "你好！" (Nǐ hǎo!) is a common form of greeting. It can be used to address strangers upon first introduction or between old acquaintances. To respond, simply repeat the greeting: "你好！" (Nǐ hǎo!). "你好嗎？" (Nǐ hǎo ma? How are you?) is a question usually asked of people you already know. The answer is usually "我很好" (Wǒ hěn hǎo; I am fine).

▲3▲ According to an etymological speculation, the character 姓 (xìng), with a woman radical on the left side and an ideographic component on the right that can mean "to give birth," suggests the matriarchal nature of the society at the time of the character's conception, when family names were inherited matrilineally.

▲4▲ In Chinese, family names (姓 xìng) always precede personal or given names (名 míng). Personal names usually carry auspicious or positive meanings. They can be either monosyllabic, written in one character, or disyllabic, written in two characters. In Chinese a person is seldom referred to by his or her family name alone, especially if the family name is monosyllabic. For example, Wang Peng (王朋 Wáng Péng), should not be referred to simply as Wang.

▲5▲ In China, when you meet someone, it is polite to ask for his or her family name first, rather than his/her full name. Then the question "你叫什麼名字？" (Nǐ jiào shénme míngzi? What is your name?) can be asked to find out his or her given name or full name.

Culture Notes

In China the use of given names often suggests a much higher degree of intimacy than in the West. If one's given name is monosyllabic, its use is even more limited, usually confined to writing. For example, Wang Peng's parents can address him as Peng in their letters to him, but at home they would most likely call him Wang Peng, instead of Peng. If he is still a child, they might call him Xiao Peng (lit. Little Peng) or Pengpeng (duplicating the syllable).

▼▼▼▼▼▼▼▼▼▼▼▼▼▼▼▼▼▼▼▼▼▼▼▼▼▼▼▼▼▼▼▼▼▼▼▼▼

Do you know anybody with the following surnames?

畢 (Bì); 蔡 (Cài); 陳 (Chén); 高 (Gāo); 黃 (Huáng); 李 (Lǐ); 林 (Lín); 劉 (Liú); 羅 (Luó); 毛 (Máo); 史 (Shǐ); 王 (Wáng); 吳 (Wú); 謝 (Xiè); 徐 (Xú); 許 (Xǔ); 楊 (Yáng); 姚 (Yáo); 葉 (Yè); 張 (Zhāng); 鄭 (Zhèng); 周 (Zhōu)

Dialogue II: Asking One's Status

VOCABULARY

1.	是	shì	v	to be
2.	老師	lǎoshī	n	teacher
3.	嗎	ma	qp	(an interrogative particle)
4.	不	bù	adv	not; no
5.	學生	xuésheng	n	student
6.	也	yě	adv	too; also
7.	中國人	Zhōngguórén	n	Chinese people/person
	中國	Zhōngguó	n	China
	人	rén	n	people; person
8.	美國人	Měiguórén	n	American people/person
	美國	Měiguó	n	America

DIALOGUE II

Lǐ Xiǎojie:	Wáng Xiānsheng, nǐ <u>shì</u>(G4) lǎoshī <u>ma</u>(G5)?
Wáng Xiānsheng:	<u>Bù</u>(G6), wǒ bú(1) shì lǎoshī, wǒ shì xuésheng. Lǐ Xiǎojie, nǐ ne?
Lǐ Xiǎojie:	Wǒ <u>yě</u>(G7) shì xuésheng. Nǐ shì Zhōngguórén ma?
Wáng Xiānsheng:	Shì, wǒ shì Zhōngguórén. Nǐ shì Měiguórén ma?
Lǐ Xiǎojie:	Wǒ shì Měiguórén.

DIALOGUE II

李小姐：　王先生，你是^(G4)老師嗎^(G5)？

王先生：　不^(G6)，我不⁽¹⁾是老師，我是學生。李小姐，你呢？

李小姐：　我也^(G7)是學生。你是中國人嗎？

王先生：　是，我是中國人。你是美國人嗎？

李小姐：　我是美國人。

Notes

▲1▲ The basic pronunciation of 不 is "bù" with fourth tone. However, when it is placed before another fourth tone syllable, 不 is pronounced in the second tone instead of the fourth. Therefore, 不是 is pronounced "bú shì" rather than "bù shì." In this textbook, the tone for 不 is marked as it is actually pronounced.

Can you identify the "老師" (lǎoshī) and "學生" (xuésheng) in this picture?

SUPPLEMENTARY VOCABULARY

1.	朋友	péngyou	n	friend
2.	太太	tàitai	n	wife; Mrs.
3.	英國	Yīngguó	n	Britain; England
4.	法國	Fǎguó	n	France
5.	日本	Rìběn	n	Japan
6.	德國	Déguó	n	Germany
7.	英國人	Yīngguórén	n	British people/person
8.	法國人	Fǎguórén	n	French people/person
9.	日本人	Rìběnrén	n	Japanese people/person
10.	德國人	Déguórén	n	German people/person
11.	韓國人	Hánguórén	n	Korean people/person
12.	越南人	Yuènánrén	n	Vietnamese people/person

Can you tell their nationalities by their costumes?

What are they saying to each other?

Grammar

[Note: In the grammar explanations in this textbook, the sign * indicates an example sentence that illustrates a grammatical or syntactic mistake.]

1. The Verb 姓 (xìng)

姓 (xìng) is both a noun and a verb. When it is used as a verb, an object must follow it. For example:

(1) A: 您貴姓？

Nín guì xìng?

(What is your surname? lit. Your honorable surname is...?)

B: 我姓王。

Wǒ xìng Wáng.

(My surname is Wang.)

(2) A: 你姓什麼？

Nǐ xìng shénme?

(What is your surname? lit. You are surnamed what?)

B: 我姓李。

Wǒ xìng Lǐ.

(My surname is Li.)

姓 (xìng) is usually negated with 不 (bù). [See G.6 below.]

(3) A: 你姓李嗎？

Nǐ xìng Lǐ ma?

(Is your family name Li?)

B: 我不姓李。

Wǒ bú xìng Lǐ.

(My surname is not Li.)

Note: When 姓 (xìng; to be surnamed) is used as a verb, an object must follow it. One should therefore never say *我姓 (*Wǒ xìng) or *我不姓 (*Wǒ bú xìng) as a short answer to the question: 你姓李嗎？ (Nǐ xìng Lǐ ma? Is your family name Li?)

2. Questions Ending with 呢 (ne)

呢 (ne) often follows a noun or pronoun to form a question when the content of the question is already clear from the context.

For example:

(1) 我姓李，你呢？

Wǒ xìng Lǐ, nǐ ne?

(My surname is Li. How about you?)

(2) 我是中國人，你呢？

Wǒ shì Zhōngguórén, nǐ ne?

(I am Chinese. How about you?)

(3) 我是老師，你呢？

Wǒ shì lǎoshī, nǐ ne?

(I am a teacher. How about you?)

Note: When 呢 (ne) is used in this way, there must be some context. In sentence (2) the context is provided by the preceding sentence, "我是中國人" (Wǒ shì Zhōngguórén). Likewise in sentence (3) "我是老師" (Wǒ shì lǎoshī) provides the context.

3. The Verb 叫 (jiào)

The verb 叫 (jiào) has several meanings. It means "to be called" in this lesson. It must be followed by an object.

For example:

(1) A: 你叫什麼名字？

Nǐ jiào shénme míngzi?

(What is your name?)

B: 我叫王朋。

Wǒ jiào Wáng Péng.

(My name is Wang Peng.)

叫 (jiào) is usually negated with 不 (bù). [See G.6 below.]

(2) A: 你叫李生嗎？

Nǐ jiào Lǐ Shēng ma?

(Is your name Li Sheng?)

B: 我不叫李生。

Wǒ bú jiào Lǐ Shēng.

(My name is not Li Sheng.)

Note: Like 姓 (xìng; to be surnamed), when 叫 (jiào; to be called) is used as a verb, it must take an object. One should therefore never say *我叫 (*Wǒ jiào) or *我不叫 (*Wǒ bú jiào).

From the examples above, we can see that the basic word order in a Chinese sentence runs like this:

Subject + Verb + Object

The word order remains the same in statements and questions. Remember that you don't place the question word at the beginning of a question as you do in English, unless that question word serves as the subject. (See more on word order in Grammar Note 1 in Lesson 4.)

4. The Verb 是 (shì)

In Chinese, 是 (shì) is a verb that can be used to link two nouns, pronouns, or noun phrases that are in some way equivalent.

For example:

(1) A: 你是老師嗎？

Nǐ shì lǎoshī ma?

(Are you a teacher?)

B: 我是老師。

Wǒ shì lǎoshī.

(I am a teacher.)

(2) A: 李友是學生。

Lǐ Yǒu shì xuésheng.

(Li You is a student.)

B: 你是美國人嗎？

Nǐ shì Měiguórén ma?

(Are you an American?)

是 (shì) is usually negated with 不 (bù). [See G.6 below.]

(3)   A: 李友不是中國人。

       Lǐ Yǒu bú shì Zhōngguórén.

       (Li You is not Chinese.)

     B: 王朋不是老師。

       Wáng Péng bú shì lǎoshī.

       (Wang Peng is not a teacher.)

5. Questions Ending with 嗎 (ma)

When 嗎 (ma) is added to the end of a declarative statement, that statement is turned into a question. The person who asks a question that ends with 嗎 (ma) often has some expectation of the answer. In sentence (1) below, the questioner may expect that the other person is a teacher, and in sentence (2) the questioner may expect that the other person is a student. To answer the question in the affirmative, 是 (shì) is used, while 不 (bù) is used if the answer is negative.

For example:

(1)   A: 你是老師嗎？

       Nǐ shì lǎoshī ma?

       (Are you a teacher?)

     B: 是，我是老師。

       Shì, wǒ shì lǎoshī.

       (Yes, I am a teacher.)

     C: 不，我不是老師。

       Bù, wǒ bú shì lǎoshī.

       (No, I am not a teacher.)

     D: 不，我是學生。

       Bù, wǒ shì xuésheng.

       (No, I am a student.)

(2)   A: 王友是學生嗎？

Wáng Yǒu shì xuésheng ma?

(Is Wang You a student?)

B: 是，王友是學生。

Shì, Wáng Yǒu shì xuésheng.

(Yes, Wang You is a student.)

C: 不，王友不是學生。

Bù, Wáng Yóu bú shì xuésheng.

(No, Wang You is not a student.)

D: 不，王友是老師。

Bù, Wáng Yǒu shì lǎoshī.

(No, Wang You is a teacher.)

(3)   A: 李朋是美國人嗎？

Lǐ Péng shì Měiguórén ma?

(Is Li Peng an American?)

B: 是，李朋是美國人。

Shì, Lǐ Péng shì Měiguórén.

(Yes, Li Peng is an American.)

C: 不，李朋不是美國人。

Bù, Lǐ Péng bú shì Měiguórén.

(No, Li Peng is not an American.)

D: 不，李朋是中國人。

Bù, Lí Péng shì Zhōngguórén.

(No, Li Peng is Chinese.)

6. The Negative Adverb 不 (bù)

In Chinese there are two main negative adverbs. One of the two, 不 (bù), occurs in this lesson.

For example:

(1) 不，我不是老師。

Bù, wǒ bú shì lǎoshī.

(No, I am not a teacher.)

(2) 李友不是中國人。

Lǐ Yǒu bú shì Zhōngguórén.

(Li You is not Chinese.)

(3) 老師不姓王。

Lǎoshī bú xìng Wáng.

(The teacher's surname is not Wang.)

(4) 我不叫李中。

Wǒ bú jiào Lǐ Zhōng.

(My name is not Li Zhong.)

7. The Adverb 也 (yě)

The adverb 也 (yě) basically means "too, also" in English. In Chinese, adverbs normally appear after subjects and in front of verbs. They usually cannot precede subjects or follow verbs. The adverb 也 (yě) cannot be put before the subject or at the very end of a sentence.

For example:

(1) 我也是學生。

Wǒ yě shì xuésheng.

(I am a student, too.)

(2) 王朋是學生，李友也是學生。

Wáng Péng shì xuésheng, Lǐ Yǒu yě shì xuésheng.

(Wang Peng is a student. Li You is a student, too.)

(3) 你是中國人，我也是中國人。

Nǐ shì Zhōngguórén, wǒ yě shì Zhōngguórén.

(You are Chinese. I am Chinese, too.)

The following sentences are **incorrect**:

(3) a. *你是中國人，我是中國人也。

Nǐ shì Zhōngguórén, wǒ shì Zhōngguórén yě.

(3) b. *你是中國人，也我是中國人。

Nǐ shì Zhōngguórén, yě wǒ shì Zhōngguórén.

When the adverb 也 (yě) is used together with the negative adverb 不 (bù), 也 (yě) is placed before 不 (bù).

For example:

(4) 王朋不是學生，李友也不是學生。

Wáng Péng bú shì xuésheng, Lǐ Yǒu yě bú shì xuésheng.

(Wang Peng is not a student. Li You is not a student either.)

(5) 你不是中國人，我也不是中國人。

Nǐ bú shì Zhōngguórén, wǒ yě bú shì Zhōngguórén.

(You are not Chinese, and I am not Chinese either.)

PATTERN DRILLS

All the exercises in the Pattern Drills section of each lesson are meant to be **Substitution Drills** unless otherwise noted. The teacher first says a sentence, then gives one or two words. The student uses the word(s) to form a new sentence.

A. 是 (shì)

Example: Teacher: Wǒ <u>shì</u> lǎoshī. (xuésheng)

Student: Wǒ <u>shì</u> xuésheng.

Teacher: 我<u>是</u>老師。(學生)

Student: 我<u>是</u>學生。

1. Wǒ   <u>shì</u>   Zhōngguó xuésheng.
2. Nǐ   lǎoshī.
3. Lǐ Xiǎojie   xuésheng.
4. Wáng Xiānsheng   lǎoshī.
5. Wáng Péng   Zhōngguórén.
6. Lǐ Yǒu   Měiguórén.

1. 我   <u>是</u>   中國學生。

2. 你   老師。

3. 李小姐   學生。

4. 王先生   老師。

5. 王朋   中國人。

6. 李友   美國人。

B. 是...嗎 (shì...ma)

1. Wáng Xiānsheng   <u>shì</u>   xuésheng   ma?
2. Lǐ Yǒu   Zhōngguórén
3. Wáng Péng   Měiguórén
4. Lǐ Xiǎojie   Zhōngguó xuésheng
5. Wáng Xiānsheng   Měiguó lǎoshī

1. 王先生   是   學生   嗎？

2. 李友   中國人

3. 王朋   美國人

4. 李小姐   中國學生

5. 王先生   美國老師

▼▼▼▼▼▼▼▼▼▼▼▼▼▼▼▼▼▼▼▼▼▼▼▼▼▼▼▼▼▼▼▼▼▼▼▼

C. 嗎 **(ma)**

Provide appropriate questions for speaker A for the answers given by speaker B.

Example: A: <u>Nǐ jiaò Wáng Péng ma</u>?   B: Bù, wǒ bú jiaò Wáng Péng.

A: <u>你叫王朋嗎？</u>   B: 不，我不叫王朋。

1. A: _____? B: Bù, Wáng Péng bú shì lǎoshī.

2. A: _____? B: Lǐ Yǒu shì xuésheng.

3. A: _____? B: Wáng Péng shì Zhōngguórén.

4. A: _____? B: Bù, Lǐ Yǒu bú shì Zhōngguórén.

5. A: _____? B: Bù, wǒ bú xìng Lǐ.

6. A: _____? B: Bù, wǒ bú jiào Lǐ Yǒu, wǒ jiào Wáng Yǒu.

1. A: _____? B: 不，王朋不是老師。

2. A: _____? B: 李友是學生。

3. A: _____? B: 王朋是中國人。

4. A: _____? B: 不，李友不是中國人。

5. A: _____? B: 不，我不姓李。

6. A: _____? B: 不，我不叫李友，我叫王友。

D. 也 (yě)

1.	<u>Nǐ shì</u>	xuésheng,	wǒ	<u>yě shì</u>	xuésheng.
2.		lǎoshī,	Wáng Xiānsheng		lǎoshī.
3.		Zhōngguórén,	Lǐ Xiǎojie		Zhōngguórén.
4.		Měiguórén,	Wáng Xiǎojie		Měiguórén.
5.		xuésheng,	Wáng Xiānsheng		xuésheng.
6.		lǎoshī,	Lǐ Xiānsheng		lǎoshī.

1.	<u>你是</u>	學生，	我	<u>也是</u>	學生。
2.		老師，	王先生		老師。
3.		中國人，	李小姐		中國人。
4.		美國人，	王小姐		美國人。
5.		學生，	王先生		學生。
6.		老師，	李先生		老師。

E. 不 (bù)

Answer questions with 不.

Example: Nǐ shì lǎoshī ma?   →   Wǒ <u>bú</u> shì lǎoshī.

你是老師嗎？   →   我<u>不</u>是老師。

1. Lǐ Yǒu shì Zhōngguórén ma?
2. Nǐ shì Wáng Lǎoshī ma?
3. Wáng Péng shì Měiguórén ma?
4. Nǐ jiào Lǐ Yǒu ma?
5. Lǎoshī xìng Wáng ma?

1. 李友是中國人嗎？

2. 你是王老師嗎？

3. 王朋是美國人嗎？

4. 你叫李友嗎？

5. 老師姓王嗎？

F. 是...不是... (shì … bú shì...)

1. <u>Wǒ shì</u>	Lǐ Yǒu,	<u>bú shì</u>	Wáng Péng.
2.	Zhōngguórén,		Měiguórén.
3.	xuésheng,		lǎoshī.
4.	Zhōngguó xuésheng,		Měiguó xuésheng.
5.	Wáng Xiānsheng,		Lǐ Xiānsheng.
6.	Lǐ Xiǎojie,		Wáng Xiǎojie.
7.	Lǐ Lǎoshī,		Wáng Lǎoshī.

1. <u>我是</u>　李友，　<u>不是</u>　王朋。

2. 　　　中國人，　　　美國人。

3. 　　　學生，　　　老師。

4. 　　　中國學生，　　　美國學生。

5. 　　　王先生，　　　李先生。

6. 　　　李小姐，　　　王小姐。

7. 　　　李老師，　　　王老師。

G. 不是…, 也不是 (bú shì…, yě bú shì…)

1.	Wǒ	bú shì	lǎoshī,	nǐ	yě bú shì	lǎoshī.
2.			Měiguórén,			Měiguórén.
3.			xuésheng,			xuésheng.
4.	Wǒ	bú xìng	Wáng,	nǐ	yě bú xìng	Wáng.
5.	Wǒ	bú jiào	Lǐ Yǒu,	nǐ	yě bú jiào	Lǐ Yǒu.

1. 我　　不是　　老師，　你　　也不是　　老師。
2. 　　　　　　美國人，　　　　　　　　美國人。
3. 　　　　　　學生，　　　　　　　　　學生。
4. 我　　不姓　　王，　　你　　也不姓　　王。
5. 我　　不叫　　李友，　你　　也不叫　　李友。

H. 呢 (ne)

1.	Wǒ shì	Zhōngguórén,	nǐ	ne?
2.		Měiguórén,	Wáng Xiǎojie	
3.		xuésheng,	Lǐ Xiānsheng	
4.		Měiguórén,	Wáng Lǎoshī	
5.		lǎoshī,	Lǐ Xiǎojie	

1. 我是　　中國人，　你　　呢？
2. 　　　　美國人，　王小姐
3. 　　　　學生，　　李先生
4. 　　　　美國人，　王老師
5. 　　　　老師，　　李小姐

▼▼▼

PRONUNCIATION EXERCISES

A. Practice the following initials:

1. **b**	**p**	**d**	**t**
bǎo	pǎo	dā	tā
bān	pān	dí	tí
bù	pù	duì	tuì
bō	pō	dīng	tīng
bēng	pēng	děng	téng

2. **j**	**q**	**z**	**c**
jiǎo	qiǎo	zāi	cāi
jǐng	qǐng	zǎo	cǎo
jīn	qīn	zì	cì
jiě	qiě	zé	cè
jiàn	qiàn	zhè	chè

3. **sh**	**s**	**x**
shēn	sēn	xīn
shēng	sēng	xīng
shàn	sàn	xiàn
shà	sà	xià

B. Practice the following tones:

tiāntiān	jīnnián	jīnglǐ	shēngqì
xīngqī	fādá	fāzhǎn	shēngdiào

C. Practice the following syllables with neutral tones:

xiānsheng	míngzi	xiǎojie	shénme
wǒ de	nǐ de	tā de	shéi de

D. Practice the following tones:

nǐ hǎo	Lǐ Yǒu	lǎohǔ	zhǎnlǎn
hǎo duō	nǐ lái	hǎo shū	qǐng wèn

English Texts

DIALOGUE I

Mr. Wang:	How do you do? (lit. You well?)
Miss Li:	How do you do?
Mr. Wang:	What's your family name, please? (lit. Please, may I ask... your honorable surname is...?)
Miss Li:	My family name is Li. What's yours? (lit. I am surnamed Li, and you?)
Mr. Wang:	My family name is Wang. My name is Wang Peng. What's your name?
Miss Li:	My name is Li You.

DIALOGUE II

Miss Li:	Mr. Wang, are you a teacher?
Mr. Wang:	No, I'm not a teacher. I'm a student. How about you, Miss Li?
Miss Li:	I'm a student, too. Are you Chinese?
Mr. Wang:	Yes, I'm Chinese. Are you American?
Miss Li:	I'm American.

LESSON 2 ▲ Family
第二課 ▲ 家庭
Dì èr kè ▲ *Jiātíng*

我家有六個人。
Wǒ jiā yǒu liù ge rén.

Dialogue I: Looking at a Family Photo

VOCABULARY

1.	那	nà/nèi	pr	that
2.	張	zhāng	m	(a measure word for flat objects)
3.	照片	zhàopiàn	n	picture; photo
4.	的	de	p	(a possessive, modifying, or descriptive particle)
5.	這	zhè/zhèi	pr	this
6.	爸爸	bàba	n	father; dad

7.	媽媽	māma	n	mother; mom
8.	這個	zhège	pr	this
	個	gè, -ge	m	(a common measure word)
9.	男孩子	nánháizi	n	boy
	男	nán	adj	male
	孩子	háizi	n	child
10.	誰	shéi	qpr	who
11.	他	tā	pr	he; him (May mean either "he/him" or "she/her" when the sex of the person is unknown.)
12.	弟弟	dìdi	n	younger brother
13.	女孩子	nǚháizi	n	girl
	女	nǚ	adj	female
14.	妹妹	mèimei	n	younger sister
15.	她	tā	pr	she
16.	女兒	nǚ'ér	n	daughter
17.	有	yǒu	v	to have; to exist
18.	兒子	érzi	n	son
19.	沒 (没)**	méi	adv	not

Note: In the vocabulary section, a hyphen is placed before or after the *pinyin* of a syllable (e.g. "-ge") to indicate a bound form (i.e., something less than an independent word), which is not used alone.

Proper Nouns

20.	小高	Xiǎo Gāo	pn	Little Gao
	小	xiǎo	adj	small; little
	高	gāo	adj	(a surname); tall

**Note that the character méi (not) appears in two forms, 沒 and 没. In writing it, you should use the latter form (没).

DIALOGUE I

(Wang Peng is in Little Gao's room pointing to a picture on the wall.)

Wáng Péng: Xiǎo Gāo[1], nà <u>zhāng</u>[G1] zhàopiàn shì nǐ de ma?

(They both walk toward the picture and then stand in front of it.)

Xiǎo Gāo: Shì. Zhè shì wǒ bàba, zhè shì wǒ māma.
Wáng Péng: Zhège nánháizi shì <u>shéi</u>[G2]?
Xiǎo Gāo: Tā shì wǒ dìdi.
Wáng Péng: Zhège nǚháizi shì nǐ mèimei ma?
Xiǎo Gāo: Bú shì, tā shì Lǐ Xiānsheng de[2] nǚ'ér.
Wáng Péng: Lǐ Xiānsheng <u>yǒu</u> [G3] érzi ma?
Xiǎo Gāo: Tā méiyǒu érzi.

DIALOGUE I

(Wang Peng is in Little Gao's room pointing to a picture on the wall.)

王朋： 小高[1]，那<u>張</u>[G1]照片是你的嗎？

(They both walk toward the picture and then stand in front of it.)

小高： 是。這是我爸爸，這是我媽媽。

王朋： 這個男孩子是<u>誰</u>[G2]？

小高： 他是我弟弟。

王朋： 這個女孩子是你妹妹嗎？

小高： 不是，她是李先生的[2]女兒。

王朋： 李先生<u>有</u>[G3]兒子嗎？

小高： 他沒有兒子。

The picture on the wall in Little Gao's room.

Notes

▲1▲ A familiar and affectionate way of addressing a young person is to add 小 (xiǎo, little; small) to the surname, e.g., 小王 (Xiǎo Wáng, Little Wang), 小李 (Xiǎo Lǐ, Little Li), 小高 (Xiǎo Gāo, Little Gao), etc. Similarly, to address an older peer, 老 (lǎo, old) can be used with the surname, e.g., 老王 (Lǎo Wáng, Old Wang), 老李 (Lǎo Lǐ, Old Li), 老高 (Lǎo Gāo, Old Gao), etc. However, such terms are rarely used to address a relative or a superior.

▲2▲ The particle 的 (de), as an indicator of a possessive relationship, always follows the "possessor" and precedes the "possessed." To that extent, it is equivalent to the "apostrophe + s" structure in English.

Chinese Kinship Terms

Chinese kinship terms are not only gender-specific but also seniority rank-specific, which makes them more precise than their Western counterparts in defining the relationship. If you are interested in learning more about Chinese kinship terms, see the chart in Lesson 22 in Integrated Chinese Level 1, Part 2.

▼ ▼

The Chinese School System

In China and Taiwan the school system is similar to that in the United States. A typical education consists of six years of elementary school (小學, xiǎoxué, grades 1–6), six years of middle school (中學, zhōngxué, grades 7–12), and four years of university (大學, dàxué) or college (學院, xuéyuàn). Middle school is further divided into junior high (初中, chūzhōng, grades 7–9) and senior high (高中, gāozhōng, grades 10–12). Many students also attend kindergarten before they enter the grade school, and some of them continue on to graduate school after college. Now that you have learned that a college student is called 大學生 (dàxuéshēng) in Chinese, can you guess the words for elementary school students, junior high school students, and senior high students?

Dialogue II: Asking about Someone's Family

VOCABULARY

1.	家	jiā	n	family; home
2.	幾	jǐ-	qw	how many
3.	哥哥	gēge	n	older brother
4.	兩	liǎng	nu	two; a couple of
5.	姐姐	jiějie	n	older sister
6.	和	hé	conj	and
7.	做	zuò	v	to do
8.	英文	Yīngwén	n	the English language
9.	#律師	lǜshī	n	lawyer
10.	都	dōu	adv	both; all
11.	大學生	dàxuéshēng	n	college student
	大學	dàxué	n	university; college
12.	#醫生	yīshēng	n	doctor; physician

▼▼▼▼▼▼▼▼▼▼▼▼▼▼▼▼▼▼▼▼▼▼▼▼▼▼▼▼▼▼▼

Proper Nouns

13.	小張	Xiǎo Zhāng	Little Zhang
	張	zhāng	(a surname); (a measure word for flat objects)

DIALOGUE II

Lǐ Yǒu: Xiǎo Zhāng, nǐ jiā(1) yǒu(G4) jǐge(2) rén?

Xiǎo Zhāng: Wǒ jiā yǒu liù ge rén. Wǒ bàba(3), wǒ māma, yí(4) ge(G1)
               gēge, liǎng(G5) ge jiějie hé(5) wǒ(6). Lǐ Xiǎojie, nǐ jiā yǒu jǐ ge
               rén?

Lǐ Yǒu: Wǒ jiā yǒu wǔ ge rén: bàba, māma, liǎng ge mèimei hé wǒ.
               Nǐ bàba māma shì zuò shénme de(7)?

Xiǎo Zhāng: Wǒ māma shì Yīngwén lǎoshī, bàba shì lǜshī, gēge, jiějie
               dōu(G6) shì dàxuéshēng.

Lǐ Yǒu: Wǒ māma yě shì lǎoshī, wǒ bàba shì yīshēng.

DIALOGUE II

李友： 小張，你家⑴有(G4)幾個⑵人？

小張： 我家有六個人。我爸爸⑶、我媽媽、
　　　一⑷個(G1)哥哥、兩(G5)個姐姐和⑸
　　　我⑹。李小姐，你家有幾個人？

李友： 我家有五個人。爸爸、媽媽、兩個
　　　妹妹和我。你爸爸媽媽是做什麼
　　　的⑺？

小張： 我媽媽是英文老師，爸爸是律師，
　　　哥哥、姐姐都(G6)是大學生。

李友： 我媽媽也是老師，我爸爸是醫生。

Notes

▲**1**▲ In Chinese, 家 (jiā) can refer to one's family as well as one's home. So, one can point to her family picture and say "我家有四個人" (Wǒ jiā yǒu sì ge rén; There are four people in my family), and one can also point to her house and say "這是我的家" (Zhè shì wǒ de jiā; This is my home).

▲**2**▲ For the number of people in a family, another measure word 口 (kǒu) is also used. The original tone for the measure word 個 (gè) is the falling tone. However, in actual speech it is always pronounced as a neutral tone word.

▲**3**▲ The possessive particle 的 (de) is usually omitted after a personal pronoun and before a kinship term. Therefore, we say "王朋的媽媽" (Wáng Péng de māma; Wang Peng's mother) with 的 (de) but "我媽媽" (wǒ māma; my mother) without 的 (de).

▲**4**▲ The numeral "一" (yī, one) is pronounced with the first tone "yī" when it stands alone or comes at the end of a word or sentence. Otherwise, its pronunciation changes according to the following rules: (a) "yī" before a fourth tone syllable becomes second tone. Therefore, "一個" is pronounced "yí gè" rather than "yī gè." (b) "yī" before a syllable in any tone other than the fourth tone becomes fourth tone. The above rules also apply to the numerals "七" (qī, seven) and "八" (bā, eight). However, nowadays few people change tones when pronouncing "七" (qī, seven) and "八" (bā, eight).

▲**5**▲ Although considered a conjunction and translated as "and," 和 (hé) cannot link two clauses or two sentences as "and" can in English. We say, "我爸爸是老師，我媽媽是醫生" (Wǒ bàba shī lǎoshì, wǒ māma shì yīshēng). We don't say, "*我爸爸是老師，和我媽媽是醫生" (*Wǒ bàba shì lǎoshī, hé wǒ māma shì yīsheng).

▲**6**▲ The pause mark, or "series comma," "、" is often used to link two, three or even more parallel words or phrases, e.g., 爸爸、媽媽、兩個妹妹和我 (bàba, māma, liǎng ge mèimei hé wǒ; dad, mom, two younger sisters and I). For further discussion of this punctuation mark, see Note 2 for Dialogue I in Lesson 4.

▲**7**▲ "X 是做什麼的" (X shì zuò shénme de) is often used to ask for a person's occupation, where the person is "X."

Culture Notes

In Chinese it is customary to mention the male before the female. Therefore, we say, 爸爸、媽媽，哥哥、姐姐，弟弟、妹妹 (bàba, māma, gēge, jiějie, dìdi, mèimei) instead of 媽媽、爸爸，姐姐、哥哥，妹妹、弟弟 (māma, bàba, jiějie, gēge, mèimei, dìdi), etc.

Whose family is this?

Grammar

1. Measure Words (I)

In Chinese a numeral is not usually followed immediately by a noun. Rather, a measure word is inserted between the number and the noun. There are several hundred measure words in Chinese, but you may hear only two or three dozen in everyday speech. Many nouns are associated with special measure words, which often bear a relationship to the meaning of the given noun. However, the general measure -ge can sometimes be substituted for the special measure. The following are two measure words that we have learned in this lesson.

個 (gè): This is the single most commonly used measure word in Chinese. It is also sometimes used as a substitute for other measure words.

Examples:

(1)	一個人	yí ge rén	a person
(2)	一個學生	yí ge xuésheng	a student
(3)	一個老師	yí ge lǎoshī	a teacher

張 (zhāng): This measure word is associated with objects with flat surfaces.

Examples:

(1)	一張照片	yì zhāng zhàopiàn	a photo
(2)	一張紙 (zhǐ)	yì zhāng zhǐ	a piece of paper
(3)	一張床 (chuáng)	yì zhāng chuáng	a bed

2. Interrogative Pronouns

Interrogative pronouns include 誰 (shéi, who), 什麼 (shénme, what), 哪 (nǎ/něi, which) [see L.6], 哪兒 (nǎr, where) [see L.5], 幾 (jǐ-, how many), etc. In a question with an interrogative pronoun, the word order is exactly the same as that in a non-interrogative statement. Therefore, when learning to compose a question in Chinese, we can start with a statement and then replace the part of the statement that is in question with the appropriate interrogative pronoun.

For example:

(1) 她是李友。

Tā shì Lǐ Yǒu.

(She is Li You.)

One can replace 她 (tā) with 誰 (shéi):

(2) 誰是李友？

Shéi shì Lǐ Yǒu?

(Who is Li You?)

Here 誰 (shéi) appears in the predicate of the sentence and occupies the same position as 她 (tā) in the corresponding statement. Or one can replace 李友 (Lǐ Yǒu) with 她 (tā):

(3)   她是誰？

Tā shì shéi?

(Who is she?)

誰 (shéi) functions as the object of the sentence and occupies the same position as 李友 (Lǐ Yǒu).

Other examples:

(4)   A: 我媽媽是醫生。

Wǒ māma shì yīshēng.

(My mother is a doctor.)

B: 你媽媽是做什麼的？

Nǐ māma shì zuò shénme de?

(What does your mother do?)

Examples with the verb 有 *(yǒu).*

(5)   A: 王朋有妹妹。

Wáng Péng yǒu mèimei.

(Wang Peng has a younger sister.)

B: 誰有妹妹？

Shéi yǒu mèimei?

(Who has any younger sisters?)

(6)   A: 我有三個姐姐。

Wǒ yǒu sān ge jiějie.

(I have three older sisters.)

B: 你有幾個姐姐？

Nǐ yǒu jǐ ge jiějie?

(How many older sisters do you have?)

Can you name the family members in Chinese?

3. 有 (yǒu) in the Sense of "to Have" or "to Possess"

有 (yǒu) is always negated with 沒 (méi).

Examples:

(1) A: 王先生有一個弟弟。

Wáng Xiānsheng yǒu yí ge dìdi.

(Mr. Wang has a younger brother.)

  B: 王先生沒有弟弟。

Wáng Xiānsheng méiyǒu dìdi.

(Mr. Wang doesn't have any younger brothers.)

(2) A: 我有兩張照片。

Wǒ yǒu liǎng zhāng zhàopiàn.

(I have two photos.)

  B: 我沒有照片。

Wǒ méiyǒu zhàopiàn.

(I don't have any photos.)

4. 有 (yǒu) in the Sense of "to Exist"

Examples:

(1) 我家有五個人。

Wǒ jiā yǒu wǔ ge rén.

(There are five people in my family.)

(2) 小張家有兩個大學生。

Xiǎo Zhāng jiā yǒu liǎng ge dàxuéshēng.

(There are two college students in Little Zhang's family.)

5. The Usage of 二 (èr) and 兩 (liǎng)

二 (èr) and 兩 (liǎng) both mean "two," but they differ in usage. 兩 (liǎng) is used in front of common measure words to express a quantity, e.g., 兩個人 (liǎng ge rén, two persons). In counting, one uses "二" (èr): "一，二，三，四……" (yī, èr, sān, sì; one, two, three, four…). "二" (èr) is also used in compound numerals, e.g., 二十二 (èrshí'èr, twenty-two) and 一百二十五 (yìbǎi èrshíwǔ, 125).

Cases involving quadruple digit numbers will be introduced later.

6. 都 (dōu, both; all)

The word 都 (dōu) indicates inclusiveness. As it always occurs in front of a verb, it is classified as an adverb. However, because it refers to something that has been mentioned earlier in the sentence, or in a preceding sentence, it also has a pronoun-like flavor and it must be used at the end of an enumeration.

Examples:

(1) 王朋、高生和李友都是律師。

Wáng Péng, Gāo Shēng hé Lǐ Yǒu dōu shì lǜshī.

(Wang Peng, Gao Sheng and Li You are all lawyers.)

(lit. Wang Peng, Gao Sheng and Li You *all are* lawyers.)

[都 (dōu) refers back to Wang Peng, Gao Sheng and Li You and therefore appears *after* they are mentioned.]

(2) 王朋和李友都不是老師。

Wáng Péng hé Lǐ Yǒu dōu bú shì lǎoshī.

(Neither Wang Peng nor Li You is a teacher.)

(3) 王朋和李友都有弟弟。

Wáng Péng hé Lǐ Yǒu dōu yǒu dìdi.

(Both Wang Peng and Li You have younger brothers.)

(lit. Wang Peng and Li You both have younger brothers.)

(4) 高生和張中都沒有妹妹。

Gāo Shēng hé Zhāng Zhōng dōu méi yǒu mèimei.

(Neither Gao Sheng nor Zhang Zhong has younger sisters.)

Note: 沒 (méi) is always used to negate 有 (yǒu). However, to say "not all of...have," we say in Chinese "不都有" (bù dōu yǒu) rather than "*沒都有" (méi dōu yǒu). Whether the negation word precedes or follows the word 都 (dōu) makes the difference between partial negation and complete negation.

Compare:

A. 他們不都是中國人。

(Tāmen bù dōu shì Zhōngguórén.)

(Not all of them are Chinese.)

B. 他們都不是中國人。

(Tāmen dōu bú shì Zhōngguórén.)

(None of them are Chinese.)

C. 他們不都有弟弟。

(Tāmen bù dōu yǒu dìdi.)

(Not all of them have younger brothers.)

D. 他們都沒有弟弟。

(Tāmen dōu méi yǒu dìdi.)

(None of them have younger brothers.)

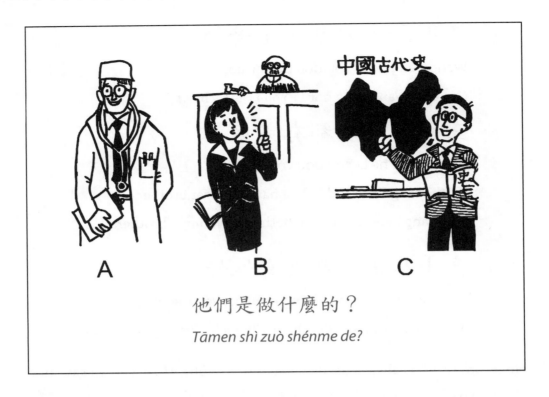

A   B   C

他們是做什麼的？

Tāmen shì zuò shénme de?

PATTERN DRILLS

A. 有 (yǒu, to have) with Measure Words

1.	Wǒ	yǒu	yí	ge	gēge.
2.	Tā		liǎng		jiějie.
3.	Xiǎo Wáng		sān		mèimei.
4.	Xiǎo Lǐ		yí		dìdi.
5.	Xiǎo Zhāng		liǎng		Zhōngguó lǎoshī.
6.	Gāo Lǎoshī		sān		érzi.
7.	Wǒ		liù	zhāng	zhàopiàn.

1.	我	有	一	個	哥哥。
2.	他		兩		姐姐。
3.	小王		三		妹妹。
4.	小李		一		弟弟。
5.	小張		兩		中國老師。

▼▼▼▼▼▼▼▼▼▼▼▼▼▼▼▼▼▼▼▼▼▼▼▼▼▼▼▼▼▼▼▼▼

6. 高老師　　　　三　　　　　　兒子。

7. 我　　　　　　六　　　張　　照片。

B. 沒有 (méiyǒu, have not)

1.	<u>Lǎo Wáng yǒu</u>	gēge,	<u>méiyǒu</u>	dìdi.
2.		jiějie,		mèimei.
3.		Zhōngguó péngyǒu,		Měiguó péngyǒu.
4.	<u>Xiǎo Lǐ yǒu</u>	gēge,		jiějie.
5.		dìdi,		mèimei.
6.	<u>Wáng Xiánsheng yǒu</u>	mèimei,		jiějie.
7.		jiějie,		dìdi.
8.		nǚ'ér,		érzi.

1.	<u>老王有</u>	哥哥，	<u>沒有</u>	弟弟。
2.		姐姐，		妹妹。
3.		中國朋友，		美國朋友。
4.	<u>小李有</u>	哥哥，		姐姐。
5.		弟弟，		妹妹。
6.	<u>王先生有</u>	妹妹，		姐姐。
7.		姐姐，		弟弟。
8.		女兒，		兒子。

C. 有 (yǒu, there is/are)

1.	Wǒ jiā	<u>yǒu</u>	liù	<u>ge rén</u>.
2.	Xiǎo Lǐ jiā		sān	
3.	Zhāng Lǎoshī jiā		liǎng	
4.	Wáng Xiānsheng jiā		sì	

How many children do they have?

5.	Gāo Xiǎojie jiā	bā
6.	Xiǎo Zhāng jiā	wǔ

1. 我家　　　　　<u>有</u>　　　六　　　<u>個人</u>。

2. 小李家　　　　　　　　　三

3. 張老師家　　　　　　　　兩

4. 王先生家　　　　　　　　四

5. 高小姐家　　　　　　　　八

6. 小張家　　　　　　　　　五

D. Interrogative Pronouns 誰 (shéi, who); 幾個 (jǐge, how many);
什麼 (shénme, what)

Formulate a question for each of the sentences below using the appropriate interrogative pronoun.

Example:　A:　<u>Zhè shì shéi?</u>　　　B:　Zhè shì wǒ bàba.

　　　　　A:　<u>這是誰？</u>　　　B:　這是我爸爸。

▼▼▼▼▼▼▼▼▼▼▼▼▼▼▼▼▼▼▼▼▼▼▼▼▼▼▼▼▼▼▼▼▼▼▼▼▼

Can you describe this photo in Chinese?

1.   A: _____ ?   B: Nà shì wǒ jiějie.

2.   A: _____ ?   B: Xiǎo Zhāng jiā yǒu liù ge rén.

3.   A: _____ ?   B: Xiǎo Gāo yǒu sān ge jiějie.

4.   A: _____ ?   B: Wǒ bàba shì lǜshī.

5.   A: _____ ?   B: Wǒ yǒu liǎng ge Zhōngguó lǎoshī.

6.   A: _____ ?   B: Tā gēge shì yīshēng.

7.   A: _____ ?   B: Tā jiào Zhāng Yǒuzhōng.

1.   A: _____ ?   B: 那是我姐姐。

2.   A: _____ ?   B: 小張家有六個人。

3.   A: _____ ?   B: 小高有三個姐姐。

4.   A: _____ ?   B: 我爸爸是律師。

5.   A: _____ ?   B: 我有兩個中國老師。

6. A: _____? B: 他哥哥是醫生。

7. A: _____? B: 他叫張有中。

E. 都 (dōu, both, all)

Rephrase the sentences with 都.

Example: Wǒ bàba shì yīshēng, tā bàba yě shì yīshēng.

→ Wǒ bàba hé tā bàba dōu shì yīshēng.

我爸爸是醫生，他爸爸也是醫生。

→ 我爸爸和他爸爸都是醫生。

1. Wǒ gēge shì lǜshī, wǒ jiějie yě shì lǜshī. →

2. Wáng Péng shì xuésheng, Lǐ Yǒu yě shì xuésheng. →

3. Wǒ bàba shì lǎoshī, tā bàba yě shì lǎoshī. →

4. Wǒ jiā yǒu sān ge rén, Xiǎo Zhāng jiā yě yǒu sān ge rén. →

5. Wǒ yǒu liǎng ge dìdi, tā yě yǒu liǎng ge dìdi. →

6. Zhège xuésheng shì Zhōngguórén, nàge xuésheng yě shì Zhōngguórén. →

7. Zhè zhāng zhàopiàn shì nǐ de, nà zhāng zhàopiàn yě shì nǐ de. →

8. Wǒ māma xìng Gāo, tā māma yě xìng Gāo. →

1. 我哥哥是律師，我姐姐也是律師。→

2. 王朋是學生，李友也是學生。→

3. 我爸爸是老師，他爸爸也是老師。→

4. 我家有三個人，小張家也有三個人。→

5. 我有兩個弟弟，他也有兩個弟弟。→

6. 這個學生是中國人，那個學生也是中國人。→

7. 這張照片是你的，那張照片也是你的。→

8. 我媽媽姓高，他媽媽也姓高。 →

F. 都 (dōu, all, both) with 不 (bù, not) or 沒有 (méiyǒu, have not)

Rephrase the sentences with 都 plus 不 or 沒有.

Examples: Wáng Zhōng shì lǎoshī. Lǐ Shēng shì lǎoshī. Gāo Péng shì yīshēng. (lǜshī)
　　→ Wáng Zhōng, Lǐ Shēng, Gāo Péng dōu bú shì lǜshī.

　　Xiǎo Zhāng méiyǒu gēge. Xiǎo Lǐ méiyǒu gēge. Xiǎo Wáng yě méiyǒu gēge.
　　→ Xiǎo Zhāng, Xiǎo Lǐ, Xiǎo Wáng dōu méiyǒu gēge.

王中是老師。李生是老師。高朋是醫生。
　(律師)

→王中、李生、高朋都不是律師。

小張沒有哥哥。小李沒有哥哥。小王也沒有哥哥。
　→小張、小李、小王都沒有哥哥。

1. Wǒ bàba shì lǎoshī. Wǒ jiějie shì lǜshī. Wǒ gēge shì yīshēng. (xuésheng)
2. Xiǎo Wáng méiyǒu mèimei. Xiǎo Lǐ méiyǒu mèimei. Xiǎo Zhāng yě méiyǒu mèimei. (mèimei)
3. Wáng Zhōng shì Měiguórén. Lǐ Yǒu shì Měiguórén. Gāo Guì yě shì Měiguórén. (Zhōngguórén)
4. Lǐ Zhōng shì lǎoshī. Wáng Péng bú shì lǎoshī. Gāo Yǒu yě bú shì lǎoshī. (lǎoshī)
5. Wáng Péng méiyǒu zhàopiàn. Lǐ Zhōng méiyǒu zhàopiàn. Gāo Yǒu yě méiyǒu zhàopiàn. (zhàopiàn)
6. Wǒ māma xìng Wáng. Nǐ māma xìng Gāo. Tā bàba xìng Zhāng. (Lǐ)

1. 我爸爸是老師，我姐姐是律師，我哥哥是醫生。(學生)

2. 小王沒有妹妹，小李沒有妹妹，小張也沒有妹妹。(妹妹)

3. 王中是美國人，李友是美國人，高貴也是美國人。(中
　 國人)

4. 李中是老師，王朋不是老師，高友也不是老師。(老師)

5. 王朋沒有照片，李中沒有照片，高友也沒有照片。(照片)

6. 我媽媽姓王，你媽媽姓高，她爸爸姓張。(李)

PRONUNCIATION EXERCISES

A. Initials

1. **zh**	zhè	zhǎo	zhāng	zhuāng
ch	chè	chǎo	chàng	chuáng
sh	shè	shǎo	shāng	shuāng
2. **d**	dà	duō	duì	dōu
t	tà	tuō	tuì	tōu
3. **r**	rén	rào	rì	rè

B. The Final "e"

gē	dé	zhè	hē
kē	tè	chē	shé
zé	cè	sè	rè

C. Tones

chénggōng	chángcháng	rénkǒu	xuéxiào
Chángjiāng	Chángchéng	míngxiǎn	chídào

D. The Neutral Tone

māma	shéi de	jiějie	mèimei
tā de	fángzi	nǐ de	dìdi

English Texts

DIALOGUE I

(Wang Peng is in Little Gao's room pointing to a picture on the wall.)

Wang Peng: Little Gao, is that picture yours?

(They both walk toward the picture and then stand in front of it.)

Little Gao: Yes. This is my dad. This is my mom.

Wang Peng: Who is this boy?

Little Gao: This is my younger brother.

Wang Peng: Is this girl your younger sister?

Little Gao: No, she's Mr. Li's daughter.

Wang Peng: Does Mr. Li have any sons?

Little Gao: He has no sons.

DIALOGUE II

Li You: Little Zhang, how many people are there in your family?

Little Zhang: There are six people in my family: my dad, my mom, an older brother, two older sisters and I. How many people are there in your family, Miss Li?

Li You: There are five people in my family: my dad, my mom, my two younger sisters and I. What do your dad and mom do?

Little Zhang: My mom is an English teacher. My dad is a lawyer. My older brother and sisters are all college students.

Li You: My mom is also a teacher. My dad is a doctor.

LESSON 3 ▲ Dates and Time
第三課 ▲ 時間
Dì sān kè ▲ *Shíjiān*

我請你吃晚飯，怎麼樣？

Wǒ qǐng nǐ chī wǎnfàn, zěnmeyàng?

Dialogue I: Taking Someone Out to Eat on His/Her Birthday

VOCABULARY

1.	九月	jiǔyuè	n	September
	月	yuè	n	month
2.	十二	shí'èr	nu	twelve
3.	#號	hào	m	number in a series; day of the month
4.	星期四	xīngqīsì	n	Thursday

	星期	xīngqī	n	week
5.	天	tiān	n	day
6.	生日	shēngrì	n	birthday
	生	shēng	v	to give birth to; to be born
	日	rì	n	day; the sun
7.	今年	jīnnián	t	this year
	年	nián	n	year
8.	多大	duō dà	ce	how old
	多	duō	adv	how many/much; to what extent
	大	dà	adj	big; old
9.	十八	shíbā	nu	eighteen
10.	#歲	suì	n	year (of age)
11.	請	qǐng	v	to treat (somebody); to invite [see also L.1]
12.	吃	chī	v	to eat
13.	晚飯	wǎnfàn	n	dinner; supper
	晚	wǎn	adj	evening; night; late
	飯	fàn	n	meal; (cooked) rice
14.	吃飯	chī fàn	vo	to eat (a meal)
15.	怎麼樣	zěnmeyàng	qpr	Is it O.K.? What is it like? How does that sound?
16.	太...(了)	tài...(le)		too; extremely
17.	#謝謝	xièxie	ce	thank you
18.	喜歡	xǐhuan	v	to like, like to; to prefer, prefer to
19.	還是	háishi	conj	or

20.	可是	kěshì	conj	but
21.	好	hǎo	adj	good; O.K.
22.	我們	wǒmen	pr	we
23.	點#鐘	-diǎnzhōng	m	o'clock
	點	diǎn	m	o'clock (lit. point, thus "points on the clock")
	鐘	zhōng	n	clock
24.	半	bàn	nu	half; half an hour
25.	晚上	wǎnshang	t/n	evening; night
26.	見	jiàn	v	to see
27.	再見	zàijiàn	ce	goodbye; see you again
	再	zài	adv	again

Proper Noun

28.	小白	Xiǎo Bái	pn	Little Bai
	白	bái	adj	white; (a surname)

DIALOGUE I

(Little Gao is talking to Little Bai.)

Xiǎo Gāo:	Xiǎo Bái, jiǔyuè <u>shí'èr</u>(1) (G1) <u>hào</u>(G2.3) shì <u>xīngqījǐ</u>(G2.1)?
Xiǎo Bái:	Shì xīngqīsì.
Xiǎo Gāo:	Nà tiān shì wǒ <u>de</u>(G3) shēngrì.
Xiǎo Bái:	Shì ma? Nǐ jīnnián duō dà(2)?
Xiǎo Gāo:	Shíbā suì(3).
Xiǎo Bái:	Xīngqīsì <u>wǒ qǐng nǐ chī wǎnfàn</u>(G4), zěnmeyàng?
Xiǎo Gāo:	Tài hǎo le. Xièxie, xièxie(4).
Xiǎo Bái:	Nǐ xǐhuan chī Zhōngguó fàn <u>háishi</u>(G5) Měiguó fàn?
Xiǎo Gāo:	Wǒ shì Zhōngguórén, kěshì wǒ xǐhuan chī Měiguó fàn.
Xiǎo Bái:	Hǎo, wǒmen chī Měiguó fàn.

Xiǎo Gāo: Xīngqīsì jǐ diǎnzhōng?

Xiǎo Bái: <u>Qīdiǎn bàn</u>(G2.6) zěnmeyàng?

Xiǎo Gāo: Hǎo, xīngqīsì wǎnshang jiàn.

Xiǎo Bái: Zàijiàn.

DIALOGUE I

(Little Gao is talking to Little Bai.)

小高：小白，九月<u>十二</u>(1)(G1)號(G2.3)是<u>星期幾</u>(G2.1)？

小白：是星期四。

小高：那天是我<u>的</u>(G3)生日。

小白：是嗎？你今年多大(2)？

小高：十八歲(3)。

小白：星期四<u>我請你吃晚飯</u>(G4)，怎麼樣？

小高：太好了。謝謝，謝謝(4)。

小白：你喜歡吃中國飯<u>還是</u>(G5)美國飯？

小高：我是中國人，可是我喜歡吃美國飯。

小白：好，我們吃美國飯。

小高：星期四幾點鐘？

小白：<u>七點半</u>(G2.6)怎麼樣？

小高：好，星期四晚上見。

小白：再見！

	九　月					
日	一	二	三	四	五	六
1	2	3	4	5	6	7
8	9	10	11	12	13	14
15	16	17	18	19	20	21
22	23	24	25	26	27	28
29	30					

Circle Little Gao's birthday.

Notes

▲**1**▲ Chinese time expressions proceed from the largest to the smallest unit, e.g., 二零零三年九月十二日晚上七點 (èr-líng-líng-sān nián jiǔyuè shí'èr rì wǎnshang qīdiǎn; literally, the year 2003, the ninth month, the twelfth day, the evening, seven o'clock).

▲**2**▲ To find out someone's age, we ask, 你今年多大？ (Nǐ jīnnián duō dà?). If the person is a child who appears to be under ten, we change the question to 你今年幾歲？ (Nǐ jīnnián jǐ suì?). To find out an older person's age, it would be more polite to ask, 您多大年紀/歲數了？ (Nín duō dà niánjì/suìshù le?).

▲**3**▲ To give one's age, it is correct to say "我十八歲" (Wǒ shíbā suì), but the word 歲 (suì, year of age) can often be dropped. If one is ten years old or younger, however, the word 歲 cannot be dropped. It is **incorrect** to say "*我十" (*Wǒ shí) or "*我八" (*Wǒ bā).

▲**4**▲ To show gratitude, one can say "謝謝" (xièxie), or "謝謝, 謝謝" (xièxie, xièxie) by repeating the word. The latter one is obviously more polite and exuberant.

Xiao Gao's birthday celebration.

Culture Notes

The traditional Chinese manner of counting age, which is still in use among many (mainly older) people on non-official occasions, is based on the number of the calendar years one has lived *in*, rather than the length of time in actual years that one has lived. For example, a child born in January 2001 can be said to be two years old in January 2002, as he or she has by then lived in two calendar years, 2001 and 2002. But for official purposes, for instance on the census, the child would still be considered as one year old, as that is the actual length of time he or she has lived.

▼ ▼

Dialogue II: Inviting Someone to Dinner

VOCABULARY

1.	現在	xiànzài	t	now
2.	刻	-kè	m	quarter (hour); 15 minutes
3.	事	shì	n	matter; affair; business
4.	明天	míngtiān	t	tomorrow
5.	忙	máng	adj	busy
6.	今天	jīntiān	t	today
7.	很	hěn	adv	very
8.	為什麼	wèishénme	qpr	why
	為 (爲)**	wèi	prep	for
9.	因為	yīnwei	conj	because
10.	還有	hái yǒu		also there are
	還	hái	adv	also; too; as well
11.	同學	tóngxué	n	classmate
12.	認識	rènshi	v	to know (someone); to recognize

Proper Noun

13.	小李	Xiǎo Lǐ	pn	Little Li

**Note that the character wèi appears in two different forms. "爲" is the printed form, while "為" is the handwritten form.

Culture Notes

The traditional Chinese equivalent of the birthday cake is noodles. Because noodles are long, they are considered a symbol of longevity. That is why they are called 長壽麵 (chángshòu miàn, longevity noodles). Among the younger generations in urban areas birthday cakes are also becoming quite common.

DIALOGUE II

(Wang Peng and Little Bai are talking to each other.)

Wáng Péng:	Xiǎo Bái, xiànzài jǐ diǎnzhōng?
Xiǎo Bái:	Wǔ diǎn sān kè.
Wáng Péng:	Wǒ liù diǎn yí kè yǒu shì.
Xiǎo Bái:	Wáng Péng, nǐ míngtiān <u>máng bu máng</u>(G6)?
Wáng Péng:	Wǒ jīntiān hěn máng(1), kěshì míngtiān bù máng. Yǒu shì ma?
Xiǎo Bái:	Míngtian wǒ qǐng nǐ chī wǎnfàn, zěnmeyàng?
Wáng Péng:	Wèishénme qǐng wǒ chī fàn?
Xiǎo Bái:	Yīnwei míngtiān shì Xiǎo Gāo de shēngrì.
Wáng Péng:	Shì ma? Hǎo, <u>hái yǒu</u>(G7) shéi?
Xiǎo Bái:	Hái yǒu wǒ de tóngxué Xiǎo Lǐ.
Wáng Péng:	Nà tài hǎo le! Wǒ yě rènshi Xiǎo Lǐ. Jǐ diǎnzhōng?
Xiǎo Bái:	Míngtiān wǎnshang qī diǎn bàn.
Wáng Péng:	Hǎo, míngtiān qī diǎn bàn jiàn.

DIALOGUE II

(Wang Peng and Little Bai are talking to each other.)

王朋： 小白，現在幾點鐘？

小白： 五點三刻。

王朋： 我六點一刻有事。

小白： 王朋，你明天忙不忙(G6)？

王朋： 我今天很忙(1)，可是明天不忙。有
事嗎？

小白： 明天我請你吃晚飯，怎麼樣？

王朋： 為什麼請我吃飯？

▼▼▼▼▼▼▼▼▼▼▼▼▼▼▼▼▼▼▼▼▼▼▼▼▼▼▼▼▼▼▼▼▼▼▼▼

小白：因為明天是小高的生日。

王朋：是嗎？好。<u>還有</u>(G7)誰？

小白：還有我的同學小李。

王朋：那太好了，我也認識小李。幾點
　　　鐘？

小白：明天晚上七點半。

王朋：好，明天七點半見。

Notes

▲1▲ Although usually translated as "very," the Chinese adverb 很 (hěn) is not quite as strong as its English equivalent. Therefore, the sentence 我很忙 (Wǒ hěn máng)—unless the word 很 (hěn) is stressed—is closer to "I am busy" than "I am *very* busy." There is a tendency in Modern Chinese to compound a monosyllabic adjective with 很, e.g., 很好 (hěn hǎo), 很忙 (hěn máng), etc. Accordingly, we usually say "我很好" (Wǒ hěn hǎo; I am fine) instead of "我好" (Wǒ hǎo) and "她很忙" (Tā hěn máng; She is busy) instead of "她忙" (Tā máng). Also see Grammar Note 2 in Lesson 5.

SUPPLEMENTARY VOCABULARY

1.	分	fēn	m	minute
2.	差	chà	v	to be short of; to be lacking
3.	昨天	zuótiān	t	yesterday
4.	前天	qiántiān	t	the day before yesterday
5.	後天	hòutiān	t	the day after tomorrow
6.	明年	míngnián	t	next year

▼▼▼▼▼▼▼▼▼▼▼▼▼▼▼▼▼▼▼▼▼▼▼▼▼▼▼▼▼▼▼▼

7.	去年	qùnián	t	last year
8.	前年	qiánnián	t	the year before last
9.	後年	hòunián	t	the year after next
10.	下(個)月	xià(ge)yuè	t	next month
11.	錶	biǎo	n	watch
12.	早飯	zǎofàn	n	breakfast
13.	中飯	zhōngfàn	n	lunch

Time Expressions Involving Year and Day

大前天	前天	昨天	今天	明天	後天	大後天
大前年	前年	去年	今年	明年	後年	大後年

Note that the above expressions with 天 (tiān, day) and 年 (nián, year) form two parallel series except for 昨天 (zuótiān, yesterday) and 去年 (qùnián, last year).

Time Expressions Involving Month and Week

上上個月	上個月	這個月	下個月	下下個月
上上個星期	上個星期	這個星期	下個星期	下下個星期

Note that the above expressions with 月 (yuè, month) and 星期 (xīngqī, week) form two parallel series.

Grammar

1. Numbers (0, 11–100)

0: 零 (líng, zero)

11–99: 十一 (shíyī, eleven), 十二 (shí'èr, twelve), 十三 (shísān, thir-teen)...二十 (èrshí, twenty), 二十一 (èrshíyī, twenty-one), 二十二 (èrshí'èr, twenty-two), 二十三 (èrshísān, twenty-three)...三十 (sānshí, thirty), 九十一 (jiǔshíyī, ninety-one)...九十九 (jiǔshíjiǔ, ninety-nine)

100, 200, etc.: 一百 (yìbǎi, one hundred), 二百 (èrbǎi, two hundred)

2. Dates and Time

(1) Days of the week

星期一	xīngqīyī	Monday
星期二	xīngqī'èr	Tuesday
星期三	xīngqīsān	Wednesday
星期四	xīngqīsì	Thursday
星期五	xīngqīwǔ	Friday
星期六	xīngqīliù	Saturday
星期日 (天)	xīngqīrì (tiān)	Sunday

While 星期 (xīngqī, week) is commonly used in spoken Chinese, 週 (zhōu, week) is usually used in written Chinese. Monday can also be called 週一 (zhōuyī), Tuesday 週二 (zhōu'èr), etc. Weekend is 週末 (zhōumò) in both spoken and written Chinese, and in written Chinese 週日 (zhōurì) is sometimes used to refer to Sunday. In China the week starts on Monday. The question 星期幾？(xīngqījǐ?) is used to ask the day of the week. To answer this question, simply replace the word 幾 (jǐ, what, how many) with the number indicating the day of the week, such as 星期四 (xīngqīsì, Thursday), meaning the fourth day of the week. In spoken Chinese the expression 禮拜 (lǐbài, week) is also used. Therefore, 禮拜四 (lǐbàisì) also means Thursday. Both 星期日 (xīngqīrì) and 星期天 (xīngqītiān) mean Sunday. 星期日 (xīngqīrì) is used more in written Chinese whereas 星期天 (xīngqītiān) is used more in spoken Chinese.

(2) Months

一月	yīyuè	January
二月	èryuè	February
三月	sānyuè	March
四月	sìyuè	April
五月	wǔyuè	May
六月	liùyuè	June
七月	qīyuè	July
八月	bāyuè	August
九月	jiǔyuè	September
十月	shíyuè	October
十一月	shíyīyuè	November
十二月	shí'èryuè	December

(3) Days of the month

In spoken Chinese 號 (hào, number) is used to refer to the days of the month. However, in written Chinese 日 (rì, day) is always used.

Examples:

二月五號	èryuè	wǔ hào	February 5	(spoken)
二月五日	èryuè	wǔ rì	February 5	(written)

(4) Year

年 (nián, year) is always included with numbers referring to a year.

Examples:

一七七六年	yī-qī-qī-liù nián	1776
一九九五年	yī-jiǔ-jiǔ-wǔ nián	1995

Note: Unlike in English, where the two years given above are read "seventeen seventy-six" and "nineteen ninety-five" respectively, years in Chinese are pronounced one digit at a time.

(5) Word Order for Dates

To give a date in Chinese, observe the following order (progression from larger to smaller unit):

year	month	day	day of the week
年	月	日	星期
nián	yuè	rì	xīngqī

Example:

一九九五年七月二十六日星期三

(Wednesday, July 26, 1995)

yī jiǔ jiǔ wǔ nián qīyuè èrshíliù rì xīngqīsān

(6) Telling Time

These terms are used to tell time in Chinese: 點鐘 (diǎnzhōng, o'clock), 半 (bàn, half hour), 刻 (kè, quarter hour), and 分 (fēn, minute).

Examples:

a. o'clock:

三點鐘	sān diǎnzhōng	three o'clock
十一點	shíyī diǎn	eleven o'clock
七、八點鐘	qī, bā diǎnzhōng	seven or eight o'clock

Note that 鐘 (zhōng) can be omitted from 點鐘 (diǎnzhōng).

b. minute:

一點十八 (分)	yī diǎn shíbā (fēn)	1:18
兩點零七分	liǎng diǎn líng qī fēn	2:07

三點零五 (分)   sān diǎn líng wǔ (fēn)   3:05

五點二十 (分)   wǔ diǎn èrshí (fēn)   5:20

差十分九點   chà shí fēn jiǔ diǎn   8:50 (ten till nine)

Note: The term 零 (líng, zero) is usually added before a single-digit number of 分 (fēn, minute), e.g., 三點零五分 (sān diǎn líng wǔ fēn). 分 (fēn) can be omitted from the end of the expression if the number for the minutes appears in two syllables. Thus one can say "一點十八" (yī diǎn shíbā) and "三點零五" (sān diǎn líng wǔ), but not "*兩點七" (*liǎng diǎn qī) or "*一點十" (*yī diǎn shí).

c. quarter hour:

兩點一刻   liǎng diǎn yí kè   2:15   (a quarter past two)

差一刻四點   chà yí kè sì diǎn   3:45   (a quarter till four)

十一點三刻   shíyī diǎn sān kè   11:45   (a quarter till twelve)

d. half hour:

兩點半   liǎng diǎn bàn   2:30   (half past two)

八點半   bā diǎn bàn   8:30   (half past eight)

十二點半   shí'èr diǎn bàn   12:30   (half past twelve)

Note that *兩刻 (*liǎng kè, two quarters) is *not* used.

e. evening time:

晚上七點 (鐘)   wǎnshang qī diǎn (zhōng)   7:00 p.m.

晚上八點零五 (分)   wǎnshang bā diǎn líng wǔ (fēn)   8:05 p.m.

晚上九點一刻   wǎnshang jiǔ diǎn yí kè   9:15 p.m.

晚上十點半   wǎnshang shí diǎn bàn   10:30 p.m.

晚上差四分十一點   wǎnshang chà sì fēn shíyī diǎn   10:56 p.m.

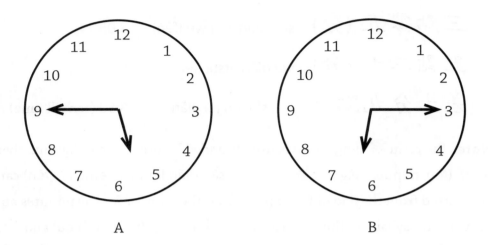

Can you say the times in the pictures above in Chinese?

3. Pronouns as Modifiers and the Usage of 的 (de)

When the personal pronouns 我 (wǒ, I), 你 (nǐ, you), and 他 (tā, he) are followed by a term indicating a close personal relationship such as 媽媽 (māma, mother), 弟弟 (dìdi, younger brother), and 老師 (lǎoshī, teacher), the word 的 (de) can be omitted; e.g., 我媽媽 (wǒ māma, my mother), 你弟弟 (nǐ dìdi, your younger brother), 我們老師 (wǒmen lǎoshī, our teacher). Otherwise 的 (de) is generally required; e.g., 我的生日 (wǒ de shēngrì, my birthday).

4. Pivotal Sentences

In the sentence "我請你吃晚飯" (Wǒ qǐng nǐ chī wǎnfàn; I will treat you to dinner), 你 (nǐ, you) is the object of the verb 請 (qǐng, to treat) as well as the subject of the second verb 吃 (chī, to eat). Therefore, 你 (nǐ, you) can be considered the pivot of the sentence. That is why some people consider this sentence as a type of "pivotal sentence."

Examples:

(1) 明天李生請你吃中國飯。

Míngtiān Lǐ Shēng qǐng nǐ chī Zhōngguófàn.

(Li Sheng is inviting you to eat Chinese food tomorrow.)

(2) 今天晚上我請你和你妹妹吃美國
飯，好嗎？

Jīntiān wǎnshang wǒ qǐng nǐ hé nǐ mèimei chī Měiguó fàn, hǎo
ma?

(How about if I invite you and your younger sister to eat
American food tonight?)

5. Alternative Questions

The structure (是)…還是…(shì…háishi…, …or…) is used to form an alternative
question. If there is another verb used in the predicate, the first 是 (shì) can
be omitted.

(1) 你是中國人，還是美國人？

Nǐ shì Zhōngguórén, háishi Měiguórén?

(Are you Chinese or American?)

(2) 你哥哥是老師，還是學生？

Nǐ gēge shì lǎoshī, háishi xuésheng?

(Is your older brother a teacher or a student?)

(3) (是)你請我吃飯，還是他請我吃飯？

(Shì) nǐ qǐng wǒ chīfàn, háishi tā qǐng wǒ chīfàn?

(Are you taking me to dinner, or is he?)

(4) A: 他(是)喜歡吃中國飯，還是喜歡吃
美國飯？

Tā (shì) xǐhuan chī Zhōngguó fàn, háishi xǐhuan chī Měiguó
fàn?

(Does he like to eat Chinese or American food?)

B: 中國飯美國飯他都喜歡。

Zhōngguó fàn Měiguó fàn tā dōu xǐhuan.

(He likes both Chinese food and American food.)

▼▼▼▼▼▼▼▼▼▼▼▼▼▼▼▼▼▼▼▼▼▼▼▼▼▼▼▼▼▼

6. Affirmative + Negative (A-not-A) Questions (I)

Besides adding the interrogative particle 嗎 (ma) to a declarative sentence, another common way of forming a question in Chinese is to repeat the verb or adjective in its affirmative and negative form.

Example:

(1) 你忙不忙?

Nǐ máng bu máng?

(Are you busy or not?)

(2) 媽媽喜歡不喜歡吃中國飯？

Māma xǐhuan bu xǐhuan chī Zhōngguó fàn?

(Does mother like to eat Chinese food or not?)

(3) 王太太今天有沒有事？

Wáng Tàitai jīntiān yǒu méiyǒu shì?

(Does Mrs. Wang have anything to do today or not?)

7. 還有 (hái yǒu, also, too, in addition) + Noun

The word 還有 (hái yǒu) can signify addition. For instance,

(1) 我家有爸爸、媽媽，還有一個妹妹。

Wǒ jiā yǒu bàba, māma, hái yǒu yí ge mèimei.

(In my family there's Dad, Mom, and a younger sister.)

(2) A: 誰喜歡吃美國飯？

Shéi xǐhuan chī Měiguó fàn?

(Who likes to eat American food?)

B: 我、我弟弟，還有我姐姐。

Wǒ, wǒ dìdi, hái yǒu wǒ jiějie.

(I, my younger brother, and also my older sister.)

▼▼▼▼▼▼▼▼▼▼▼▼▼▼▼▼▼▼▼▼▼▼▼▼▼▼▼▼▼▼▼▼▼▼▼

PATTERN DRILLS

A. Days of the week

(Provide the correct answers based on the calendar below.)

			March			
Su	M	Tu	W	Th	F	Sa
12	13	14	15	16	17	18

Example: (Sānyuè shíwǔ hào)

A: <u>Sānyuè shíwǔ hào</u> shì xīngqī jǐ?

B: <u>Sānyuè shíwǔ hào</u> shì xīngqīsān.

(三月十五號)

A: <u>三月十五號</u>是星期幾？

B: <u>三月十五號</u>是星期三。

1. Sānyuè shísān hào

2. Sānyuè shíliù hào

3. Sānyuè shí'èr hào

4. Sānyuè shíqī hào

5. Sānyuè shíbā hào

6. Sānyuè shísì hào

1. 三月十三號

2. 三月十六號

3. 三月十二號

幾點鐘？

Jǐ diǎnzhōng?

4. 三月十七號

5. 三月十八號

6. 三月十四號

B. Time

1.	<u>Wǒmen</u>	wǔ diǎnzhōng	<u>jiàn.</u>
2.		liù diǎn èrshí fēn	
3.		jiǔ diǎn	
4.		qī diǎn bàn	
5.		bā diǎn shí fēn	
6.		shíyī diǎn sìshí fēn	

1.	<u>我們</u>	五點鐘	<u>見</u>。
2.		六點二十分	
3.		九點	
4.		七點半	
5.		八點十分	
6.		十一點四十分	

A Chinese teahouse.

C. 還是 (háishi, or)

Form 還是 *questions with the information given.*

1.	Tā shì xuésheng,	háishi	lǎoshī?
2.	Xiǎo Gāo xǐhuan chī Zhōngguó fàn,		xǐhuan chī Měiguó fàn?
3.	Nǐ de lǎoshī xìng Gāo,		xìng Zhāng?
4.	Nǐ jīnnián shì shíjiǔ,		èrshí?
5.	Tā gēge shì yīshēng,		lǜshī?
6.	Nǐ qǐng wǒ chīfàn,		wǒ qǐng nǐ chīfàn?

1. 他是學生　　　　　還是　　　老師？

2. 小高喜歡吃中國飯，　　　　喜歡吃美國飯？

3. 你的老師姓高，　　　　　　姓張？

4. 你今年是十九，　　　　　　二十？

5. 他哥哥是醫生，　　　　　　律師？

6. 你請我吃飯，　　　　　　　我請你吃飯？

What time was this photo taken?

D. 可是 (kěshì, but)

Rephrase the sentences with 可是.

Example: Xiǎo Gāo shì Zhōngguórén. Xiǎo Gāo xǐhuan chī Měiguó fàn.

→ Xiǎo Gāo shì Zhōngguórén, <u>kěshì</u> xǐhuan chī Měiguó fàn.

小高是中國人。小高喜歡吃美國飯。

→ 小高是中國人，<u>可是</u>喜歡吃美國飯。

1.   Wǒ xǐhuan Zhāng Xiǎojie. Wǒ bù xǐhuan Bái Xiǎojie.

2.   Wǒ rènshi Wáng Lǎoshī. Wǒ bú rènshi Lǐ Lǎoshī.

3.   Wǒ yǒu liǎng ge gēge. Wǒ méiyǒu dìdi.

4.   Gāo Lǜshī jīntiān hěn máng. Gāo Lǜshī míngtiān bù máng.

5.   Wǒ dìdi shì lǎoshī. Wǒ shì xuésheng.

6.   Wǒ qǐng tā chīfàn. Tā bù qǐng wǒ chīfàn.

1.   我喜歡張小姐。我不喜歡白小姐。

2.   我認識王老師。我不認識李老師。

3.   我有兩個哥哥。我沒有弟弟。

4. 高律師今天很忙。 高律師明天不忙。

5. 我弟弟是老師。 我是學生。

6. 我請他吃飯。 他不請我吃飯。

E. Affirmative + Negative (A-not-A) Questions

Change the questions below into A-not-A questions.

Example: Nǐ shì xuésheng ma?

→Nǐ shì bu shì xuésheng?

你<u>是</u>學生嗎？

→ 你<u>是 不 是</u>學生？

1. Tā gēge <u>shì</u> yīshēng ma? →

2. Shíyuè wǔ hào <u>shì</u> xīngqīsì ma? →

3. Nǐ <u>qǐng</u> wǒ chī wǎnfàn ma? →

4. Gāo Yīshēng <u>xǐhuan</u> chī Měiguó fàn ma? →

5. Wǒmen jīntiān wǎnshang <u>chī</u> Zhōngguó fàn ma? →

6. Zhāng Lǎoshī jīntiān <u>máng</u> ma? →

7. Wáng Lǜshī <u>rènshì</u> Lǐ Xiǎojie ma? →

8. Xiǎo Bái <u>shì</u> nǐ de tóngxué ma? →

1. 他哥哥<u>是</u>醫生嗎？ →

2. 十月五號<u>是</u>星期四嗎？ →

3. 你<u>請</u>我吃晚飯嗎？ →

4. 高醫生<u>喜歡</u>吃美國飯嗎？ →

5. 我們今天晚上<u>吃</u>中國飯嗎？→

6. 張老師今天<u>忙</u>嗎？→

7. 王律師<u>認識</u>李小姐嗎？→

8. 小白<u>是</u>你的同學嗎？→

F. 還有 (háiyǒu, also; in addition)

Answer the questions using 還有 *and the information in parentheses.*

Example: Nǐ rènshi shéi? (Wáng Péng, Xiǎo Gāo)

→ Wǒ rènshi Wáng Péng, háiyǒu Xiǎo Gāo.

你認識誰？(王朋，小高)

→ 我認識王朋，<u>還有</u>小高。

1.	Nǐ qǐng shéi chīfàn?	(Zhāng Yīshēng, Lǐ Lǎoshī, Bái Lǜshī)
2.	Nǐ xǐhuan chī shénme fàn?	(Měiguó fàn, Zhōngguó fàn)
3.	Shéi qǐng nǐ chīfàn?	(Xiǎo Gāo, Xiǎo Lǐ, Xiǎo Wáng)
4.	Shéi xǐhuan chī Zhōngguó fàn?	(Wǒ bàba, wǒ māma, wǒ dìdi)

1. 你請誰吃飯？   (張醫生、李老師、白律師)

2. 你喜歡吃什麼飯？ (美國飯，中國飯)

3. 誰請你吃飯？   (小高，小李，小王)

4. 誰喜歡吃中國飯？ (我爸爸，我媽媽，我弟弟)

PRONUNCIATION EXERCISES

A. The Initial r

shēngrì	rìjì	rèqíng	rénmín
réngrán	ránhòu	ruìlì	ràngbù

B. Finals

1. **ie**	jiè	xiě	dié	tiě
ue	jué	xué	quē	qiē
2. **uo**	duō	tuō	zuò	cuò
ou	dōu	tóu	zǒu	còu
3. **u**	dū	tū	zū	cū

C. Two-syllable Words

bàngōng	gànhuó	rìjì	xiànzài
dìqū	dìtú	dàxiě	jiǎozhà

D. The Neutral Tone

yí ge	sān ge	zhè ge	nà ge
tā de	shéi de	wǒ de	nǐ de

E. Tone Sandhi [See Sec. D.2 in the Introduction]

zhǎnlǎn	lǚguǎn	yǔsǎn	děngděng
shǒufǎ	yǔnxǔ	xuǎnjǔ	guǎngchǎng

English Texts

DIALOGUE I

(Little Gao is talking to Little Bai.)

Little Gao:	Little Bai, what day is September 12?
Little Bai:	It's a Thursday.
Little Gao:	That (day) is my birthday.
Little Bai:	Really? How old are you this year?
Little Gao:	Eighteen.
Little Bai:	I'll treat you to dinner on Thursday. How's that?
Little Gao:	That would be great. Thank you very much!
Little Bai:	Do you like Chinese food or American food?
Little Gao:	I'm Chinese, but I like American food.
Little Bai:	All right. Let's have American food.

Little Gao:	Thursday at what time?
Little Bai:	How about seven thirty?
Little Gao:	All right. See you Thursday evening.
Little Bai:	See you.

DIALOGUE II

(Wang Peng and Little Bai are talking to each other.)

Wang Peng:	Xiao Bai, what time is it now?
Little Bai:	A quarter to six.
Wang Peng:	I have something to do at a quarter after six.
Little Bai:	Wang Peng, are you busy tomorrow?
Wang Peng:	I'm very busy today, but I won't be tomorrow. What is it?
Little Bai:	I'd like to take you to dinner tomorrow. What do you think?
Wang Peng:	Why are you taking me to dinner?
Little Bai:	Because tomorrow is Little Gao's birthday.
Wang Peng:	Really? Great. (Are you taking) anyone else?
Little Bai:	My classmate Little Li.
Wang Peng:	That's fantastic! I know Little Li, too. At what time?
Little Bai:	Seven thirty tomorrow night.
Wang Peng:	O.K., I'll see you at seven thirty tomorrow.

Can you describe this picture in Chinese?

LESSON 4 ▲ Hobbies

第四課 ▲ 愛好

Dì sì kè ▲ *Aìhào*

你喜歡做什麼？

Nǐ xǐhuan zuò shénme?

Dialogue I: Talking about Hobbies

VOCABULARY

1.	週末	zhōumò	n	weekend
2.	打球	dǎ qiú	vo	to play ball
	打	dǎ	v	to hit; to strike
	球	qiú	n	ball
3.	看	kàn	v	to watch; to look
4.	電視	diànshì	n	TV

	電	diàn	n	electricity
	視	-shì	n	vision
5.	唱歌(兒)	chàng gē(r)	vo	to sing (a song)
	唱	chàng	v	to sing
	歌	gē	n	song
6.	跳#舞	tiào wǔ	vo	to dance
	跳	tiào	v	to jump
	舞	wǔ	n	dance
7.	#聽	tīng	v	to listen
8.	音樂	yīnyuè	n	music
9.	對	duì	adj	right; correct
10.	有時候	yǒu shíhou	ce	sometimes
	時候	shíhou	n	(a point in) time; moment; (a duration of) time
11.	看書	kàn shū	vo	to read books; to read
	書	shū	n	book
12.	電影	diànyǐng	n	movie
	影	yǐng	n	shadow
13.	常常	chángcháng	adv	often
14.	那	nà	conj	in that case; then
15.	去	qù	v	to go
16.	外國	wàiguó	n	foreign country
17.	請客	qǐng kè	vo	to invite someone to dinner; to be the host
18.	昨天	zuótiān	t	yesterday
19.	所以	suǒyǐ	conj	so

DIALOGUE I

(Little Bai is talking to Little Gao.)

Xiǎo Bái: Xiǎo Gāo, nǐ zhōumò[1] xihuan zuò shénme[G1]?

Xiǎo Gāo: Wǒ xǐhuan dǎ qiú, kàn diànshì[2]. Nǐ ne?

Xiǎo Bái: Wǒ xǐhuan chàng gē, tiào wǔ, hái xǐhuan tīng yīnyuè.

Xiǎo Gāo: Nǐ yě xǐhuan kàn shū, duì bu duì?

Xiǎo Bái: Duì, yǒu shíhou yě xǐhuan kàn shū.

Xiǎo Gāo: Nǐ xǐhuan bu xǐhuan[G2] kàn diànyǐng?

Xiǎo Bái: Xǐhuan. Wǒ zhōumò chángcháng kàn diànyǐng.

Xiǎo Gāo: Nà[G3] wǒmen jīntiān wǎnshang qù kàn[G4] yí ge wàiguó
             diànyǐng, zěnmeyàng?

Xiǎo Bái: Hǎo. Jīntiān wǒ qǐngkè.

Xiǎo Gāo: Wèishénme nǐ qǐngkè?

Xiǎo Bái: Yīnwei zuótiān nǐ qǐng wǒ chīfàn, suǒyǐ jīntiān wǒ qǐng nǐ
             kàn diànyǐng.

DIALOGUE I

(Little Bai is talking to Little Gao.)

小白：小高，你週末[1]喜歡做什麼[G1]？

小高：我喜歡打球、看電視[2]。你呢？

小白：我喜歡唱歌、跳舞，還喜歡聽音樂。

小高：你也喜歡看書，對不對？

小白：對，有時候也喜歡看書。

小高：你喜歡不喜歡[G2]看電影？

小白：喜歡。我週末常常看電影。

小高：那[G3]我們今天晚上去看[G4]一個外國
　　　電影，怎麼樣？

小白：好。今天我請客。

小高：為什麼你請客？

小白：因為昨天你請我吃飯，所以今天我
　　　請你看電影。

Name the hobby depicted in each of the pictures above.

Notes

▲**1**▲ The concept of 週末 (zhōumò) has not always been exactly the same in China and Taiwan as it is in the United States. Until the mid-90s, office workers in China and Taiwan had to work on Saturdays and students had to go to class on Saturday mornings.

▲**2**▲ The series comma (、) is very useful in Chinese. When three or more nouns or pronouns occur in a series, this punctuation mark is used to sepa-

▼▼▼▼▼▼▼▼▼▼▼▼▼▼▼▼▼▼▼▼▼▼▼▼▼▼▼▼▼▼▼▼▼▼▼▼

Karaoke.

rate them, while the conjunction 和 (hé) connects the last two items in the series, e.g., 我、你和她 (wǒ, nǐ hé tā; you, she and I); 中國、美國、英國和法國 (Zhōngguó, Měiguó, Yīngguó hé Fǎguó; China, the United States, England and France). The series comma can also be used between two or more verbs, as for example in 我喜歡唱歌、跳舞 (Wǒ xǐhuan chàng gē, tiào wǔ; I like singing and dancing).

Dialogue II: Inviting Someone to Play Ball

VOCABULARY

1.	好久	hǎo jiǔ	ce	a long time
	久	jiǔ	adj	a long time; for a long time
2.	不錯	búcuò	adj	not bad; pretty good
	錯	cuò	adj	wrong
3.	想	xiǎng	av	to want to; to think

▼▼▼▼▼▼▼▼▼▼▼▼▼▼▼▼▼▼▼▼▼▼▼▼▼▼▼▼▼▼▼▼▼▼▼▼▼▼

Can you name this sport in Chinese?

4.	覺得*	juéde	v	to feel/think that...
5.	有意思	yǒuyìsi	adj	interesting
	意思	yìsi	n	meaning
6.	只	zhǐ	adv	only
7.	睡#覺*	shuì jiào	vo	to sleep
	睡	shuì	v	to sleep
8.	算了	suàn le	ce	Forget it. Never mind.
9.	找	zhǎo	v	to look for
10.	別人	biérén	n	others; other people; another person
	別 (的)	bié (de)	adv	other

*Note that the character 覺 is pronounced in two different ways and has two different meanings: jué "to feel," and jiào "to sleep."

Culture Notes

The Chinese are known for their hospitality, which often finds its strongest expression in connection with meals. After a meal at a restaurant Chinese people often compete with

今天誰請客？

Jīntiān shéi qǐngkè?

their friends or relatives to pay the bill, with everyone insisting that it's their treat today: "今天我請客" (Jīntiān wǒ qǐngkè). For further discussion of Chinese food culture, see Culture Notes in Dialogue I of Lesson 12, in Level 1 Part 2.

DIALOGUE II

(Wang Peng is talking to Little Zhang.)

Wáng Péng:	Xiǎo Zhāng, hǎo jiǔ bú jiàn⁽¹⁾, nǐ hǎo ma?
Xiǎo Zhāng:	Wǒ hěn hǎo. Nǐ zěnmeyàng?
Wáng Péng:	Wǒ yě búcuò. Zhège zhōumò nǐ <u>xiǎng</u>^(G5) zuò shénme? Xiǎng bu xiǎng qù dǎ qiú?
Xiǎo Zhāng:	Dǎ qiú? Wǒ bù xǐhuan dǎ qiú.
Wáng Péng:	Nà wǒmen qù kàn diànyǐng, <u>hǎo ma</u>^(G6)?
Xiǎo Zhāng:	Kàn diànyǐng? Wǒ juéde kàn diànyǐng yě méiyǒu yìsi⁽²⁾.
Wáng Péng:	Nà nǐ xǐhuan zuò shénme?
Xiǎo Zhāng:	Wǒ zhǐ xǐhuan chī fàn, shuì jiào.
Wáng Péng:	Nà suàn le^(F). Wǒ qù zhǎo biérén.

DIALOGUE II

(Wang Peng is talking to Little Zhang.)

王朋： 小張，好久不見⁽¹⁾，你好嗎？

小張： 我很好。你怎麼樣？

王朋： 我也不錯。這個週末你想⁽ᴳ⁵⁾做什麼？想不想去打球？

小張： 打球？我不喜歡打球。

王朋： 那我們去看電影，好嗎⁽ᴳ⁶⁾？

小張： 看電影？我覺得看電影也沒有意思⁽²⁾。

王朋： 那你喜歡做什麼？

小張： 我只喜歡吃飯、睡覺。

王朋： 那算了⁽ꟳ⁾。我去找別人。

Note: The ⁽ꟳ⁾ sign indicates an idiomatic expression of which more examples are given below, in "Functional Expressions."

FUNCTIONAL EXPRESSIONS

算了 **(suàn le; forget it, never mind)**

  1. A: 明天我們去打球，怎麼樣？

       (We'll go to play ball tomorrow, how does that sound?)

       Míngtiān wǒmen qù dǎ qiú, zěnmeyàng?

     B: 明天我很忙。 (I'll be busy tomorrow.)

       Míngtiān wǒ hěn máng.

▼▼▼▼▼▼▼▼▼▼▼▼▼▼▼▼▼▼▼▼▼▼▼▼▼▼▼▼▼▼▼▼▼▼▼

A traditional dance of the Uighur people from Xinjiang Province.

A: 那算了。(Oh, then never mind.)

Nà suàn le.

2.　A: 你今年多大了？(How old are you this year?)

Nǐ jīnnián duō dà le?

B: 你為什麼問我多大了？

(Why do you ask how old I am?)

Nǐ wèishénme wèn wǒ duō dà le?

A: 算了，我不問了。(Forget it. I'll ask no more.)

Suàn le, wǒ bú wèn le.

Notes

▲1▲ To English speakers, 好久不見 (hǎo jiǔ bú jiàn) may be vaguely reminiscent of the pidgin English expression, "Long time no see," which is said to have had its origin in a word-for-word translation of the Chinese greeting.

▲2▲ The position of negatives in Chinese is not always the same as their counterparts in English. An English speaker would say: "I *don't* think going to the movies is interesting," but Chinese uses the more logical order of negation, as in "我覺得看電影沒有意思" (Wǒ juéde kàn diànyǐng méiyou yìsi), which literally means, "I think going to the movies is *not* interesting."

SUPPLEMENTARY VOCABULARY

1.	對了	duì le	ce	That's right!
2.	籃球	lánqiú	n	basketball
3.	網球	wǎngqiú	n	tennis
4.	橄欖球	gǎnlǎnqiú	n	American style football (used in Taiwan)
	橄欖	gǎnlǎn	n	olive
5.	美式足球	Měishì zúqiú	n	American style football (used in mainland China)
6.	棒球	bàngqiú	n	baseball
7.	足球	zúqiú	n	soccer
8.	排球	páiqiú	n	volleyball

Grammar

1. Word Order in Chinese

The basic word order in a Chinese sentence is:

Subject + Adverbial + Verb + Object

Subject (agent of the action) + Adverbial (time, place, manner, etc.) + Verb + Object (receiver of the action)

Examples:

	Subject	Adv. of time		Verb	Object
(1)	他	今天		吃	中國飯。
	Tā	jīntiān		chī	Zhōngguó fàn.

(He is eating Chinese food today.)

(2)	我	週末	常常	看	電影。
	Wǒ	zhōumò	chángcháng	kàn	diànyǐng.

(I often watch movies on weekends.)

This is the most common word order in a Chinese sentence. (Also see Grammar Note 3 in Lesson 1.) Of course, varying discourse contexts may affect this norm.

2. Affirmative + Negative Questions (II)

In this type of question there can be no adverbials before the verb other than time words. If there is an adverbial—such as 很 (hěn, very), 都 (dōu, all), or 常常 (chángcháng, often)—before the verb, the 嗎 type question must be used instead.

(1) 你明天去不去？

Nǐ míngtiān qù bu qù?

(Are you going tomorrow?)

(2) 她今天晚上看不看電視？

Tā jīntiān wǎnshang kàn bu kàn diànshì?

(Is she going to watch TV tonight?)

(3) 他們都是學生嗎？

Tāmen dōu shì xuésheng ma?

(Are they all students?)

(3a) *他們都是不是學生？

*Tāmen dōu shì bu shì xuésheng?

(4) 你常常看電影嗎？

Nǐ chángcháng kàn diànyǐng ma?

(Do you often go to the movies?)

(4a) *你常常看不看電影？

*Nǐ chángcháng kàn bu kàn diànyǐng?

(5) 張醫生很忙嗎？

Zhāng Yīshēng hěn máng ma?

(Is Dr. Zhang very busy?)

Having dinner at home.

(5a) *張醫生很忙不忙？

*Zhāng Yīshēng hěn máng bu máng?

3. 那(麼) (nà{me}) as a Cohesive Device

那 (麼) (nà{me}) can function as a cohesive device in a dialogue. In other words, 那 (麼) shows the relationship between a previously-discussed sentence and the current sentence.

For example:

(1) 你今天晚上不想打球，那麼我們去看一個外國電影，怎麼樣？

Nǐ jīntiān wǎnshang bù xiǎng dǎ qiú, nàme wǒmen qù kàn yí ge wàiguó diànyǐng, zěnmeyàng?

(You don't feel like playing ball this evening. Then let's go and see a foreign movie. How does that sound?)

(2) A: 我今天很忙，不想去吃晚飯。

Wǒ jīntiān hěn máng, bù xiǎng qù chī wǎnfàn.

(I'm very busy today. I don't want to go to dinner.)

B: 那明天呢？

Nà míngtiān ne?

(How about tomorrow?)

(3) A: 你喜歡不喜歡吃美國飯？

Nǐ xǐhuan bu xǐhuan chī Měiguó fàn?

(Do you like to eat American food or not?)

B: 不喜歡。

Bù xǐhuan.

(No, I don't.)

C: 那我們吃中國飯，怎麼樣？

Nà wǒmen chī Zhōngguó fàn, zěnmeyàng?

(Then let's eat Chinese food. How's that sound?)

D: 我也不喜歡。

Wǒ yě bù xǐhuan.

(I don't like it either.)

4. 去 (qù, to go) + Verb

To indicate that the performance of an action involves moving away from the speaker, the 去 (qù) + V construction must be used.

For example:

(1) 我們去看電影。

Wǒmen qù kàn diànyǐng.

(We are going to see a movie.)

(2) 晚上我不去跳舞。

Wǎnshang wǒ bú qù tiào wǔ.

(I will not go dancing tonight.)

(3) 今天我想去打球，你去不去？

Jīntiān wǒ xiǎng qù dǎ qiú, nǐ qù bu qù?

(I would like to play ball today. Do you want to go?)

5. The Auxiliary Verb 想 (xiǎng, to want to)

想 (xiǎng) has several meanings. In this lesson it is a modal verb indicating a desire to do something. It must be followed by a verb, a clause or a whole sentence.

For example:

(1) 你想聽音樂嗎？

Nǐ xiǎng tīng yīnyuè ma?

(Would you like to listen to some music?)

(2) 今天白老師想打球，可是王老師不想打。

Jīntiān Bái Lǎoshī xiǎng dǎ qiú, kěshì Wáng Lǎoshī bù xiǎng dǎ.

(Today Teacher Bai felt like playing ball, but Teacher Wang didn't.)

(3) 你想不想看中國電影？

Nǐ xiǎng bu xiǎng kàn Zhōngguó diànyǐng?

(Do you feel like going to see a Chinese movie?)

(4) 你想不想聽外國音樂？

Nǐ xiǎng bu xiǎng tīng wàiguó yīnyuè?

(Do you feel like listening to some foreign music?)

6. Questions with 好嗎 (hǎo ma)

To solicit someone's opinion, we can ask 好嗎 (hǎo ma) after stating an idea or suggestion.

For example:

(1) 我們去看電影，好嗎？

Wǒmen qù kàn diànyǐng, hǎo ma?

(Let's go see a movie, all right?)

▼▼▼▼▼▼▼▼▼▼▼▼▼▼▼▼▼▼▼▼▼▼▼

(2) 我們今天晚上吃中國飯，好嗎？

Wǒmen jīntiān wǎnshang chī Zhōngguó fàn, hǎo ma?

(We'll eat Chinese food tonight, all right?)

Note: In Taiwan 好不好 (hǎo bu hǎo), instead of 好嗎 (hǎo ma), is often used to solicit opinions.

PATTERN DRILLS

A. Subject + Time + Verb + (Object)

1.	Tā dìdi	<u>zhōumò chángcháng</u>	dǎ qiú.
2.	Wáng Péng, Lǐ Yǒu		kàn Zhōngguó diànyǐng.
3.	Gāo Lǎoshī		qǐng xuésheng chī fàn.
4.	Wǒ jiějie		tiào wǔ.
5.	Xiǎo Wáng		kàn diànshì.
6.	Bái Xiǎojie		tīng yīnyuè.

1.	她弟弟	<u>週末常常</u>	打球。
2.	王朋、李友		看中國電影。
3.	高老師		請學生吃飯。
4.	我姐姐		跳舞。
5.	小王		看電視。
6.	白小姐		聽音樂。

B. 去 (qù, to go) + Verb

1.	Wǒmen jīntiān wǎnshang	<u>qù</u>	tiào wǔ.
2.			chàng gē.
3.			dǎ qiú.
4.			kàn wàiguó diànyǐng.

5.   chī Měiguó fàn.

6.   tīng Zhōngguó yīnyuè.

1. 我們今天晚上   去   跳舞。

2.   唱歌。

3.   打球。

4.   看外國電影。

5.   吃美國飯。

6.   聽中國音樂。

c. 因為...所以...(yīnwèi...suǒyǐ..., because...therefore...)

Make sentences using 因為...所以....

1.	Yīnwèi	tā shì Zhōngguórén,	suǒyǐ	tā hěn xǐhuan chī Zhōngguó fàn.
2.		tā hěn máng,		tā bú qù kàn diànyǐng.
3.		tā juéde dǎ qiú méiyǒu yìsi,		tā bù xiǎng qù dǎ qiú.
4.		jīntiān de diànshì méiyǒu yìsi,		tā Txiǎng qù kàn diànyǐng.
5.		tā xiǎng qù tiào wǔ,		tā bú qù kàn diànyǐng.
6.		tā juéde tīng yīnyuè méiyǒu yìsi,		tā bù tīng yīnyuè.

1. 因為 他是中國人，   所以 他很喜歡吃中國飯。

2.   他很忙，   他不去看電影。

3.   他覺得打球沒有意思，   他不想去打球。

4.   今天的電視沒有意思，   他想去看電影。

5.   他想去跳舞，   他不去看電影。

6.   他覺得聽音樂沒有意思，   他不聽音樂。

看電影

Kàn diànyǐng

D. 想 (xiǎng, to want to)

1. Nǐ	<u>xiǎng bu xiǎng</u>	qù dǎ qiú?
2. Tā		chī Zhōngguó fàn?
3. Gāo Yīshēng		qù tiào wǔ?
4. Xiǎo Zhāng de mèimei		tīng yīnyuè?
5. Lǐ Xiǎojie		qù kàn Měiguó diànyǐng?
6. Nǐmen		tīng yīnyuè?
7. Xiǎo Wáng de dìdi		kàn diànshì?

1. 你	<u>想不想</u>	去打球？
2. 他		吃中國飯？
3. 高醫生		去跳舞？
4. 小張的妹妹		聽音樂？
5. 李小姐		去看美國電影？
6. 你們		聽音樂？
7. 小王的弟弟		看電視？

看書

Kàn shū

E. 有意思 (yǒu yìsi, interesting)

1.	Xiǎo Zhāng	<u>juéde</u>	dǎ qiú	<u>hěn yǒu yìsi</u>.
2.	Bái Yīshēng		tiào wǔ	
3.	Zhāng Lǜshī		tīng Zhōngguó yīnyuè	
4.	Lǐ Lǎoshī		kàn wàiguó diànyǐng	
5.	Wáng Xiǎojie		kàn shū	
6.	Xiǎo Gāo de dìdi		kàn diànshì	

1. 小張　　　　覺得　　打球　　　　　　很有意思。

2. 白醫生　　　　　　跳舞

3. 張律師　　　　　　聽中國音樂

4. 李老師　　　　　　看外國電影

5. 王小姐　　　　　　看書

6. 小高的弟弟　　　　看電視

F. 好嗎？(hǎo ma? O.K.?)

1.	Wǒmen	zhège zhōumò	qù	kàn diànyǐng,	hǎo ma?
2.		míngtiān		tiào wǔ,	
3.		xīngqīsì		chàng gē,	
4.		zhège zhōumò		Gāo Lǎoshī jiā,	
5.		xīngqīliù		dǎ qiú,	
6.		xīngqīwǔ		kàn wàiguó diànyǐng,	
7.		jīntiān wǎnshang		tīng yīnyuè,	

1.	我們	這個週末	去	看電影，	好嗎？
2.		明天		跳舞，	
3.		星期四		唱歌，	
4.		這個週末		高老師家，	
5.		星期六		打球，	
6.		星期五		看外國電影，	
7.		今天晚上		聽音樂，	

English Texts

DIALOGUE I

(Little Bai is talking to Little Gao.)

Little Bai: What do you like to do on weekends?

Little Gao: I like to play ball and watch TV. How about you?

Little Bai: I like to sing, dance, and listen to music.

Little Gao: You like to read as well, right?

Little Bai: Yes, sometimes I like to read as well.

Little Gao: Do you like to watch movies?

Little Bai: Yes, I do. I often watch movies on weekends.

Little Gao: Then let's go see a foreign movie this evening. How's that sound?

Little Bai:	Fine. I'll treat today.
Little Gao:	Why is it your treat?
Little Bai:	Because you treated me to dinner yesterday, so today I'm treating you to a movie.

DIALOGUE II

(Wang Peng is talking to Little Zhang.)

Wang Peng:	Little Zhang, long time no see. How are you?
Little Zhang:	Great. How about you?
Wang Peng:	I'm fine, too. What would you like to do this weekend? Would you like to play ball?
Little Zhang:	Play ball? I don't like playing ball.
Wang Peng:	Then let's go see a movie. How's that sound?
Little Zhang:	See a movie? I don't think seeing a movie would be much fun either.
Wang Peng:	Then what do you like to do?
Little Zhang:	I only like to eat and sleep.
Wang Peng:	Then forget it. I'll ask somebody else.

我只喜歡睡覺。

Wǒ zhǐ xǐhuan shuì jiào.

LESSON 5 ▲ Visiting Friends
第五課 ▲ 看朋友
Dì wǔ kè ▲ *Kàn péngyou*

*Xiao Gao introduces Li You and Wang Peng
to his sister, Xiaoyin.*

Dialogue: Visiting a Friend's Home

VOCABULARY

1.	呀	ya	p	(an interjectory particle used to soften a question)
2.	進	jìn	v	to enter
3.	快	kuài	adj/adv	fast; quick; quickly
4.	進來	jìnlai	vc	to come in
5.	來	lái	v	to come
6.	#介#紹	jièshào	v	to introduce

7.	一下	yí xià	m	(a measure word used after a verb indicating short duration) [see G1]
8.	高#興	gāoxìng	adj	happy; pleased
9.	#漂亮	piàoliang	adj	pretty
10.	坐	zuò	v	to sit
11.	在	zài	prep	at; in; on
12.	哪兒	nǎr	qpr	where
13.	工作	gōngzuò	v/n	to work; work; job
14.	學校	xuéxiào	n	school
15.	喝	hē	v	to drink
16.	點(兒)	diǎn(r)	m	a little; a bit; some [see G1]
17.	茶	chá	n	tea
18.	#咖#啡	kāfēi	n	coffee
19.	啤酒	píjiǔ	n	beer
	酒	jiǔ	n	wine; any alcoholic beverage [see Culture Note 3]
20.	吧	ba	p	(a "suggestion" particle; softens the tone of the sentence to which it is appended)
21.	要	yào	v	to want; to have a desire for
22.	杯	bēi	m	cup; glass
23.	可樂	kělè	n	cola
24.	可以	kěyǐ	av	can; may
25.	對不起	duìbuqǐ	ce	I'm sorry.
26.	給	gěi	v	to give
27.	水	shuǐ	n	water

▼▼

Bringing gifts to a friend's house.

DIALOGUE

Xiǎo Gāo:	Shéi ya?(F)
Wáng Péng:	Shì wǒ, Wáng Péng, hái yǒu Lǐ Yǒu.
Xiǎo Gāo:	Qǐng jìn, qǐng jìn! Lǐ Yǒu, kuài jìnlai! Lái, wǒ jièshào <u>yí xià</u>(G1), zhè shì wǒ jiějie, Gāo Xiǎoyīn.
Lǐ Yǒu:	Xiǎoyīn, nǐ hǎo. Rènshi nǐ hěn gāoxìng(1).
Gāo Xiǎoyīn:	Rènshi nǐmen wǒ yě hěn gāoxìng.
Lǐ Yǒu:	Nǐmen jiā hěn <u>dà</u>(G2), yě hěn piàoliang.
Xiǎo Gāo:	Shì ma(2)(F)? Qǐng zuò, qǐng zuò.
Wáng Péng:	Xiǎoyīn, nǐ <u>zài</u> (G3) nǎr gōngzuò?
Gāo Xiǎoyīn:	Wǒ zài xuéxiào gōngzuò. Nǐmen xiǎng hē <u>diǎnr</u>(G1) shénme? Yǒu chá, kāfēi, hái yǒu píjiǔ.
Wáng Péng:	Wǒ hē píjiǔ <u>ba</u>(G4).
Lǐ Yǒu:	Wǒ bù hē jiǔ. Wǒ yào yì bēi kělè, kěyǐ ma?
Gāo Xiǎoyīn:	Duìbuqǐ, wǒmen méiyǒu kělè.
Lǐ Yǒu:	Nà gěi wǒ yì bēi shuǐ ba.

DIALOGUE

小高：　　誰呀？(F)

王朋：　　是我，王朋，還有李友。

小高：　　請進，請進！李友，快進來！來，我介紹一下(G1)，這是我姐姐，高小音。

李友：　　小音，你好。認識你很高興(1)。

高小音：認識你們我也很高興。

李友：　　你們家很大(G2)，也很漂亮。

小高：　　是嗎(2)(F) ？請坐，請坐。

王朋：　　小音，你在(G3)哪兒工作？

高小音：我在學校工作。你們想喝點兒(G1)什麼？有茶、咖啡，還有啤酒。

王朋：　　我喝啤酒吧(G4)。

李友：　　我不喝酒。我要一杯可樂，可以嗎？

高小音：對不起，我們沒有可樂。

李友：　　那給我一杯水吧。

▼▼▼▼▼▼▼▼▼▼▼▼▼▼▼▼▼▼▼▼▼▼▼▼▼▼▼▼▼▼▼▼▼▼▼▼▼

Notes

▲**1**▲ 認識你很高興 (Rènshi nǐ hěn gāoxìng) is a translation of the English "I'm happy to meet you," and may therefore sound rather western to some Chinese speakers. However, the traditional Chinese equivalent polite formulae have now generally become obsolete and this expression is often heard.

▲**2**▲ Although it takes a question mark, 是嗎 (shì ma) is not a question here but a mild expression of one's surprise on hearing something unexpected in a conversation. Here it indicates modest acceptance of a compliment, with the intended implication: "Your compliment has taken me by surprise." It could be translated as "Is that so?" "You don't say!" or "Really?" Another phrase which can be used for the same purpose is 哪裏 (nǎli). The original meaning of 哪裏 (nǎli) is "where?" When paid a compliment, some Chinese people would say, "哪裏" (nǎli) or "哪裏，哪裏" (nǎli, nǎli). In recent times, however, 哪裏 (nǎli) has become somewhat old fashioned.

你們家很大，也很漂亮。

Nǐmen jiā hěn dà, yě hěn piàoliang.

Enjoying refreshments.

FUNCTIONAL EXPRESSIONS

誰呀 (shéi ya? Who is it?)

1.   A: (敲門) (Knocking at the door.)

     (Qiāo mén.)

   B: 誰呀？ (Who is it?)

     Shéi ya?

   A: 是我，李友。 (It's me, Li You.)

     Shì wǒ, Lǐ Yǒu.

   B: 請進。 (Come in, please.)

     Qǐng jìn.

2.   A: (敲門) (Knocking at the door.)

     (Qiāo mén.)

   B: 誰呀？ (Who is it?)

     Shéi ya?

   A: 我，小王。 (It's me, Little Wang.)

     Wǒ, Xiǎo Wáng.

▼▼▼▼▼▼▼▼▼▼▼▼▼▼▼▼▼▼▼▼▼▼▼▼▼▼▼▼▼▼▼▼▼▼▼

礦泉水

Kuàngquánshuǐ

B: 進來。 (Come in.)

Jìn lai.

是嗎 (shì ma? Really?)

1. A: 王朋的女朋友很漂亮。

(Wang Peng's girlfriend is pretty.)

Wáng Péng de nǚpéngyǒu hěn piàoliang.

B: 是嗎？她是學生嗎？

(Really? Is she a student?)

Shì ma? Tā shì xuésheng ma?

2. A: 你的中文老師不是中國人。

(Your Chinese teacher is not Chinese.)

Nǐ de Zhōngwén lǎoshī búshì Zhōngguó rén.

B: 是嗎？他是哪國人？

(Really? What country is he from?)

Shì ma? Tā shì nǎ guó rén?

A: 他是美國人。

(He is American.)

Tā shì Měiguó rén.

Culture Notes

▲**1**▲ Generally speaking, in Chinese culture privacy is a less sacrosanct notion than it is in the West. One would not necessarily be considered an intruder if one drops by a friend's place without any warning. Neither are age, marital status, and salary considered off limits in polite conversation. However, all that is changing—particularly among urbanites.

▲**2**▲ Although tea is the most popular beverage in China, the number of coffee drinkers has been on the rise in recent years, as evidenced by the varieties of coffee on supermarket shelves and the surge of coffee shops, such as Starbucks (星巴克, Xīngbākè), in many Chinese cities.

▲**3**▲ Although usually translated as "wine," 酒 (jiǔ) applies to all kinds of alcoholic beverages. Among the traditional Chinese rice wines and liquors, the most celebrated is 茅台 (Máotái), a strong liquor with a heady aroma.

Narrative: At a Friend's House

VOCABULARY

1.	玩(兒)	wán(r)	v	to have fun; to play
2.	圖書館	túshūguǎn	n	library
3.	#瓶	píng	m	bottle
4.	一起	yìqǐ	adv	together
5.	#聊天 (兒)	liáo tiān(r)	vo	to chat
	#聊	liáo	v	to chat
6.	才	cái	adv	not until, only then
7.	回家	huí jiā	vo	to go home
	回	huí	v	to return

Narrative

Zuótiān wǎnshang, Wáng Péng hé Lǐ Yǒu qù Xiǎo Gāo jiā wánr. Zài Xiǎo Gāo jiā, tāmen rènshile(G5) Xiǎo Gāo de jiějie. Tā jiào Gāo Xiǎoyīn, zài xuéxiào de túshūguǎn gōngzuò. Xiǎo Gāo qǐng Wáng Péng hē(1) píjiǔ, Wáng Péng hēle liǎng píng. Lǐ Yǒu bù hē jiǔ, zhǐ hēle yì bēi shuǐ. Tāmen yìqǐ liáotiānr, kàn diànshì. Wáng Péng hé Lǐ Yǒu wǎnshang shí'èr diǎn cái(G6) huíjiā.

Narrative

昨天晚上，王朋和李友去小高家玩兒。在小高家，他們認識了(G5)小高的姐姐。她叫高小音，在學校的圖書館工作。小高請王朋喝(1)啤酒，王朋喝了兩瓶。李友不喝酒，只喝了一杯水。他們一起聊天兒、看電視。王朋和李友晚上十二點才(G6)回家。

Notes

▲1▲ 喝 (hē) is not always used in the same way as its English equivalent, "to drink." When used intransitively, the English verb often carries the connotation of "drinking alcohol." 喝 (hē), on the other hand, is a transitive verb. Unless it's clear from the context, it always takes an object; in other words, the beverage has to be specified. Therefore, "他常常喝" (Tā chángcháng hē) is a complete sentence only when the beverage has been indicated in the context, e.g.:

A: 他常常喝咖啡嗎？

Tā chángcháng hē kāfēi ma?

(Does he often drink coffee?)

B: 他常常喝。

Tā chángcháng hē.

(He often does.)

她在哪兒工作？

Tā zài nǎr gōngzuò?

SUPPLEMENTARY VOCABULARY

1.	打工	dǎ gōng	vo	to work part-time; to do manual work
2.	好吃	hǎochī	adj	good to eat; delicious
3.	好喝	hǎohē	adj	good to drink; tasty
4.	好看	hǎokàn	adj	good-looking
5.	好玩 (兒)	hǎowán(r)	adj	fun
6.	可口可樂	Kěkǒukělè	n	Coke
7.	百事可樂	Bǎishìkělè	n	Pepsi
8.	雪碧	Xuěbì	n	Sprite
9.	汽水(兒)	qìshuǐ(r)	n	soft drink; soda pop
10.	礦泉水	kuàngquánshuǐ	n	mineral water

▼▼▼

Grammar

1. 一下 (yí xià) and (一) 點兒 ({yì}diǎnr) Moderating the Tone of Voice

Following a verb, both 一下 (yí xià, lit. "once") and (一) 點兒 ({yì }diǎnr, "a bit") can soften a statement. This is similar to a moderated tone of voice in English and is therefore more polite. When used in this way, 一下 (yí xià) modifies the verb, while (一) 點兒 ({yì}diǎnr) modifies the object.

(1) 你看一下，這是誰的照片？

Nǐ kàn yí xià, zhè shì shéi de zhàopiàn?

(Take a look. Whose photo is this?)

(2) 你進來一下。

Nǐ jìnlai yí xià.

(Come in for a minute.)

(3) 你想吃點兒什麼？

Nǐ xiǎng chī diǎnr shénme?

(What would you like to eat?)

(4) 你喝一點兒茶吧。

Nǐ hē yīdiǎnr chá ba.

(Have some tea.)

2. Adjectives Used as Predicates

In Chinese an adjective can be used as a predicate without being preceded by the verb 是 (shì, to be).

(1) 我今天很高興。

Wǒ jīntiān hěn gāoxìng.

(I'm very happy today.)

(2) 他妹妹很漂亮。

Tā mèimei hěn piàoliang.

(His younger sister is very pretty.)

(3)   那個電影很好。

Nàge diànyǐng hěn hǎo.

(That movie is very good.)

(4)   你們學校很大。

Nǐmen xuéxiào hěn dà.

(Your school is very large.)

Note: When an adjective is used as a predicate, it is usually modified by 很 (hěn, very) or some other adverbial modifier. 很 (hěn) is not as strong as its English counterpart "very." In certain contexts Chinese adjectives without some sort of a modifier before them can be inherently comparative.

(5)   A: 姐姐漂亮還是妹妹漂亮？

Jiějie piàoliang háishi mèimei piàoliang?

(Who's prettier, the older sister or the younger sister?)

B: 妹妹漂亮。

Mèimei piàoliang.

(The younger sister is prettier).

(6)   妹妹的中文好，我的中文不好。

Mèimei de Zhōngwén hǎo, wǒ de Zhōngwén bù hǎo.

(My younger sister's Chinese is good. Mine is not.)

3. 在 (zài, at; in; on)

Combined with a noun, the preposition 在 (zài) indicates location. When the phrase is placed before a verb, it indicates the location of the action.

(1)   你在哪兒工作？

Nǐ zài nǎr gōngzuò?

(Where do you work?)

(2)   我在這個學校學中文。

Wǒ zài zhège xuéxiào xué Zhōngwén.

(I study Chinese at this school.)

Chinese green tea.

(3) 我不喜歡在家看電影。

Wǒ bù xǐhuan zài jiā kàn diànyǐng.

(I don't like to watch movies at home.)

4. The Particle of Mood 吧 (ba)

吧 (ba) is often used at the end of an imperative sentence to soften the tone.

(1) 你喝茶吧。

Nǐ hē chá ba.

(Have some tea.)

(2) 請進來吧。

Qǐng jìnlai ba.

(Come in, please.)

5. The Particle 了 (le) (I)

The dynamic particle 了 (le) signifies the occurrence of an action or the emergence of a situation. The action or situation usually pertains to the past, but sometimes it can refer to the future. Therefore the use of 了 (le) should not be taken as an equivalent to the past tense in English. In the current lesson, 了 (le) indicates the occurrence of an action. It can be used after a verb or at the end of a sentence.

(1) 媽媽喝了一杯水。

Māma hēle yì bēi shuǐ.

(Mom had a glass of water.)

(2) 昨天晚上我去小高家玩兒了。

Zuótiān wǎnshang wǒ qù Xiǎo Gāo jiā wánr le.

(Yesterday evening I went to Little Gao's home for a visit.)

(3) 星期一小高請我喝了一杯茶。

Xīngqīyī Xiǎo Gāo qǐng wǒ hēle yì bēi chá.

(On Monday Little Gao invited me out for tea.)

(4) 明天我吃了晚飯去看電影。

Míngtiān wǒ chīle wǎnfàn qù kàn diànyǐng.

(Tomorrow I'll go see a movie after I have eaten dinner.)

Note: There is often a specific time phrase in a sentence with the dynamic particle 了 (le)—such as 昨天晚上 (zuótiān wǎnshang, last night) in example (2), 星期一 (xīngqīyī, Monday) in example (3), and 明天 (míngtiān, tomorrow) in example (4). When 了 (le) is embedded between the verb and the object, the object must be preceded by a modifier. The following numeral + measure word is the most common type of modifier for the object:

一杯 (yì bēi, one cup; one glass) example (1)

一瓶 (yì píng, one bottle) example (3)

If there are other phrases or sentences following the object, then the object does not need a modifier. See example (4) above. Also, if the object following 了 (le) is a proper noun, it does not need a modifier, either:

我昨天看了 "Titanic," 那個電影很好。

Wǒ zuótiān kànle "Titanic." Nàge diànyǐng hěn hǎo.

(I saw *Titanic* yesterday. It was very good.)

Name these drinks in Chinese.

To say that an action did not take place in the past, use 沒 (有) (méi{yǒu}) instead of 不...了 (bù...le) or 沒有...了 (méiyǒu...le) .

For example:

(5) 昨天我沒有聽音樂。

Zuótiān wǒ méiyǒu tīng yīnyuè.

(I didn't listen to the music yesterday.)

(5a) *昨天我不聽音樂了。

Zuótiān wǒ bù tīng yīnyuè le.

(5b) *昨天我沒有聽音樂了。

Zuótiān wǒ méiyǒu tīng yīnyuè le.

Interrogative forms:

(6) A: 你吃了嗎？

Nǐ chīle ma?

(Did you eat?)

B: 我沒吃。

Wǒ méi chī.

(No, I didn't.)

(7) 你吃飯了沒有？

Nǐ chī fànle méiyǒu?

(Have you eaten?)

(8) A: 你喝了幾杯水？

Nǐ hēle jǐ bēi shuǐ?

(How many glasses of water did you drink?)

B: 我喝了一杯水。

Wǒ hēle yì bēi shuǐ.

(I drank one glass of water.)

A note on the phrase 認識了 (rènshile): 認識 (rènshi, to know; to be or become acquainted with) is a verb that usually indicates not an action but a state. Thus 認識了 (rènshile) indicates the beginning of a new state, "to become acquainted with." 了 (le) indicates the occurrence of the transition from "not knowing" to "knowing." Compare:

(9) 我認識高小音。

Wǒ rènshi Gāo Xiǎoyīn.

(I know Gao Xiaoyin.)

(10) 我昨天認識了高小音。

Wǒ zuótiān rènshile Gāo Xiǎoyīn.

(I got acquainted with Gao Xiaoyin yesterday.)

6. The Adverb 才 (cái)

才 (cái) indicates that an action or state occurs later than might have been expected.

(1) 我六點請他吃晚飯，他六點半才來。

Wǒ liù diǎn qǐng tā chī wǎnfàn, tā liù diǎn bàn cái lái.

(I invited him to dinner at six. He didn't come till six thirty.)

(2) 我昨天十二點才回家。

Wǒ zuótiān shí'èr diǎn cái huíjiā.

(I didn't go home yesterday till twelve o'clock.)

(3) 她晚上很晚才睡覺。

Tā wǎnshang hěn wǎn cái shuì jiào.

(She goes to bed very late in the evening.)

▼▼▼▼▼▼▼▼▼▼▼▼▼▼▼▼▼▼▼▼▼▼▼▼▼▼▼▼▼▼▼▼▼▼▼▼

PATTERN DRILLS

A. 一下 (yí xià)

1.	Wǒ kàn	yí xià.
2.	Nǐ jièshào	
3.	Nǐ zuò	
4.	Wǒ tīng	
5.	Nǐ qù	
6.	Nǐ lái	

1. 我看 一下。

2. 你介紹

3. 你坐

4. 我聽

5. 你去

6. 你來

B. Adjectives as Predicates

1.	Xiǎo Gāo de	jiā	hěn	piàoliang.
2.	xuéxiào			dà.
3.	yīshēng			máng.
4.	shū			yǒu yìsi.
5.	jiějie			gāoxìng.
6.	dìdi			gāo.
7.	lǎoshī			hǎo.
8.	tóngxué			hǎo.

1. 小高的 家 很 漂亮。

2. 學校 大。

3. 醫生   忙。

4. 書   有意思。

5. 姐姐   高興。

6. 弟弟   高。

7. 老師   好。

8. 同學   好。

C. 在 (zài)

C1:

1.	<u>Wáng Péng hé Lǐ Yǒu</u> <u>zài</u>	túshūguǎn	kàn shū.
2.		jiā	tīng yīnyuè.
3.		túshūguǎn	gōngzuò.
4.		jiā	kàn diànshì.
5.		Xiǎo Gāo jiā	hē kāfēi.
6.		Wáng Lǎoshī jiā	liáo tiān.
7.		Xiǎo Bái jiā	chī fàn.
8.		xuéxiào	dǎ qiú.

1.	<u>王朋和李友在</u>	圖書館	看書。
2.		家	聽音樂。
3.		圖書館	工作。
4.		家	看電視。
5.		小高家	喝咖啡。
6.		王老師家	聊天。
7.		小白家	吃飯。
8.		學校	打球。

C2: Answer questions with 在.

Example: Xiǎo Gāo zài <u>nǎr</u> gōngzuò? (xuéxiào)

        → Xiǎo Gāo zài <u>xuéxiào</u> gōngzuò.

小高在<u>哪兒</u>工作？(學校)
→小高在<u>學校</u>工作。

1. Zhāng Yīshēng zài nǎr tīng yīnyuè?   (jiā)
2. Xiǎo Wáng zài nǎr dǎ qiú?   (xuéxiào)
3. Xiǎo Gāo de mèimei zài nǎr kàn shū?   (túshūguǎn)
4. Xiǎo Lǐ hé Xiǎo Bái zài nǎr kàn diànyǐng?   (xuéxiào)
5. Wáng Péng hé Lǐ Yǒu zài nǎr liáo tiānr?   (Xiǎo Gāo jiā)
6. Xiǎo Gāo de jiějie zài nǎr gōngzuò?   (túshūguǎn)
7. Xiǎo Zhāng zài nǎr shuìjiào?   (jiā)

1. 張醫生在哪兒聽音樂？   (家)

2. 小王在哪兒打球？   (學校)

3. 小高的妹妹在哪兒看書？   (圖書館)

4. 小李和小白在哪兒看電影？   (學校)

5. 王朋和李友在哪兒聊天兒？   (小高家)

6. 小高的姐姐在哪兒工作？   (圖書館)

7. 小張在哪兒睡覺？   (家)

D. 點兒 (diǎnr)

1. Nǐ	<u>xiǎng</u>	chī	<u>diǎnr</u>	<u>shénme</u>?
2. Xiǎo Bái		tīng		
3. Nǐ		zuò		
4. Zhāng Lǜshī		chī		
5. Lǐ Yīshēng, nín		hē		

1. 你   <u>想</u>   吃   <u>點兒</u>   <u>什麼</u>？

2. 小白   聽

3. 你   做

4. 張律師   吃

5. 李醫生，您   喝

E. 了 (le)

1.	<u>Tā zuótiān wǎnshang</u>	hē	<u>le</u>	sì bēi	shuǐ.
2.		kàn		liǎng ge	diànyǐng.
3.		hē		wǔ bēi	kělè.
4.		hē		liǎng píng	píjiǔ.
5.		hē		liù bēi	chá.
6.		chàng		sān ge	gē.
7.		tiào		yí ge	wǔ.

1. <u>他昨天晚上</u> 喝   <u>了</u>   四杯   水。

2.   看   兩個   電影。

3.   喝   五杯   可樂。

4.   喝   兩瓶   啤酒。

5.   喝   六杯   茶。

6.   唱   三個   歌。

7.   跳   一個   舞。

F. 才 (cái)

1.	<u>Wǒmen</u>	liù diǎn	chī fàn,	<u>tā</u>	liù diǎn bàn	<u>cái lái.</u>
2.		jiǔ diǎn	tiào wǔ,		shí diǎn	
3.		qī diǎn	kàn diànyǐng,		bā diǎn	
4.		bā diǎn bàn	hē kāfēi,		jiǔ diǎn	
5.		qī diǎn	chī wǎnfàn,		qī diǎn bàn	
6.		jiǔ diǎn shí fēn	dǎ qiú,		jiǔ diǎn bàn	
7.		bā diǎn	tīng yīnyuè,		bā diǎn bàn	
8.		liù diǎn shíwǔ fēn	gōngzuò,		liù diǎn bàn	
9.		wǔ diǎn	qù zhǎo Gāo Lǎoshī,		liù diǎn èrshí fēn	

1	<u>我們</u>	六點	吃飯，	<u>他</u> 六點半 <u>才來</u>。
2.		九點	跳舞，	十點
3.		七點	看電影，	八點
4.		八點半	喝咖啡，	九點
5.		七點	吃晚飯，	七點半
6.		九點十分	打球，	九點半
7.		八點	聽音樂，	八點半
8.		六點十五分	工作，	六點半
9.		五點	去找高老師，	六點二十分

Make a story out of the four pictures above.
Don't forget to mention the time in each picture!

English Texts

DIALOGUE

Little Gao:	Who is it?
Wang Peng:	It's me, Wang Peng. Li You is here, too.
Little Gao:	Please come in. Please come in, Li You. Let me introduce you to one another. This is my sister, Gao Xiaoyin.
Li You:	How do you do, Xiaoyin! Pleased to meet you.
Gao Xiaoyin:	Pleased to meet you, too.
Li You:	Your home is very big, and very beautiful, too.
Little Gao:	Really? Sit down, please.
Wang Peng:	Xiaoyin, where do you work?
Gao Xiaoyin:	I work at a school. What would you like to drink? We have tea, coffee, and beer.
Wang Peng:	I'll have a beer.
Li You:	I don't drink. Could I have a glass of cola?
Miss Gao:	I'm sorry. We don't have cola.
Li You:	Then please give me a glass of water.

Describe this scene in detail.

Narrative

Last night Wang Peng and Li You went to Little Gao's home for a visit. At Little Gao's home they met Little Gao's older sister. Her name is Gao Xiaoyin. She works at a school library. Little Gao offered beer to Wang Peng. Wang Peng had two bottles of beer. Li You does not drink. She just had a glass of water. They talked and watched TV together. Wang Peng and Li You did not get home until twelve o'clock.

Use what you have learned so far to describe the picture above.
You may also write a dialogue for the conversation that is underway.

LESSON 6 ▲ Making Appointments
第六課 ▲ 約時間
Dì liù kè ▲ *Yuē shíjiān*

您什麼時候有空？

Nín shénme shíhòu yǒu kòng?

Dialogue I: Calling One's Teacher

VOCABULARY

1.	給	gěi	prep	to; for [see also L.5]
2.	打電話	dǎ diànhuà	vo	to make a phone call
	電話	diànhuà	n	telephone
	話	huà	n	speech; talk; words
3.	# 喂	wèi/wéi	interj	(on telephone) Hello! Hey!
4.	在	zài	v	to be present; to be at (a place)

5.	就	jiù	adv	the very one (indicating verification of someone mentioned before)
6.	哪	nǎ/něi	qpr	which
7.	位	wèi	m	(a polite measure for people)
8.	下午	xiàwǔ	t	afternoon
9.	時間	shíjiān	t	time
10.	幾	jǐ-	nu	some; a few (an indefinite number, usually less than ten)
11.	問題	wèntí	n	question; problem
12.	要	yào	av	will; to be going to
13.	開會	kāi huì	vo	to have a meeting
	開	kāi	v	to hold (a meeting, party, etc.)
14.	上午	shàngwǔ	t	morning
15.	節	jié	m	(a measure word for class period)
16.	課	kè	n	class; lesson
17.	年級	niánjí	n	grade in school
18.	考試	kǎoshì	v/n	to give or take a test; test
	考	kǎo	v	to give or take a test
19.	以後	yǐhòu	t	after
20.	有空(兒)	yǒu kòng(r)	vo	to have free time
21.	要是	yàoshi	conj	if
22.	方便	fāngbiàn	adj	convenient
23.	到…去	dào…qù		to go to (a place)
24.	辦公室	bàngōngshì	n	office
25.	行	xíng	adj	all right; O.K.

26.	沒問題	méi wèntí	ce	no problem
27.	等	děng	v	to wait; to wait for
28.	不客氣	bú kèqi	ce	You are welcome. Don't be (so) polite.
	客氣	kèqi	adj	polite

開會
Kāi huì

DIALOGUE I

(Lǐ Yǒu gěi(G1) *lǎoshī dǎ diànhuà.)*

Lǐ Yǒu: Wèi(F), qǐng wèn, Wáng Lǎoshī zài ma?

Wáng Lǎoshī: Wǒ jiù shì. Nín shì nǎ wèi?

Lǐ Yǒu: Lǎoshī, nín hǎo. Wǒ shì Lǐ Yǒu.

Wáng Lǎoshī: Lǐ Yǒu, nǐ hǎo, yǒu shì ma?

Lǐ Yǒu: Lǎoshī, jīntiān xiàwǔ nín yǒu shíjiān ma? Wǒ xiǎng wèn(1) nín jǐ ge wèntí.

Wáng Lǎoshī: Duìbuqǐ, jīntiān xiàwǔ wǒ yào(G2) kāi huì.

Lǐ Yǒu: Míngtiān ne?

Wáng Lǎoshī: Míngtiān shàngwǔ wǒ yǒu liǎng jié(2) kè, xiàwǔ sān diǎnzhōng yào gěi èr niánjí kǎoshì.

Lǐ Yǒu: Nín shénme shíhou yǒu kòng?

Wáng Lǎoshī: Míngtiān sì diǎn yǐhòu(3) cái yǒu kòng.

Lǐ Yǒu: Yàoshì nín fāngbiàn, sì diǎn bàn wǒ dào nín de bàngōngshì qù, xíng ma?

Wáng Lǎoshī: Sì diǎn bàn, méi wèntí(F). Wǒ zài bàngōngshì děng nǐ.
Lǐ Yǒu: Xièxie(F) nín.
Wáng Lǎoshī: Bú kèqi.

DIALOGUE I

(李友給(G1)老師打電話。)

李友： 喂(F)，請問，王老師在嗎？

王老師： 我就是。您是哪位？

李友： 老師，您好。我是李友。

王老師： 李友，你好，有事嗎？

李友： 老師，今天下午您有時間嗎？我想問(1)您幾個問題。

王老師： 對不起，今天下午我要(G2)開會。

李友： 明天呢？

王老師： 明天上午我有兩節(2)課，下午三點鐘要給二年級考試。

李友： 您什麼時候有空？

王老師： 明天四點以後(3)才有空。

李友： 要是您方便，四點半我到您的辦公室去，行嗎？

王老師： 四點半，沒問題(F)。我在辦公室等你。

李友：　　謝謝(F)您。

王老師：　不客氣。

Notes

▲**1**▲ The verb 問 (wèn, to ask) is not as versatile as its English equivalent "ask," which can be used in two semantic categories only loosely related to each other: making a request and directing a question. Thus we can say "I asked her to dance" as well as "I asked her a question." In Chinese, however, 問 (wèn) is only used in the sense of questioning. To make a request or invitation, 請 (qǐng) is used instead. For the two English sentences above, we have to say in Chinese: "我請她跳舞" (Wǒ qǐng tā tiào wǔ; I ask her to dance) and "我問她一個問題" (Wǒ wèn tā yí ge wèntí; I ask her a question).

▲**2**▲ The term 節 (jié), which literally means "segment," is here a measure word for class periods. It is not used as a measure for courses, for which the measure word is 門 (mén). Compare 三節課 (sān jié kè, three class periods) with 三門課 (sān mén kè, three courses).

▲**3**▲ While 以後 (yǐhòu) is translated as "after," it is positioned differently than in English. In English, we say "after four o'clock." The word "after" appears before the time marker "four o'clock." In the Chinese equivalent, 四點 以後 (sìdiǎn yǐhòu), the word 以後 (yǐhòu) appears after the time marker. Likewise, we say "before Monday" in English, but "星期一以前" (xīngqīyī yǐqián) in Chinese.

Use the information in Dialogue I to tell what's happening in this picture.

Use the information in Dialogue I to tell what's happening in this picture.

Use the information in Dialogue I to tell what's happening in this picture.

FUNCTIONAL EXPRESSIONS

喂 (wèi, hello) [used on the telephone]

1. A: 喂，哪位？ (Hello! May I ask who's calling?)

    Wèi. Nǎ wèi?

    B: 我是王朋。請問，李友在嗎？

    (This is Wang Peng. Is Li You in?)

    Wǒ shì Wáng Péng. Qǐng wèn Lǐ Yǒu zài ma?

    A: 在，你等等，我去叫她。

    (Yes. Just a minute, I'll go get her.)

    Zài, nǐ děngdeng, wǒ qù jiào tā.

2. A: 喂，你找誰？

    (Hello! With whom would you like to speak?)

    Wèi, nǐ zhǎo shéi?

    B: 我找小張。 (I'd like to speak to Little Zhang.)

    Wǒ zhǎo Xiǎo Zhāng.

    A: 我就是。你是誰？ (This is he. Who is this?)

    Wǒ jiù shì. Nǐ shì shéi?

    B: 我是你哥哥。 (This is your older brother.)

    Wǒ shì nǐ gēge.

沒問題 (méi wèntí, no problem)

1. 李友：王朋，你今天晚上幫助我練
    習中文，好嗎？

    (Li You: Wang Peng, would you please help me practice Chinese
      this evening?)

    Lǐ Yǒu: Wáng Péng, nǐ jīntiān wǎnshang bāngzhù wǒ liànxí
       Zhōngwén, hǎo ma?

王朋：沒問題。晚上見。

(Wang Peng: No problem. See you this evening.)

Wáng Péng: Méi wèntí. Wǎnshang jiàn.

2.　A: 你給我介紹一個女朋友，好嗎？

(Can you help find me a girlfriend?)

Nǐ gěi wǒ jièshào yíge nǚpéngyou, hǎo ma?

　　B: 沒問題。 (No problem.)

Méi wèntí.

謝謝！ **(Xièxie! Thanks!)**

1.　A: 小李，你的電話。 (Little Li, your phone call.)

Xiǎo Lǐ, nǐ de diànhuà.

　　B: 謝謝！ (Thanks!)

Xièxie!

　　A: 不客氣。 (You're welcome.)

Bú kèqi.

2.　A: 小李，請喝茶。 (Please have some tea, Little Li.)

Xiǎo Lǐ, qǐng hē chá.

　　B: 多謝！ (Thanks a lot.)

Duō xiè.

　　A: 不謝。 (No need to thank [me].)

Bú xiè.

3.　A: 小李，這是你的可樂。

(Little Li, this is your cola.)

Xiǎo Lǐ, zhèshì nǐde kělè.

　　B: 謝謝！ (Thanks!)

Xièxie.

▼▼▼▼▼▼▼▼▼▼▼▼▼▼▼▼▼▼▼▼▼▼▼▼▼▼▼▼▼▼▼▼▼▼▼▼▼▼

A: 沒事兒。 (No problem.)

Méi shìr.

4.　A: 小李，你的中文書。

(Little Li, your Chinese book.)

Xiǎo Lǐ, nǐde Zhōngwén shū.

B: 謝了。 (Thanks.)

Xiè le.

A: 不用謝。 (No need to thank [me].)

Búyòng xiè.

Use the information in Dialogue I to tell
what's happening in this picture.

Culture Notes

About Chinese phone etiquette: The receiver of the call usually does not identify herself immediately on picking up the phone as some people like to do in the United States. Instead, she would only say "喂" (wèi) and let the caller initiate the conversation.

▼▼▼▼▼▼▼▼▼▼▼▼▼▼▼▼▼▼▼▼▼▼▼▼▼▼▼▼▼▼▼▼▼▼▼▼▼

Dialogue II: Calling a Friend for Help

VOCABULARY

1.	幫忙	bāng máng	vo	to help; to do someone a favor
2.	別客氣	bié kèqi	ce	Don't be so polite!
	別	bié		don't [see G3]
3.	下個星期	xiàge xīngqī	t	next week
	下	xià		below; next
4.	中文	Zhōngwén	n	the Chinese language
	文	wén	n	language; script; written language
5.	幫	bāng	v	to help
6.	#練習	liànxí	v	to practice
7.	說	shuō	v	to say; to speak
8.	啊	a	p	(a sentence-final particle of exclamation, interrogation, etc.)
9.	但是	dànshì	conj	but
10.	得	děi	av	must; to have to
11.	知道	zhīdao	v	to know [see also Note 4 for Dialogue II below]
12.	回來	huílai	vc	to come back

DIALOGUE II

Lǐ Yǒu: Wèi, qǐng wèn, Wáng Péng zài ma?

Wáng Péng: Wǒ jiù shì. Nǐ shì Lǐ Yǒu ba[1]? Yǒu shì ma?

Lǐ Yǒu: Wǒ xiǎng qǐng nǐ bāng máng.

Wáng Péng: <u>Bié</u>[G3] kèqi, yǒu shénme shì?

Lǐ Yǒu:	Wǒ xiàge xīngqī(2) yào kǎo Zhōngwén(3), nǐ bāng wǒ liànxí shuō Zhōngwén, hǎo ma?
Wáng Péng:	Hǎo a, dànshì nǐ <u>děi</u>(G4) qǐng wǒ hē kāfēi.
Lǐ Yǒu:	Hē kāfēi, méi wèntí. Jīntiān wǎnshang nǐ yǒu kòngr ma?
Wáng Péng:	Jīntiān wǎnshang yǒu rén qǐng wǒ chīfàn, bù zhīdao(4) shénme shíhou <u>huílai</u>(G5). Wǒ huílai yǐhòu gěi nǐ dǎ diànhuà ba.
Lǐ Yǒu:	Hǎo ba, wǒ děng nǐ de diànhuà.

DIALOGUE II

李友： 喂，請問，王朋在嗎？

王朋： 我就是。你是李友吧(1)？有事嗎？

李友： 我想請你幫忙。

王朋： <u>別</u>(G3)客氣，有什麼事？

李友： 我下個星期(2)要考中文(3)，你幫我
練習說中文，好嗎？

王朋： 好啊，但是你<u>得</u>(G4)請我喝咖啡。

李友： 喝咖啡，沒問題。今天晚上你有空
兒嗎？

王朋： 今天晚上有人請我吃飯，不知道(4)
什麼時候回<u>來</u>(G5)。我回來以後給你
打電話吧。

李友： 好吧，我等你的電話。

Notes

▲**1**▲ Compare the questions "你是李友吧？" (Nǐ shì Lǐ Yǒu ba?) and "你是李友嗎？" (Nǐ shì Lǐ Yǒu ma?). While in the latter question the speaker does not lean toward either the positive or the negative answer, the use of 吧 (ba) in the former question suggests that the speaker expects a confirmation of his assumption: "I guess you are Li You. Am I right?"

▲**2**▲ The expression 下個星期 (xiàge xīngqī, next week) literally means "the week below." By the same token, 上個星期 (shàngge xīngqī, last week) literally means "the week above." The 個 (gè) in the above expressions can be omitted, e.g., 下個星期 (xiàge xīngqī) and 下星期 (xià xīngqī) both mean "next week." The same formula is used in the expressions for "next month" (下個月, xiàge yuè) and "last month" (上個月, shàngge yuè) as well, but the 個 (gè) is usually kept. To the Chinese people, the elapse of time is perceived as a downward movement. Hence the month that has passed is the one "up" and the month ahead is the one "down." However, for "last year" the term 去年 (qùnián, lit. the gone year) is used, rather than *上年 (*shàngnián). For "next year" the term 明年 (míngnián, lit. bright year) is used, rather than *下年 (*xiànián). Also, for "yesterday" and "tomorrow," 昨天 (zuótiān) and 明天 (míngtiān) are used, instead of *上天 (*shàngtiān) and *下天 (*xiàtiān). For a review of such time expressions, see the tables on page 81 in Lesson 3.

▲**3**▲ The Chinese language is referred to both as 中文 (Zhōngwén) and as 漢語 (Hànyǔ). The latter term refers to the predominant ethnic group in China, the Han. There is also a difference in nuance between 語 (yǔ, speech) and 文 (wén, writing), but 漢語 (Hànyǔ) and 中文 (Zhōngwén) are generally considered synonymous.

▲**4**▲ Although both 知道 (zhīdao) and 認識 (rènshi) translate as "to know," the two terms are not synonymous. 知道 (zhīdao) means "to know (a fact)," while 認識 (rènshi) means "to know, be acquainted with (usually a person) or a written character." The object of 知道 (zhīdao) can sometimes be a person as well, but the meaning is different. The sentence "我知道他" (Wǒ zhīdao tā) suggests knowledge about that person: "I know who he is." It does not indicate personal acquaintance as does the word 認識 (rènshi).

Tell a story based on this picture.

Tell a story based on this picture.

SUPPLEMENTARY VOCABULARY

1.	中午	zhōngwǔ	t	noon
2.	法文	Fǎwén	n	the French language
3.	日文	Rìwén	n	the Japanese language
4.	德文	Déwén	n	the German language
5.	韓國	Hánguó	n	Korea
6.	韓文	Hánwén	n	the Korean language
7.	俄國	Éguó	n	Russia
8.	俄文	Éwén	n	the Russian language
9.	西班牙	Xībānyá	n	Spain
10.	西班牙文	Xībānyáwén	n	the Spanish language
11.	意大利	Yìdàlì	n	Italy
12.	意大利文	Yìdàlìwén	n	the Italian language
13.	葡萄牙	Pútáoyá	n	Portugal
14.	葡萄牙文	Pútáoyáwén	n	the Portuguese language
15.	希臘	Xīlà	n	Greece
16.	希臘文	Xīlàwén	n	the Greek language
17.	拉丁文	Lādīngwén	n	Latin
18.	越南	Yuènán	n	Vietnam
19.	菲律賓	Fēilùbīn	n	the Philippines
20.	泰國	Tàiguó	n	Thailand
21.	馬來西亞	Mǎláixīyà	n	Malaysia
22.	夏威夷	Xiàwēiyí	n	Hawaii

Grammar

1. The Preposition 給 (gěi)

給 (gěi) can be a verb or a preposition. In Chinese, prepositions are generally combined with nouns or pronouns to form prepositional phrases, which appear before verbs as adverbials.

(1) 他給我打了一個電話。

Tā gěi wǒ dǎle yí gè diànhuà.

(He gave me a call.)

(2) 他是誰？請你給我們介紹一下。

Tā shì shéi? Qǐng nǐ gěi wǒmen jièshào yí xià.

(Who is he? Please introduce us.)

(3) 你有你姐姐的照片嗎？給我看一下，行嗎？

Nǐ yǒu nǐ jiějie de zhàopiàn ma? Gěi wǒ kàn yí xià, xíng ma?

(Do you have a picture of your older sister? Can you let me have a look?)

2. The Auxiliary Verb 要 (yào, will; be going to) (I)
[See also L.9 G1]

The auxiliary verb 要 (yào) has several meanings. In this lesson, 要 (yào) indicates a future action.

(1) 明天我要去小白家玩。

Míngtiān wǒ yào qù Xiǎo Bái jiā wán.

(Tomorrow I'm going to visit Little Bai.)

(2) 今天晚上妹妹要去看電影。

Jīntiān wǎnshang mèimei yào qù kàn diànyǐng.

(This evening my younger sister is going to see a movie.)

(3) 下午我們要開會。

Xiàwǔ wǒmen yào kāi huì.

(This afternoon we are going to have a meeting.)

A public phone in Taiwan.

3. 別 (bié, don't)

別 (bié, don't) is used to advise someone to refrain from doing something.

(1) **你別說！**

Nǐ bié shuō!

(Don't tell.)

(2) **別進來！**

Bié jìnlai!

(Don't come in.)

(3) **那個電影沒有意思，你別看。**

Nàge diànyǐng méiyǒu yìsi, nǐ bié kàn.

(That movie is boring. Don't go see it.)

An office building at a college.

4. The Auxiliary Verb 得 (děi, must)

The modal verb 得 (děi) means "need" or "must."

(1) 老師三點鐘給你打了一個電話，你
得給老師回個電話。

Lǎoshī sān diǎnzhōng gěi nǐ dǎle yí ge diànhuà, nǐ děi gěi
lǎoshī huí ge diànhuà.

(The teacher called you at three o'clock. You'd better call him
back.)

(2) 我有事，得去學校。

Wǒ yǒu shì, děi qù xuéxiào.

(I've some business [to attend to]. I must go to the school.)

Note: The negative form of 得 (děi, must) is 不用 (bú yòng, need not) or
不必 (bú bì, need not), not 不得 (bù děi). Therefore, the correct way to say
"You don't have to go to the school" in Chinese is A, and not B, below.

Did she hear 進來 (jìnlai) or 進去 (jìnqu) when she knocked at the door?

A. 你不用去學校。 (Nǐ bú yòng qù xuéxiào.)

or 你不必去學校。 (Nǐ bú bì qù xuéxiào.)

B. *你不得去學校。 (*Nǐ bù děi qù xuéxiào.)

5. Directional Complements (I)

來/去 (lái/qù, to come/go) can serve as a directional complement after such verbs as 進 (jìn, to enter) and 回 (huí, to return). 來 (lái, to come) signifies movement toward the speaker. 去 (qù, to go) signifies movement away from the speaker.

(1)   [**A** is at home on the phone.]

A: 你什麼時候回來？

Nǐ shénme shíhou huílai?

(When are you coming home?)

B: 我六點回去。

Wǒ liù diǎn huíqu.

(I'm going back home at six.)

(2)   [**A** is outside, and **B** is inside. **A** knocks on the door.]

進來。

Jìnlai. (Come in.)

(3)   [Both **A** and **B** are outside. **A** tells **B** to go inside.]

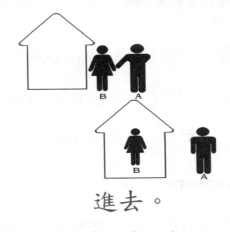

進去。

Jìnqu. (Go in.)

PATTERN DRILLS

A. 給 (gěi) as a Preposition

1.	Wǒ	<u>gěi nǐmen</u>	jièshào yí xià.
2.	Lǐ Lǎoshī		kàn tā de shū.
3.	Xiǎo Gāo		kàn tā bàba māma de zhàopiàn.
4.	Xiǎo Wáng		tīng Zhōngguó yīnyuè.
5.	Tā		jièshào yí ge péngyou.
6.	Gāo Xiǎoyīn		hē Zhōngguó chá.

▼▼▼▼▼▼▼▼▼▼▼▼▼▼▼▼▼▼▼▼▼▼▼▼▼▼▼▼▼▼▼▼▼▼▼▼▼

1. 我　　　　　　<u>給你們</u>　　介紹一下。

2. 李老師　　　　　　　　看她的書。

3. 小高　　　　　　　　　看他爸爸媽媽的照片。

4. 小王　　　　　　　　　聽中國音樂。

5. 她　　　　　　　　　　介紹一個朋友。

6. 高小音　　　　　　　　喝中國茶。

B. 要 (yào) Indicating a Future Action

1. Míngtiān　　　　　　<u>wǒ yào</u>　　qù tiào wǔ.

2. Zhège zhōumò　　　　　　　qù zhǎo Gāo Xiǎoyīn.

3. Jīntiān wǎnshang　　　　　　qǐng Wáng Péng hē kāfēi.

4. Míngtiān xiàwǔ　　　　　　qù Lǐ Lǎoshī de bàngōngshì.

5. Jīntiān xiàwǔ　　　　　　wèn Xiǎo Bái yí ge wèntí.

6. Míngtiān wǎnshang　　　　qù Xiǎo Zhāng de xuéxiào kàn diànyǐng.

7. Míngtiān shàngwǔ　　　　qù Xiǎo Gāo jiā liànxí Zhōngwén.

8. Zhège zhōumò　　　　　gěi Wáng Lǎoshī dǎ diànhuà.

9. Zhège zhōumò　　　　　gěi Xiǎo Gāo jièshào yí ge péngyou.

1. 明天　　　　　　<u>我要</u>　　去跳舞。

2. 這個週末　　　　　　　去找高小音。

3. 今天晚上　　　　　　　請王朋喝咖啡。

4. 明天下午　　　　　　　去李老師的辦公室。

5. 今天下午　　　　　　　問小白一個問題。

6. 明天晚上　　　　　　　去小張的學校看電影。

7. 明天上午　　　　　　　去小高家練習中文。

8. 這個週末　　　　　　　給王老師打電話。

9. 這個週末　　　　　　　給小高介紹一個朋友。

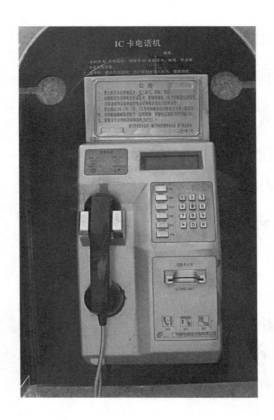

A public phone in China.

C. 要是 (yàoshi, if)

1. <u>Yàoshi</u>	nǐ jīntiān méiyǒu kòngr, míngtiān	<u>zěnmeyàng</u>?
2.	nǐ bù xiǎng kàn diànshì, wǒmen tīng yīnyuè,	
3.	nǐ juéde dǎ qiú méiyǒu yìsi, wǒmen qù kàn diànyǐng,	
4.	nǐ bù xǐhuan tiào wǔ, wǒmen liáo tiānr,	
5.	jīntiān bù fāngbiàn, míngtiān,	
6.	bù xǐhuan hē chá, wǒmen hē píjiǔ,	
7.	nǐ jīntiān qǐng wǒ hē kāfēi, wǒ míngtiān qǐng nǐ kàn diànyǐng,	
8.	nǐ xiǎng wèn wǒ wèntí, xiàwǔ lái wǒ de bàngōngshì,	

1. <u>要是</u> 你今天沒有空兒，明天　　　　　　　　<u>怎麼樣</u>？

2. 你不想看電視，我們聽音樂，

3. 你覺得打球沒有意思，我們去看電影，

4. 你不喜歡跳舞，我們聊天兒，

5. 今天不方便，明天

6. 不喜歡喝茶，我們喝啤酒，

7. 你今天請我喝咖啡，我明天請你看電影，

8. 你想問我問題，下午來我的辦公室，

D. 別 (bié, don't) and 得 (děi, must)

1.	<u>Nǐ bié</u>	dǎ qiú,	<u>nǐ děi</u>	kàn shū.
2.		hē chá,		shuì jiào.
3.		kàn diànshì,		gěi Wáng Lǎoshī dǎ diànhuà.
4.		shuì jiào,		kàn shū.
5.		liáo tiān,		qù kāi huì.
6.		hē píjiǔ,		kǎo shì.
7.		chī fàn,		dǎ qiú.
8.		qù Xiǎo Gāo jiā,		zài jiā děng nǐ bàba māma de diànhuà.
9.		liáo tiānr,		liànxí Zhōngwén.

1. <u>你別</u>　打球，　<u>你得</u>　看書。

2. 　喝茶，　睡覺。

3. 　看電視，　給王老師打電話。

4. 　睡覺，　看書。

5. 　聊天，　去開會。

6. 　喝啤酒，　考試。

7. 　吃飯，　打球。

8. 　去小高家，　在家等你爸爸媽媽的電話。

9. 　聊天兒，　練習中文。

Using a 手機 (shǒujī), cellular phone.

E. 得 (děi, have to, must)

1.	Jīntiān	<u>wǒ děi</u>	qù zhǎo Wáng Lǎoshī.
2.	Jīntiān wǎnshang		qù Xiǎo Gāo jiā liànxí Zhōngwén.
3.	Zhège zhōumò		qù túshūguǎn kàn shū.
4.	Jīntiān xiàwǔ		qù xuéxiào kāi huì.
5.	Míngtiān wǎnshang		qù Xiǎo Bái jiā chī wǎnfàn.
6.	Míngtiān shàngwǔ		qù Wáng Lǎoshī de bàngōngshì.
7.	Míngtiān xiàwǔ		hé Wáng Péng liànxí Zhōngwén.
8.	Míngtiān wǎnshang		qù xuéxiào liànxí chàng gē.
9.	Jīntiān wǎnshang		zài jiā liànxí tiào wǔ.

1. 今天　　　　　我得　　去找王老師。

2. 今天晚上　　　　　　去小高家練習中文。

3. 這個週末　　　　　　去圖書館看書。

4. 今天下午　　　　　　去學校開會。

5. 明天晚上　　　　　　去小白家吃晚飯。

6. 明天上午　　　　　去王老師的辦公室。

7. 明天下午　　　　　和王朋練習中文。

8. 明天晚上　　　　　去學校練習唱歌。

9. 今天晚上　　　　　在家練習跳舞。

English Texts

DIALOGUE I

(Li You is on the phone with her teacher.)

Li You:　　　　Hello, is Teacher Wang in?

Teacher Wang:　This is he. Who's this, please?

Li You:　　　　Teacher, how are you? This is Li You.

Teacher Wang:　Li You, how are you? What can I do for you?

Li You:　　　　Teacher, are you free this afternoon? I'd like to ask you a few questions.

Teacher Wang:　I'm sorry. This afternoon I have to go to a meeting.

Li You:　　　　What about tomorrow?

Teacher Wang:　Tomorrow morning I have two classes. Tomorrow afternoon at three o'clock I have to give an exam to the second-year class.

Li You:　　　　When will you be free?

Teacher Wang:　I won't be free until after four o'clock tomorrow.

Li You:　　　　If it's convenient for you, I'll go to your office at four thirty. Is that all right?

Teacher Wang:　Four thirty? No problem. I'll wait for you in my office.

Li You:　　　　Thank you.

Teacher Wang:　You're welcome.

DIALOGUE II

(Li You and Wang Peng are talking on the phone.)

Li You:　　　　Hello, is Wang Peng there?

Wang Peng:　　This is he. Is this Li You? What's up?

Li You:　　　　I'd like to ask you a favor.

Wang Peng:	Don't be so polite. What is it?
Li You:	Next week I have a Chinese exam. Could you help me practice speaking Chinese?
Wang Peng:	Sure, but you must invite me to drink some coffee.
Li You:	Invite you to drink some coffee? No problem. Are you free this evening?
Wang Peng:	This evening someone is taking me to dinner. I don't know when I'll be back. Why don't I call you after I get back?
Li You:	O.K. I'll wait for your call.

LESSON 7 ▲ Studying Chinese
第七課 ▲ 學中文
Dì qī kè ▲ Xué Zhōngwén

我中國字寫得太慢！

Wǒ Zhōngguó zì xiě de tài màn!

Dialogue I: Asking about an Examination

VOCABULARY

1. 跟	gēn	conj	and
2. 說話	shuō huà	vo	to talk
3. 上個星期	shàngge xīngqī	t	last week [see Note 2 for Dialogue 2 in L.6]
4. 得	de	p	(a structural particle) [see G1]
5. 幫助	bāngzhù	v	to help
6. #復習	fùxí	v	to review

7.	字	zì	n	character
8.	寫	xiě	v	to write
9.	慢	màn	adj	slow
10.	教	jiāo	v	to teach
11.	怎麼	zěnme	qpr	how
12.	就	jiù	adv	(indicates that something takes place sooner than expected)
13.	學	xué	v	to study
14.	筆	bǐ	n	pen
15.	難	nán	adj	difficult
16.	快	kuài	adj	quick; fast
17.	哪裏	nǎli	ce	You flatter me. Not at all. (a polite reply to a compliment) [also see Note 2 for the Dialogue in L.5]
18.	第	dì	prefix	(a prefix for ordinal numbers)
19.	#預習	yùxí	v	to preview
20.	語法	yǔfǎ	n	grammar
21.	容易	róngyì	adj	easy
22.	多	duō	adj	many; much
23.	懂	dǒng	v	to understand
24.	生詞	shēngcí	n	new words
25.	漢字	Hànzì	n	Chinese character
26.	有一點兒	yǒu yìdiǎnr	ce	a little; somewhat [also see G5]
27.	不謝	bú xiè	ce	Don't mention it. Not at all. You're welcome.

DIALOGUE I

(Wáng Péng gēn Lǐ Yǒu shuōhuà.)

Wáng Péng: Lǐ Yǒu, nǐ shàngge xīngqī kǎoshì kǎo <u>de</u>(G1) zěnmeyàng?

Lǐ Yǒu: Kǎo de búcuò, yīnwèi nǐ bāngzhù(1) wǒ fùxí, suǒyǐ kǎo de búcuò. Dànshì lǎoshī shuō wǒ Zhōngguó zì xiě de <u>tài</u>(G2) màn!

Wáng Péng: Shì ma? Yǐhòu wǒ gēn nǐ yìqǐ liànxí xiě zì, jiāo nǐ zěnme xiě, hǎo bu hǎo(2)?

Lǐ Yǒu: Nà tài hǎo le! Wǒmen xiànzài <u>jiù</u>(G3) xiě. Gěi nǐ bǐ.

Wáng Péng: Hǎo, wǒ jiāo nǐ xiě "nán" zì.

Lǐ Yǒu: Nǐ xiě zì xiě de hěn hǎo, yě hěn kuài.

Wáng Péng: Nǎli, nǎli(F). Nǐ míngtiān yǒu Zhōngwén kè ma?

Lǐ Yǒu: Yǒu, míngtiān wǒmen xué <u>dì qī</u>(G4) kè.

Wáng Péng: Nǐ yùxí le ma?

Lǐ Yǒu: Yùxí le. Dì qī kè de yǔfǎ hěn róngyì, wǒ dōu dǒng, kěshì shēngcí tài duō, hànzì yě <u>yǒu yìdiǎnr</u>(G5) nán.

Wáng Péng: Jīntiān wǎnshang wǒ gēn nǐ yìqǐ liànxí ba.

Lǐ Yǒu: Hǎo, xièxie nǐ.

Wáng Péng: Bú xiè, wǎnshang jiàn.

DIALOGUE I

(王朋跟李友說話。)

王朋： 李友，你上個星期考試考<u>得</u>(G1)怎麼樣？

李友： 考得不錯，因為你幫助(1)我復習，所以考得不錯。但是老師說我中國字寫得<u>太</u>(G2)慢！

王朋： 是嗎？以後我跟你一起練習寫字，教你怎麼寫，好不好(2)？

李友： 那太好了！我們現在就(G3)寫。給你
　　　　筆。

王朋： 好，我教你寫"難"字。

李友： 你寫字寫得很好，也很快。

王朋： 哪裏，哪裏(F)。你明天有中文課
　　　　嗎？

李友： 有，明天我們學第七(G4)課。

王朋： 你預習了嗎？

李友： 預習了。第七課的語法很容易，我
　　　　都懂，可是生詞太多，漢字也有一
　　　　點兒(G5)難。

王朋： 今天晚上我跟你一起練習吧。

李友： 好，謝謝你。

王朋： 不謝，晚上見。

Notes

▲**1**▲ 幫助 (bāngzhù), like 幫 (bāng), takes an object. 幫忙 (bāng máng) does not. Therefore, we say "他幫我練習中文 (Tā bāng wǒ liànxí Zhōngwén)" or "他幫助我練習中文 (Tā bāngzhù wǒ liànxí Zhōngwén)." We don't say "*他幫忙我練習中文 (*Tā bāng máng wǒ liànxí Zhōngwén)." Remember that 幫忙 (bāng máng) is a verb + object compound. It already has an object built into it.

▲**2**▲ The expression 好不好 (hǎo bu hǎo), like 行嗎 (xíng ma), means "Is it O.K.?" They are both used to seek approval.

Based on Dialogue I, tell what's happening in this picture.

FUNCTIONAL EXPRESSIONS

哪裏，哪裏 (nǎli, nǎli; You flatter me.)

1. A: 你今天很漂亮。 (You are very pretty today.)

    Nǐ jīntiān hěn piàoliang.

    B: 哪裏，哪裏。 (You flatter me.)

    Nǎli, nǎli.

2. A: 你寫漢字寫得很漂亮。

    (You write Chinese characters beautifully.)

    Nǐ xiě Hànzì xiě de hěn piàoliang.

    B: 哪裏，哪裏。 (You flatter me.)

    Nǎli, nǎli.

Simplified and Traditional Characters

In the 1950s, as part of the campaign to raise the nation's literacy rate, the government of the People's Republic of China set out to simplify some of the more complex characters, or 漢字 (Hànzì). That accounts for the bifurcation of 簡體字 (jiǎntǐzì, simplified

考 試

Kǎo shì

characters) and 繁體字 (fántǐzì, traditional characters, or, literally, complex charac-ters). Currently, simplified characters are used in Mainland China and Singapore. However, people in Taiwan, Hong Kong, and most Chinese diasporas still write traditional characters. Most of the simplified characters were actually not new inventions. They had been used at different times in China's long history, and a few of them even have a longer history than their *fantizi* counterparts. The additional burden on Chinese learners caused by this bifur-cation is actually not as onerous as it may appear. After all, most of the characters were not affected.

Direction of Chinese Script

Traditionally, the Chinese wrote vertically from top to bottom, and from right to left. Now almost everyone in China writes horizontally from left to right. But the traditional way of writing is still kept alive in calligraphy.

Chinese Writing Brushes

For many centuries the Chinese wrote with a 毛筆 (máobǐ), or "writing brush," as it is called in English. But nowadays people have switched to more convenient Western-style writing instruments such as the 鉛筆 (qiānbǐ, pencil), the 鋼筆 (gāngbǐ, foun-tain pen), and the 圓珠筆 (yuánzhūbǐ, ballpoint pen), which is also known in Taiwan

Name these writing instruments.

as 原子筆 (yuánzǐbǐ). The traditional 毛筆 (máobǐ) is now used almost exclusively in calligraphy.

Complex vs. Simplified: *Examples*

問	學	幾	號	話	寫	難	筆	電	聽
问	学	几	号	话	写	难	笔	电	听

Dialogue II: Preparing for a Chinese Class

VOCABULARY

1.	平常	píngcháng	adv	usually
2.	早	zǎo	adj	early
3.	怎麼	zěnme	qpr	how come (used to inquire about the cause of something, implying a degree of surprise or disapproval)
4.	這麼	zhème	pr	so; such
5.	半夜	bànyè	t	midnight
	夜	yè	n	night
6.	功課	gōngkè	n	schoolwork; homework

7.	朋友	péngyou	n	friend
8.	真	zhēn	adv	really
9.	大家	dàjiā	pr	everybody
10.	早	zǎo		Good morning!
11.	開始	kāishǐ	v	to start
12.	上課	shàng kè	vo	to go to class; to start a class
13.	念	niàn	v	to read aloud
14.	課文	kèwén	n	text of a lesson
15.	#錄音	lùyīn/lù yīn	n/vo	sound recording; to record
16.	男的	nán de		male
17.	#帥	shuài	adj	handsome

DIALOGUE II

(Lǐ Yǒu gēn Xiǎo Bái shuō huà.)

Lǐ Yǒu: Xiǎo Bái, nǐ píngcháng lái de hěn zǎo, jīntiān <u>zěnme</u>(G6) lái de zhème wǎn?

Xiǎo Bái: Wǒ zuótiān yùxí Zhōngwén, bànyè yì diǎn <u>cái</u>(G3) shuì jiào, nǐ yě shuì de hěn wǎn ma?

Lǐ Yǒu: Wǒ zuótiān shí diǎn <u>jiù</u>(G3) shuì le. Yīnwèi Wáng Péng bāng wǒ liànxí Zhōngwén, suǒyǐ wǒ gōngkè zuò de hěn kuài.

Xiǎo Bái: Yǒu ge Zhōngguó péngyou <u>zhēn</u>(G2) hǎo.

(Shàng Zhōngwén kè.)

Lǎoshī: Dàjiā zǎo(1), xiànzài wǒmen kāishǐ shàng kè. Dì qī kè nǐmen dōu yùxí le ma?

Xuésheng: Yùxí le.

Lǎoshī: Lǐ Yǒu, qǐng nǐ niàn kèwén….Nǐ niàn de hěn hǎo. Nǐ zuótiān wǎnshang tīng lùyīn le ba?

Lǐ Yǒu:	Wǒ méi tīng.
Xiǎo Bái:	Dànshì tā de péngyou chángcháng bāngzhù tā.
Lǎoshī:	Nǐ de péngyou shì Zhōngguórén ma?
Lǐ Yǒu:	Shì de.
Xiǎo Bái:	<u>Tā shì yí ge nán de</u>(2), <u>hěn shuài</u>(3), <u>jiào Wáng Péng</u>(G7).

DIALOGUE II

（李友跟小白說話。）

李友： 小白，你平常來得很早，今天<u>怎麼</u>
(G6)來得這麼晚？

小白： 我昨天預習中文，半夜一點<u>才</u>(G3)睡
覺，你也睡得很晚嗎？

李友： 我昨天十點<u>就</u>(G3)睡了。因為王朋
幫我練習中文，所以我功課做得很
快。

小白： 有個中國朋友<u>真</u>(G2)好。

（上中文課。）

老師： 大家早(1)，現在我們開始上課。<u>第
七</u>(G4)課你們都預習了嗎？

學生： 預習了。

老師： 李友，請你念課文。...你念得很
好。你昨天晚上聽錄音了吧？

李友： 我沒聽。

小白： 但是她的朋友常常幫助她。

老師： 你的朋友是中國人嗎？

李友： 是的。

小白： <u>他是一個男的</u>(2)，<u>很帥</u>(3)，<u>叫王</u>
<u>朋</u>(G7)。

Notes

▲**1**▲ 早 (Zǎo! Good morning!), and the more formal 早安 (Zǎo ān! Good morning!) may strike some people in mainland China as rather Western, but these greetings are gradually gaining acceptance among young and educated people.

▲**2**▲ If the referent is obvious from the context, the noun following the particle 的 (de) can often be omitted, as in the sentence: 他是一個男的 (Tā shì yí ge nán de). It is understood from the context that 男的 (nán de, male) refers to 朋友 (péngyou, friend). The word 朋友 is left out. Another example: 我寫了十個字，五個難的，五個容易的。 (Wǒ xiěle shí ge zì, wǔ ge nán de, wǔ ge róngyì de; I wrote ten characters, five difficult ones and five easy ones). See Lesson 9, Grammar Note 3.

▲**3**▲ 帥 (shuài) is used to describe a handsome—usually young—man. To describe an attractive girl one uses the word 漂亮 (piàoliang, pretty). The term 好看 (hǎokàn, good looking), is gender neutral, and can be used for either sex.

What is Little Bai telling Li You?   *What is Li You telling Little Bai?*

What is Li You doing?

What is Little Bai trying to tell the teacher?

SUPPLEMENTARY VOCABULARY

1. 鉛筆	qiānbǐ	n	pencil
2. 鋼筆	gāngbǐ	n	fountain pen
3. 毛筆	máobǐ	n	writing brush
4. 紙	zhǐ	n	paper
5. 本子	běnzi	n	notebook
6. 午覺	wǔjiào	n	nap

Grammar

1. Descriptive Complements (I)

The particle 得 (de) can be used after a verb or an adjective. This lesson mainly deals with 得 (de) as it appears after a verb. What follows 得 (de) in the construction introduced in this lesson is called a descriptive complement, which can be an adjective, an adverb, or a verb phrase. In this lesson, the words that function as descriptive complements are all adjectives. These complements serve as comments on the actions expressed by the verbs that precede 得 (de).

(1)   他寫字寫得很好。

　　　 Tā xiě zì xiě de hěn hǎo.

　　　 (He writes characters well.)

[很好 (hěn hǎo, very well) is a comment on the action 寫 (xiě, to write).]

(2)   他昨天睡覺睡得很晚。

　　　 Tā zuótiān shuì jiào shuì de hěn wǎn.

　　　 (He went to bed late last night.)

[很晚 (hěn wǎn, very late) is a comment on the action 睡覺 (shuì jiào, to sleep).]

(3)   妹妹歌唱得很好。

　　　 Mèimei gē chàng de hěn hǎo.

　　　 (My younger sister sings beautifully.)

[很好 (hěn hǎo, very well) is a comment on the action 唱 (chàng, to sing).]

If the complement is an adjective, it is usually preceded by 很 (hěn, very), as is the case when an adjective is used as a predicate. If the verb is followed by an object, the verb has to be repeated before it can be followed by the "得 (de) + Complement" structure, e.g., 寫字寫得 (xiě zì xiě de) in (1). By repeating the verb, the "verb + object" combination preceding it becomes a "topic" and the complement that follows serves as a comment on it. The first verb can be omitted if the meaning is clear from the context. See (3).

2. 太 (tài, too) and 真 (zhēn, really)

When the adverbs 太 (tài, too) and (zhēn, really) are used in exclamatory sentences, they convey in most cases not new factual information but the speaker's approval, disapproval, or other emotional reaction. If the speaker wants to make a more "objective" statement or description, other intensifiers such as 很 (hěn, very), or 特別 (tèbié, especially) are often used in place of 太 (tài, too) or (zhēn, really).

(1)   A: 他寫字寫得怎麼樣？

      Tā xiě zì xiě de zěnmeyàng?

      (How well does he write characters?)

One would normally answer:

      B: 他寫字寫得很好。

      Tā xiě zì xiě de hěn hǎo.

      (He writes characters very well.)

Compare "B" with "C" below:

      C: 小張: 小李，你寫字寫得真好！你可以幫助我嗎？

      Xiǎo Zhāng: Xiǎo Lǐ, nǐ xiě zì xiě de zhēn hǎo! Nǐ kěyǐ bāngzhù wǒ ma?

      (Xiao Zhang: Xiao Li, you write characters really well! Could you help me?)

When 太 (tài, too) is used in an exclamatory sentence, 了 (le) usually appears at the end of the sentence:

(2)   這本書太有意思了！

      Zhè běn shū tài yǒu yìsi le!

      (This book is really interesting!)

(3)   我的語法太不好了！我得多練習。

      Wǒ de yǔfǎ tài bù hǎo le! Wǒ děi duō liànxí.

      (My grammar is indeed awful! I have to practice more.)

Can you describe this photo in Chinese?

(4)   你跳舞跳得太好了。

   Nǐ tiào wǔ tiào de tài hǎo le!

   (You really dance beautifully!)

3. The Adverb 就 (jiù) (I)

The adverb 就 (jiù) is used before a verb to suggest the earliness, briefness, or quickness of the action.

(1)   他明天早上八點就得上課。

   Tā míngtiān zǎoshang bā diǎn jiù děi shàng kè.

   (He has to go to class [as early as] at 8 o'clock tomorrow morning.)

(2)   他昨天就來了。

   Tā zuótiān jiù lái le.

   (He came [as early as] yesterday.)

就 (jiù) and 才 (cái) Compared [See also L.5 G6]

The adverb 就 (jiù) suggests the earliness or promptness of an action in the speaker's judgment. The adverb 才 (cái) is the opposite. It suggests the tardiness or lateness of an action as perceived by the speaker.

(1) A: 八點上課，他七點就來了。

Bā diǎn shàng kè, tā qī diǎn jiù lái le.

(Class starts at eight, but he came [as early as] seven.)

B: 八點上課，他八點半才來。

Bā diǎn shàng kè, tā bā diǎn bàn cái lái.

(Class started at eight, but he didn't come until eight thirty.)

(2) A: 我昨天五點鐘就回家了。

Wǒ zuótiān wǔ diǎnzhōng jiù huí jiā le.

(Yesterday I went home when it was only five o'clock.)

B: 我昨天五點才回家。

Wǒ zuótiān wǔ diǎn cái huí jiā.

(Yesterday I didn't go home until five o'clock.)

Note: When commenting on a past action, 就 (jiù) is always used with 了 (le) to indicate promptness, but not 才 (cái).

4. Ordinal Numbers

Ordinal numbers in Chinese are formed by placing 第 (dì) before the cardinal numbers, e.g., 第一 (dì yī; the first)、第二杯茶 (dì èr bēi chá; the second cup of tea)、第三個月 (dì sān ge yuè; the third month)....However, 第 (dì) is not used in names of months: 一月、二月、三月 (yīyuè, èryuè, sānyuè; January, February, March)....Neither is it used to indicate the birth order of siblings: 大哥、二哥、三哥 (dàgē, èrgē, sāngē; oldest brother, second oldest brother, third oldest brother)...;大姐、二姐、三姐 (dàjiě, èrjiě, sānjiě; oldest sister, second oldest sister, third oldest sister)....

5. 有(一)點兒 (yǒu {yì}diǎnr, somewhat, rather; a little bit)

The phrase 有一點兒 (yǒu yìdiǎnr) precedes adjectives or verbs, indicating a slight degree. It often carries a negative tone. The 一 in the phrase is optional.

(1) 我覺得中文有(一)點兒難。

Wǒ juéde Zhōngwén yǒu (yì)diǎnr nán.

(I think Chinese is a little bit difficult.)

*我覺得中文有(一)點兒容易。

*Wǒ juéde Zhōngwén yǒu (yì)diǎnr róngyì.

*(I think Chinese is a little bit easy.)

(2) 我覺得這一課生詞有點兒多。

Wǒ juéde zhè yí kè shēngcí yǒu diǎnr duō.

(I think there are a few too many new words in this lesson.)

[The speaker complains about it.]

(3) 我有(一)點兒不喜歡他。

Wǒ yǒu (yī)diǎnr bù xǐhuan tā.

(I somewhat dislike him.)

*我有(一)點兒喜歡他。

*Wǒ yǒu (yī)diǎnr xǐhuan tā.

*(I somewhat like him.)

However, when the sentence suggests a change of the situation, the phrase 有一點兒 (yǒu yìdiǎnr) can carry a positive tone, e.g.:

(4) 我以前不喜歡他, 現在有(一)點兒喜歡他了。

Wǒ yǐqián bù xǐhuan tā, xiānzāi yǒu (yī)diǎnr xǐhuan tā le.

(I used to dislike him, but now I somewhat like him.)

Note: 以前 yǐqián = previously or before. See "An Entry from Li You's Diary" in L.8.

Take care not to confuse 有一點兒 (yǒu yìdiǎnr, a little), which is an adverbial used to modify adjectives, with 一點兒 (yìdiǎnr, a little), which usually modifies nouns. In the above sentences, 有一點兒 (yǒu yìdiǎnr) cannot be replaced by 一點兒 (yìdiǎnr). Compare:

Learning to read Chinese characters.

(5) 給我一點兒咖啡。

Gěi wǒ yìdiǎnr kāfēi.

(Give me a little coffee.)

(6) 給我一點兒時間。

Gěi wǒ yìdiǎnr shíjiān.

(Give me a little time.)

(7) 我有一點兒忙。

Wǒ yǒu yìdiǎnr máng.

(I am kind of busy.)

*我一點兒忙。

*Wǒ yìdiǎnr máng.

(8) 她有一點兒不高興。

Tā yǒu yìdiǎnr bù gāoxìng.

(She is a little bit unhappy.)

*她一點兒不高興。

*Tā yìdiǎnr bù gāoxìng.

6. 怎麼 (zěnme, how come) in Questions

怎麼 (zěnme, how come) is an interrogative adverb. It is often used to ask about the manner—and sometimes the reason or the cause—of an action.

(1) 你怎麼才來？

Nǐ zěnme cái lái?

(How come you've just arrived?)

(2) 你怎麼沒去看電影？

Nǐ zěnme méi qù kàn diànyǐng?

(Why didn't you go to the movie?)

(3) 怎麼，你不認識他？他不是你的老師嗎？

Zěnme, nǐ bú rènshi tā? Tā bú shì nǐ de lǎoshī ma?

(What? You don't know him? Isn't he your teacher?)

Both 怎麼 (zěnme, how come) and 為什麼 (wèishénme, why) are used to ask about the cause of or reason for something. However, 怎麼 (zěnme, how come) conveys the speaker's bewilderment or surprise whereas 為什麼 (wèishénme, why) does not.

怎麼 (zěnme, how come) can stand alone as a clause, as in (3).

7. The Use of Nouns and Pronouns in Continuous Discourse

If the subject remains the same in a continuous discourse, it is to be substituted with an appropriate pronoun in the second clause or sentence. In the third clause or sentence, even the pronoun can sometimes be omitted.

小白很喜歡學中文。她晚上預習課文，常常半夜一點才睡覺。

Xiǎo Bái hěn xǐhuan xué Zhōngwén. Tā wǎnshang yùxí kèwén, chángcháng bànyè yì diǎn cái shuì jiào.

(Little Bai likes to study Chinese very much. She previews the text at night, and often doesn't sleep until 1:00 a.m.)

If we keep repeating the subject, the sentence will become choppy and read like a bunch of unrelated sentences.

小白很喜歡學中文。小白晚上預習
課文。小白常常半夜一點才睡覺。

Xiǎo Bái hěn xǐhuan xué Zhōngwén. Xiǎo Bái wǎnshang yùxí kèwén. Xiǎo Bái chángcháng bànyè yì diǎn cái shuì jiào.

(Little Bai likes to study Chinese very much. Little Bai previews the text at night. Little Bai often doesn't sleep until 1:00 a.m.)

PATTERN DRILLS

A. Verb + 得 (de) + Complement

1.	Tā kǎo	de	hěn hǎo.
2.	Xiǎo Gāo zuótiān shuì		hěn wǎn.
3.	Nàge xuésheng yùxí		búcuò.
4.	Wǒ dìdi chī		hěn duō.
5.	Lǎoshī lái		hěn zǎo.

1.	她考	得	很好。
2.	小高昨天睡		很晚。
3.	那個學生預習		不錯。
4.	我弟弟吃		很多。
5.	老師來		很早。

B. Verb + Object + Verb + 得 (de) + Complement

1.	Wáng Péng shuō huà	shuō	de	hěn kuài.
2.	Xiǎo Bái hē píjiǔ	hē		hěn duō.
3.	Tā niàn kèwén	niàn		búcuò.
4.	Wǒ xiě Zhōngguó zì	xiě		bú tài hǎo.
5.	Nǐ mèimei chàng gē	chàng		hěn hǎo.

1. 王朋說話　　　　　說　　　　__得__　　　　很快。
2. 小白喝啤酒　　　　喝　　　　　　　　　很多。
3. 他念課文　　　　　念　　　　　　　　　不錯。
4. 我寫中國字　　　　寫　　　　　　　　　不太好。
5. 你妹妹唱歌　　　　唱　　　　　　　　　很好。

C. 太 (tài, too)

1.	Zhège zì	__tài__	nán	__le__.
2.	Wáng Lǎoshī		máng	
3.	Zhè yí kè de shēngcí		duō	
4.	Wǒ de jiā		xiǎo	
5.	Nǐ		kèqi	
6.	Zhège diànyǐng		yǒuyìsi	
7.	Xiǎo Gāo de jiā		piàoliang	
8.	Jīntiān de Zhōngwén kè		róngyì	

1. 這個字　　　__太__　難　　　__了__。
2. 王老師　　　　　忙
3. 這一課的生詞　　多
4. 我的家　　　　　小
5. 你　　　　　　　客氣
6. 這個電影　　　　有意思
7. 小高的家　　　　漂亮
8. 今天的中文課　　容易

▼▼▼▼▼▼▼▼▼▼▼▼▼▼▼▼▼▼▼▼▼▼▼▼▼▼▼▼▼▼▼▼▼▼▼▼▼

D. 有一點兒 (yǒu yì diǎnr, a little bit) + Adjective

1.	Jīntiān de yǔfǎ	<u>yǒu yì diǎnr</u>	nán.
2.	Dì wǔ kè de shēngcí		duō.
3.	Wáng Lǎoshī míngtiān		máng.
4.	Wǔ diǎnzhōng chī wǎnfàn		zǎo.
5.	Bànyè yì diǎn cái shuìjiào		wǎn.
6.	Lǐ Xiǎojie shuō huà		kuài.

1. 今天的語法　　　<u>有一點兒</u>　難。

2. 第五課的生詞　　　　　　　多。

3. 王老師明天　　　　　　　　忙。

4. 五點鐘吃晚飯　　　　　　　早。

5. 半夜一點才睡覺　　　　　　晚。

6. 李小姐說話　　　　　　　　快。

E. 怎麼 (zěnme, how come)

1.	Zuótiān de diànyǐng hěn hǎo,	<u>nǐ zěnme</u>	méi qù kàn?
2.	Shí diǎn shàngkè,		shí diǎn bàn cái lái?
3.	Zuótiān shì Xiǎo Gāo de shēngrì		méiyǒu lái?
4.	Jīntiān de kǎoshì hěn róngyì		kǎo de zhème bù hǎo?
5.	Míngtiān yǒu kǎoshì		bú fùxí?
6.	Gāo Xiǎoyīn zài túshūguǎn gōngzuò		bú rènshi tā?
7.	Bā diǎn bàn cái kāi huì		qī diǎn jiù lái le?
8.	Jīntiān shì xīngqīyī		méi qù shàng kè?

1. 昨天的電影很好，　　<u>你怎麼</u>　沒去看？

2. 十點上課，　　　　　　　　十點半才來？

3. 昨天是小高的生日   沒有來？

4. 今天的考試很容易   考得這麼不好？

5. 明天有考試   不復習？

6. 高小音在圖書館工作   不認識她？

7. 八點半才開會   七點就來了？

8. 今天是星期一   沒去上課？

F. 才 (cái; indicating that something takes place later than expected)

1. Māma hěn wǎn   <u>cái</u>   huílai.
2. Xiǎo Gāo shí diǎn   chī zǎofàn.
3. Wǒ gēge zuótiān wǎnshang bā diǎn   chī wǎnfàn.
4. Tā de tóngxué zuótiān bànyè   shuì jiào.
5. Bā diǎn bàn kǎoshì, tā jiǔ diǎn   lái.
6. Bàba jīntiān hěn máng, zhōumò   yǒu kòngr.
7. Wǒ yào zài xuéxiào tīng lùyīn, wǔ diǎnzhōng   huí jiā.

1. 媽媽很晚   <u>才</u>   回來。

2. 小高十點   吃早飯。

3. 我哥哥昨天晚上八點   吃晚飯。

4. 他的同學昨天半夜   睡覺。

5. 八點半考試，他九點   來。

6. 爸爸今天很忙，週末   有空兒。

7. 我要在學校聽錄音，五點鐘   回家。

▼▼

G. 就 (jiù; indicating that something takes place sooner than expected)

1.	Wǒ zuótiān wǎnshang shí diǎn	<u>jiù</u>	shuì le.
2.	Tā zǎoshang qī diǎn bàn		kāishǐ fùxí kèwén le.
3.	Xiǎo Wáng zǎoshang wǔ diǎn		qù xuéxiào le.
4.	Tā chī fàn yǐhòu		qù túshūguǎn kàn shū le.
5.	Jiǔ diǎn kǎoshì, Xiǎo Bái bā diǎn		lái le.
6.	Tā píngcháng liù diǎn chī wǎnfàn, jīntiān wǔ diǎn		chī le.

1. 我昨天晚上十點　　　　　　　<u>就</u>　　睡了。

2. 他早上七點半　　　　　　　　　　開始復習課文了。

3. 小王早上五點　　　　　　　　　　去學校了。

4. 她吃飯以後　　　　　　　　　　　去圖書館看書了。

5. 九點考試，小白八點　　　　　　　來了。

6. 他平常六點吃晚飯，今天五點　　　吃了。

H. 真 (zhēn, really)

1.	Zhège xuéxiào	<u>zhēn</u>	hǎo.
2.	Jīntiān de fàn		bù hǎo chī.
3.	Wáng Lǎoshī		máng.
4.	Zhège zì		nán.
5.	Nǐ de Zhōngwén		búcuò.
6.	Zhè yí kè de yǔfǎ		róngyì.
7.	Zhège diànyǐng		yǒu yìsi.
8.	Zuótiān de gōngkè		duō.

1. 這個學校　　　<u>真</u>　　好。

2. 今天的飯　　　　　　不好吃。

3. 王老師   忙。

4. 這個字   難。

5. 你的中文   不錯。

6. 這一課的語法   容易。

7. 這個電影   有意思。

8. 昨天的功課   多。

English Texts

DIALOGUE I

(Wang Peng is talking with Li You.)

Wang Peng:	How did you do on last week's exam?
Li You:	Pretty well. Because you helped me review, I did pretty well, but the teacher said I was too slow at writing the Chinese characters.
Wang Peng:	Really? I'll practice writing characters with you from now on. I'll teach you how to write Chinese characters. How's that sound?
Li You:	That would be great! Let's do it right now. Here's a pen.
Wang Peng:	O.K., I'll teach you how to write the character "nán" (difficult).
Li You:	You write characters really well, and fast, too.
Wang Peng:	You flatter me. Do you have Chinese tomorrow?
Li You:	Yes. Tomorrow we'll study Lesson Seven.
Wang Peng:	Have you prepared it?
Li You:	Yes, I have. The grammar in Lesson Seven is very easy. I can understand all of it, but there are too many new words, and the Chinese characters are rather difficult, too.
Wang Peng:	Let me practice with you tonight.
Li You:	Great. Thank you.
Wang Peng:	Don't mention it. See you tonight.

Tell a story based on this picture.

DIALOGUE II

(Li You is talking with Xiao Bai.)

Li You: Xiao Bai, you usually come very early. How come you got here so late today?

Xiao Bai: Yesterday I was preparing Chinese. I didn't go to bed till one o'clock. Did you go to bed very late, too?

Li You: No, yesterday I went to bed at ten. Because Wang Peng helped me practice Chinese, I finished my homework very quickly.

Xiao Bai: It's great to have a Chinese friend.

(In the Chinese class.)

Teacher: Good morning, everyone. Let's begin. Have you all prepared Lesson Seven?

Students: Yes, we have.

Teacher: Li You, would you please read the text aloud?...You read very well. Did you listen to the tape recording last night?

Li You: No, I didn't.

Xiao Bai: But her friend often helps her.

Teacher: Is your friend Chinese?

Li You: Yes.

Xiao Bai: It's a he. He's really handsome. His name is Wang Peng.

LESSON 8 ▲ School Life
第八課 ▲ 學校生活
Dì bā kè ▲ *Xuéxiào shēnghuó*

下課以後，你想去打球嗎？

Xià kè yǐhòu, nǐ xiǎng qù dǎ qiú ma?

A Diary: A Typical School Day

VOCABULARY

1.	#篇	piān	m	(a measure for essays, articles, etc.)
2.	日記	rìjì	n	diary
3.	早上	zǎoshang	t	morning
4.	起床	qǐ chuáng	vo	to get up
	床	chuáng	n	bed
5.	洗#澡	xǐ zǎo	vo	to take a bath/shower

6.	早飯	zǎofàn	n	breakfast
7.	一邊…一邊	yìbiān…yìbiān		(a parallel construction indicating two simultaneous actions)
8.	教室	jiàoshì	n	classroom
9.	發音	fāyīn	n	pronunciation
10.	新	xīn	adj	new
11.	電#腦	diànnǎo	n	computer
	腦	nǎo	n	brain
12.	中午	zhōngwǔ	n	noon
13.	#餐#廳	cāntīng	n	dining room; cafeteria
14.	午飯	wǔfàn	n	lunch; midday meal
15.	報	bào	n	newspaper
16.	#宿#舍	sùshè	n	dormitory
17.	到	dào	v	to arrive
18.	那兒	nàr	pr	there
19.	…的時候	…de shíhou		when…; at the time of…
20.	正在	zhèngzài	adv	in the middle of (doing something)
21.	以前	yǐqián	t	before; ago; previously
22.	告訴	gàosu	v	to tell
23.	已經	yǐjīng	adv	already

李友的一天

Lǐ Yǒu de yì tiān

AN ENTRY FROM LI YOU'S DIARY

Lǐ Yǒu de yì piān rìjì

Bāyuè jiǔrì, xīngqīyī

Wǒ jīntiān zǎoshang[1] <u>qī diǎn bàn qǐ chuáng</u>[G1], xǐle zǎo yǐhòu <u>jiù</u>[G2] chī zǎofàn. Wǒ <u>yìbiān</u> chī fàn, <u>yìbiān</u>[G3] tīng lùyīn. Jiǔ diǎnzhōng <u>dào jiàoshì qù shàng kè</u>[G4].

Dì yī jié kè shì Zhōngwén, <u>lǎoshī jiāo wǒmen fāyīn</u>[G5], shēngcí hé yǔfǎ, yě jiāo wǒmen xiě zì, hái gěi<u>le</u>[G6] wǒmen yì piān xīn kèwén[2], zhè piān kèwén hěn yǒu yìsi. Dì èr jié kè shì diànnǎo[3] kè, hěn nán. Zhōngwǔ wǒ hé tóngxuémen yìqǐ dào cāntīng qù chī wǔfàn. Wǒmen yìbiān chī, yìbiān liànxí shuō Zhōngwén. Xiàwǔ wǒ dào túshūguǎn qù kàn bào. Sì diǎnzhōng Wáng Péng lái zhǎo wǒ qù dǎ qiú. Wǔ diǎn sān kè chī wǎnfàn. Qī diǎn bàn wǒ qù Xiǎo Bái de sùshè gēn tā liáo tiān(r). Dào nàr <u>de shíhou</u>, tā <u>zhèngzài</u>[G7] zuò gōngkè. Wǒ bā diǎn bàn huí jiā. Shuì jiào yǐqián, gěi Wáng Péng dǎle yí ge diànhuà, gàosu tā míngtiān yào kǎoshì. Tā shuō tā yǐjīng zhīdao le.

▼▼

AN ENTRY FROM LI YOU'S DIARY

李友的一篇日記

八月九日　星期一

我今天早上⁽¹⁾七點半起床^(G1)，洗了澡以後就^(G2)吃早飯。我一邊吃飯，一邊^(G3)聽錄音。九點鐘到教室去上課^(G4)。

　　第一節課是中文，老師教我們發音^(G5)、生詞和語法，也教我們寫字，還給了^(G6)我們一篇新課文⁽²⁾，這篇課文很有意思。第二節課是電腦⁽³⁾課，很難。中午我和同學們一起到餐廳去吃午飯。我們一邊吃，一邊練習說中文。下午我到圖書館去看報。四點鐘王朋來找我去打球。五點三刻吃晚飯。七點半我去小白的宿舍跟他聊天(兒)。到那兒的時候，他正在^(G7)做功課。我八點半回家。睡覺以前，給王朋打了一個電話，告訴他明天要考試。他說他已經知道了。

Notes

▲1▲ Both 早上 (zǎoshang) and 上午 (shàngwǔ) are usually translated as "morning," but the two Chinese words are not interchangeable. 早上 (zǎoshang) refers to the early morning; and 上午 (shàngwǔ) to the latter part of the morning or to the first half of the day (until noon).

▲2▲ When a disyllabic adjective modifies a noun, the particle 的 (de) is usually inserted between the adjective and the noun, e.g. 漂亮的學校 (piàoliang

Describe what Li You did yesterday. Don't forget to mention the time!

de xuéxiào, beautiful school), 容易的漢字 (róngyì de Hànzì, easy characters). However, with monosyllabic adjectives, 的 (de) is often omitted, e.g., 新課文 (xīn kèwén, new lesson text), 新電腦 (xīn diànnǎo, new computer), 大教室 (dà jiàoshì, big classroom), and 好老師 (hǎo lǎoshī, good teacher). If the adjective is preceded by 很 (hěn), however, 的 (de) cannot be dropped, e.g., 很新的電腦 (hěn xīn de diànnǎo, very new computer); 很大的教室 (hěn dà de jiàoshì, very big classroom); 很好的老師 (hěn hǎo de lǎoshī, very good teacher).

▲**3**▲ The usual colloquial term for computer is 電腦 (diànnǎo), literally "electric brain." A more formal term, especially in mainland China, is 電子計算機 (diànzǐ jìsuànjī) or "electronic computing machine" or simply 計算機 (jìsuànjī).

A Letter: Talking about Studying Chinese

VOCABULARY

1.	封	fēng	m	(a measure word for letters)
2.	信	xìn	n	letter (mail)
3.	最近	zuìjìn	tw	recently
	最	zuì	adv	(an adverb of superlative degree; most, -est)
	近	jìn	adj	near
4.	學期	xuéqī	n	school term; semester/quarter
5.	除了…以外	chúle…yǐwài	conj	in addition to; besides [see G8]
6.	專#業	zhuānyè	n	major (in college); specialty
7.	會	huì	av	can; to know how to [see G9]
8.	開始	kāishǐ	n/v	in the beginning; to begin; to start
9.	習#慣	xíguàn	v/adj/n	to be accustomed to; habit
10.	後來	hòulái	t	later
11.	清#楚	qīngchu	adj	clear
12.	進步	jìnbù	v/n	to make progress; progress
13.	音樂會	yīnyuèhuì	n	concert
14.	希望	xīwàng	v/n	to hope; hope
15.	能	néng	av	can; be able to
16.	用	yòng	v/n	to use; use
17.	笑	xiào	v	to laugh; to laugh at
18.	#祝	zhù	v	to express good wishes

Proper Noun

| 19. | 意文 | Yìwén | n | (a given name) |

A Letter

YÌ FĒNG XÌN

Zhāng Xiǎojie:

   Nǐ hǎo! Hǎo jiǔ bú jiàn, zuìjìn zěnmeyàng?

   Zhège xuéqī wǒ hěn máng, <u>chúle</u> zhuānyè kè <u>yǐwài, hái</u>(G8) děi xué Zhōngwén. Wǒmen de Zhōngwén kè hěn yǒu yìsi. Yīnwei wǒmen de Zhōngwén lǎoshī zhǐ <u>huì</u>(G9) shuō Zhōngwén, bú huì shuō Yīngwén, suǒyǐ shàngkè de shíhou wǒmen zhǐ shuō Zhōngwén, bù shuō Yīngwén. Kāishǐ wǒ bù xíguàn, hòulái, wǒ yǒule yí ge Zhōngguó péngyou, tā shuō huà shuō de hěn qīngchu, chángcháng gēn wǒ yìqǐ liànxí shuō Zhōngwén, suǒyǐ wǒ de Zhōngwén jìnbù de hěn kuài.

   Nǐ xǐhuan tīng yīnyuè ma? Xià xīngqīliù, wǒmen xuéxiào yǒu yí ge yīnyuèhuì, xīwàng nǐ <u>néng</u>(G9) lái. Wǒ yòng Zhōngwén xiě xìn xiě de hěn bù hǎo, qǐng bié xiào wǒ. Zhù

   Hǎo

                                          Nǐ de péngyou

                                          Yìwén

                                          Bāyuè shírì

Culture Notes

Colleges and universities in China and Taiwan are on the semester system. Typically, the fall semester starts in late August or early September, and ends in mid January. The winter break lasts about a month. Since the Chinese New Year usually falls in late January or early February, college students can take advantage of the break to go home and celebrate the most important holiday of the year with their families. The spring semester starts around

▼▼▼▼▼▼▼▼▼▼▼▼▼▼▼▼▼▼▼▼▼▼▼▼▼▼▼▼▼▼▼▼▼▼▼▼▼▼▼

mid February and lasts till early July. A semester at a Chinese college is about three weeks longer than that at an American college.

一封信

張小姐：

你好！好久不見，最近怎麼樣？

這個學期我很忙，<u>除了</u>專業課<u>以外</u>，<u>還</u>(G8)得學中文。我們的中文課很有意思。因為我們的中文老師只<u>會</u>(G9)說中文，不會說英文，所以上課的時候我們只說中文，不說英文。開始我不習慣，後來，我有了一個中國朋友，他說話說得很清楚，常常跟我一起練習說中文，所以我的中文進步得很快。

你喜歡聽音樂嗎？下星期六，我們學校有一個音樂會，希望你<u>能</u>(G9)來。我用中文寫信寫得很不好，請別笑我。祝

好

你的朋友
意文
八月十日

音樂會

Yīnyuèhuì

Grammar

1. The Position of Time-When Expressions

Time-when expressions come before the verb.

(1) 我們十點上課。

Wǒmen shí diǎn shàng kè.

(Our class starts at ten.)

(2) 我們幾點鐘去？

Wǒmen jǐ diǎnzhōng qù?

(What time are we going?)

(3) 你什麼時候睡覺？

Nǐ shénme shíhou shuì jiào?

(What time do you go to bed?)

(4) 他明天上午八點來。

Tā míngtiān shàngwǔ bā diǎn lái.

(He will come at eight tomorrow morning.)

2. 就 (jiù) (II) [See also L.7 G3]

The adverb 就 (jiù) connecting two verb phrases indicates that the second action happens as soon as the first one is completed.

(1) 他今天早上起床以後就聽中文錄音。

Tā jīntiān zǎoshang qǐchuáng yǐhòu jiù tīng Zhōngwén lùyīn.

(He listened to the Chinese recordings right after he got up this morning.)

(2) 寫了信以後就去睡覺。

Xiěle xìn yǐhòu jiù qù shuì jiào.

(Go to bed right after you finish writing the letter.)

(3) 我做了功課以後就去朋友家玩。

Wǒ zuòle gōngkè yǐhòu jiù qù péngyou jiā wán.

(I will go to my friend's for a visit right after I have done my homework.)

3. 一邊...一邊... (yìbiān...yìbiān...)

This structure denotes the simultaneity of two ongoing actions. Usually, the word or phrase for the action that started earlier follows the first 一邊 (yìbiān), while that for the action that started later follows the second 一邊 (yìbiān).

(1) 我們一邊吃飯，一邊練習說中文。

Wǒmen yìbiān chī fàn, yìbiān liànxí shuō Zhōngwén.

(We practiced speaking Chinese while having dinner.)

(2) 他常常一邊吃飯一邊看電視。

Tā chángcháng yìbiān chī fàn yìbiān kàn diànshì.

(He often watches TV while eating.)

Sometimes, the action that follows the second 一邊 (yìbiān) is slightly more important, while the first 一邊 (yìbiān) conveys the background action.

(3) 我一邊唱歌一邊寫字。

Wǒ yìbiān chàng gē, yìbiān xiě zì.

(I write characters while singing.)

(4) 我妹妹喜歡一邊聽音樂一邊看書。

Wǒ mèimei xǐhuan yìbiān tīng yīnyuè, yìbiān kàn shū.

(My younger sister loves reading while listening to music.)

4. Serial Verbs/Verb Phrases

A number of verbs or verb phrases can be used in succession to represent a
series of actions. The sequential order of these verbs or verb phrases usually
coincides with the temporal order of the actions.

(1) 他常常去餐廳吃飯。

Tā chángcháng qù cāntīng chī fàn.

(He often goes to the cafeteria to eat.)

(2) 下午我要到圖書館去看書。

Xiàwǔ wǒ yào dào túshūguǎn qù kàn shū.

(This afternoon I want to go to the library to read.)

(3) 我想找同學去打球。

Wǒ xiǎng zhǎo tóngxué qù dǎ qiú.

(I'd like to find some classmates to play ball with me.)

(4) 你明天來我家吃晚飯吧。

Nǐ míngtiān lái wǒ jiā chī wǎnfàn ba.

(Come and have dinner at my home tomorrow.)

Sometimes the first verb indicates the means or manner of the action.

(5) 他常常用中文寫信。

Tā chángcháng yòng Zhōngwén xiě xìn.

(He often writes letters in Chinese.)

A student dorm at a Chinese university.

5. Double Objects

Some verbs can take two objects. The object representing a person or persons precedes the one representing an inanimate thing.

(1) 老師教我們發音、生詞和語法。

Lǎoshī jiāo wǒmen fāyīn, shēngcí hé yǔfǎ.

(The teacher teaches us pronunciation, vocabulary, and grammar.)

(2) 哥哥給了我一張照片。

Gēge gěile wǒ yì zhāng zhàopiàn.

(My brother gave me a photo.)

(3) 你教我電腦，可以嗎？

Nǐ jiāo wǒ diànnǎo, kěyǐ ma?

(Teach me how to use a computer, O.K.?)

(4) 我想問你一個問題。

Wǒ xiǎng wèn nǐ yí ge wèntí.

(I'd like to ask you a question.)

學生餐廳

Xuésheng cāntīng

6. More on the Particle 了 (le) (II) [See also L.5 G5 and L.10 G2]

If a statement enumerates a series of realized actions or events, 了 (le) usually appears at the end of the series, rather than after each of the verbs.

昨天第一節課是中文。老師教我們
發音、生詞和語法，也教我們寫字，
還給了我們一篇新課文。那篇課文
很有意思。

Zuótiān dì yī jié kè shì Zhōngwén. Lǎoshī jiāo wǒmen fāyīn, shēngcí hé yǔfǎ, yě jiāo wǒmen xiězì, hái gěile wǒmen yì piān xīn kèwén. Nà piān kèwén hěn yǒu yìsi.

(Yesterday the first class was Chinese. Our teacher taught us pronunciation, vocabulary, and grammar. She taught us how to write the characters, and gave us a new text. That text was very interesting.)

上中文課

Shàng Zhōngwén kè

7. ...的時候，正在... (...de shíhou, zhèngzài...; when...be doing...)

This structure expresses an ongoing or progressive action at a certain point in time.

(1) 我到他宿舍的時候，他正在做功課。

Wǒ dào tā sùshè de shíhou, tā zhèngzài zuò gōngkè.

(When I got to his dorm, he was doing his homework.)

(2) 老師到教室的時候，我們正在看書。

Lǎoshī dào jiàoshì de shíhou, wǒmen zhèngzài kàn shū.

(When the teacher came into the classroom, we were reading.)

(3) 我進他的宿舍的時候，他正在聽音樂。

Wǒ jìn tā de sùshè de shíhou, tā zhèngzài tīng yīnyuè.

(When I entered his dorm, he was listening to music.)

(4) 我給他打電話的時候，他正在練習發音。

Wǒ gěi tā dǎ diànhuà de shíhou, tā zhèngzài liànxí fāyīn.

(When I called him, he was practicing pronunciation.)

8. 除了...以外,還 (chúle...yǐwài, hái, in addition to..., also...)

(1) 我除了學中文以外，還學日文。

Wǒ chúle xué Zhōngwén yǐwài, hái xué Rìwén.

(Besides Chinese, I also study Japanese.)

(2) 上個週末我們除了看電影以外，還聽了音樂。

Shàngge zhōumò wǒmen chúle kàn diànyǐng yǐwài, hái tīngle yīnyuè.

(Last weekend, besides seeing a movie we also listened to some music.)

(3) 他除了喜歡聽音樂以外，還喜歡打球。

Tā chúle xǐhuan tīng yīnyuè yǐwài, hái xǐhuan dǎ qiú.

(In addition to listening to music, he also likes to play ball.)

9. 能 (néng) and 會 (huì) (I) Compared

Both 能 (néng) and 會 (huì) have several meanings. The basic meaning of 能 (néng) is "to be capable of (the action named by the following verb)." It can also be an indication of whether circumstances allow the execution of an action. Additional meanings will be introduced in subsequent lessons.

(1) 我能喝十杯咖啡。

Wǒ néng hē shí bēi kāfēi.

(I can drink ten cups of coffee.)

What is the student in the middle doing?

(2) 今天下午我要開會，不能去聽音樂。

Jīntiān xiàwǔ wǒ yào kāi huì, bù néng qù tīng yīnyuè.

(I have a meeting this afternoon. I cannot go to listen to music.)

(3) 我的宿舍沒有電話，所以不能打電話。

Wǒ de sùshè méiyǒu diànhuà, suǒyǐ bù néng dǎ diànhuà.

(There's no phone in my dorm, so I cannot make any phone calls.)

會 (huì), as used in this lesson, means having the skill to do something through learning or instruction. However, when referring to particular language skills, we can also use 能 (néng): 我能用中文寫信 (Wǒ néng yòng Zhōngwén xiě xìn; I can write letters in Chinese).

(4) 小張會說英文。

Xiǎo Zhāng huì shuō Yīngwén.

(Little Zhang can speak English.)

(5) 李友會唱很多美國歌。

Lǐ Yǒu huì chàng hěn duō Měiguó gē.

(Li You can sing many American songs.)

(6) 誰會打球？

Shéi huì dǎ qiú?

(Who can play ball?)

PATTERN DRILLS

A. Time Expression + Verb

Rephrase the sentences below using the words in parentheses.

Example:　　Wǒmen shàngwǔ jiǔ diǎn shàngkè. (qī diǎn bàn qǐchuáng)

　　　　→ Wǒmen qī diǎn bàn qǐchuáng.

我們上午九點上課。(七點半，起床)

→ 我們七點半起床。

1.	Wáng Péng wǎnshang shí diǎn shuì jiào.	(shàngwǔ bā diǎn, shàng kè)
2.	Wǒmen shàng kè yǐqián yùxí kèwén.	(huí jiā yǐqián, tīng lùyīn)
3.	Wǒde péngyou míngtiān xiàwǔ lái.	(míngtiān shàngwǔ, lái)
4.	Xià kè yǐhòu, wǒ xiǎng qù dǎ qiú.	(wǎnfàn yǐhòu, kàn diànyǐng)
5.	Wǒ huí jiā yǐqián gēn péngyou liáo tiān.	(shàng kè yǐqián, liànxí Zhōngwén)
6.	Nǐ shénme shíhou kàn diànyǐng?	(jǐ diǎnzhōng, kǎoshì)
7.	Wǒ shí'èr diǎn bàn dào cāntīng chī fàn.	(liǎngdiǎn, dào túshūguǎn kàn shū)

1. 王朋晚上十點睡覺。　　　(上午八點，上課)

2. 我們上課以前預習課文。　　(回家以前，聽錄音)

3. 我的朋友明天下午來。　　　(明天上午，來)

4. 下課以後，我想去打球。　　(晚飯以後，看電影)

5. 我回家以前跟朋友聊天。　　(上課以前，練習中文)

6. 你什麼時候看電影？　　　　(幾點鐘，考試)

7. 我十二點半到餐廳吃飯。　　(兩點，到圖書館看書)

▼▼

看中文報

Kàn Zhōngwén bào

B. 一邊…一邊… (yìbiān…yìbiān…)

Use the groups of words below to create sentences with 一邊…一邊….

Example: Wǒ dìdi   zuò gōngkè   kàn diànshì

→ Wǒ dìdi yìbiān zuò gōngkè yìbiān kàn diànshì.

我 弟 弟　　做 功 課　　看 電 視

→ 我 弟 弟 一 邊 做 功 課 一 邊 看 電 視 。

1.	Wǒ mèimei chángcháng	chī fàn	shuō huà
2.	Wáng Xiānsheng chángcháng	xǐ zǎo	chàng gē
3.	Wǒ dìdi xǐhuan	xiě Hànzì	tīng lùyīn
4.	Xiǎo Gāo yǒu shíhou	kàn bào	hē kāfēi
5.	Wǒ hé Lǎo Lǐ	liáo tiānr	hē kělè
6.	Tāmen	chī wǔfàn	liànxí shuō Zhōngwén
7.	Wǒ gēn wǒde tóngxué	dǎ qiú	liáo tiānr
8.	Wáng Péng hé Lǐ Yǒu	hē chá	tīng yīnyuè

在圖書館

Zài túshūguǎn

1. 我妹妹常常   吃飯   說話
2. 王先生常常   洗澡   唱歌
3. 我弟弟喜歡   寫漢字   聽錄音
4. 小高有時候   看報   喝咖啡
5. 我和老李   聊天兒   喝可樂
6. 他們   吃午飯   練習說中文
7. 我跟我的同學   打球   聊天兒
8. 王朋和李友   喝茶   聽音樂

▼▼▼▼▼▼▼▼▼▼▼▼▼▼▼▼▼▼▼▼▼▼▼▼▼▼▼▼▼▼▼▼▼▼▼

C. Subject + Verb 1 + Verb 2

Rephrase the sentences below using the words in parentheses.

Example: Wáng Péng qù xuéxiào shàng kè. (dào Xiǎo Gāo jiā, chī fàn)

         → Wáng Péng dào Xiǎo Gāo jiā chī fàn.

王朋去學校上課。(到小高家，吃飯)

→ 王朋到小高家吃飯。

1.	Wǒ dìdi chángcháng dào péngyou jiā kàn diànshì.	(qù túshūguǎn, kàn shū)
2.	Tā xǐhuan qù túshūguǎn kàn bào.	(qù jiàoshì, liànxí fāyīn)
3.	Xià kè yǐhòu tā qù zhǎo Wáng Péng dǎ qiú.	(qù zhǎo péngyou, liáo tiānr)
4.	Tā gēn péngyou qù xuéxiào tīng lùyīn.	(qù lǎoshī jiā, wèn wèntí)
5.	Wǒ de tóngxué yào lái wǒ jiā wánr.	(lái wǒmen xuéxiào, kàn diànyǐng)

1. 我弟弟常常到朋友家看電視。   (去圖書館，看書)

2. 他喜歡去圖書館看報。   (去教室，練習發音)

3. 下課以後他去找王朋打球。   (去找朋友，聊天兒)

4. 她跟朋友去學校聽錄音。   (去老師家，問問題)

5. 我的同學要來我家玩兒。   (來我們學校，看電影)

D. Verb + Object 1 + Object 2

D1:

1.	<u>Lǎoshī</u>	<u>jiāo</u>	xuésheng	shēngcí.
2.			xuésheng	hànzì.
3.			Lǐyǒu	Zhōngwén.
4.			Xiǎo Bái	fāyīn.

D1:

1.	老師	教	學生 生詞
2.			學生 漢字
3.			李友 中文
4.			小白 發音

D2:

1.	Wǒ de péngyou	gěi	lǎoshī	yì piān rìjì.
2.			tā dìdi	yí ge diànnǎo.
3.			lǎoshī	yì fēng xìn.
4.			tā bàba	yì zhāng zhàopiàn.
5.			wǒ	yì běn shū.
6.			Xiǎo Gāo	yì bēi kělè.

D2:

1.	我的朋友	給	老師	一篇日記。
2.			他弟弟	一個電腦。
3.			老師	一封信。
4.			他爸爸	一張照片。
5.			我	一本書。
6.			小高	一杯可樂。

E. …的時候，正在… (…de shíhou, zhèngzài…)

1.	Wǒ huí jiā	de shíhou,	dìdi	zhèngzài	kàn diànshì.
2.	Wǒmen qù zhǎo Lǐ Yǒu		tā		shuì jiào.
3.	Wǒ qù tā sùshè		tā		kàn diànshì.

4.	Wáng Péng gěi dìdi dǎ diànhuà	tā dìdi	xiě xìn.
5.	Lǎoshī jìn jiàoshì	wǒmen	niàn kèwén.
6.	Wǒ huí sùshè	Xiǎo Bái	gēn péngyou liáo tiānr.
7.	Wǒ dào túshūguǎn	Lǐ Yǒu	kàn shū.
8.	Lǐ Yǒu qù zhǎo Wáng Péng	Wáng Péng	yùxí gōngkè.

1. 我回家　　　　的時候，弟弟　正在　看電視。

2. 我們去找李友　　　　她　　　　睡覺。

3. 我去他宿舍　　　　他　　　　看電視。

4. 王朋給弟弟打電話　　　　他弟弟　　　　寫信。

5. 老師進教室　　　　我們　　　　念課文。

6. 我回宿舍　　　　小白　　　　跟朋友聊天兒。

7. 我到圖書館　　　　李友　　　　看書。

8. 李友去找王朋　　　　王朋　　　　預習功課。

F. 除了...以外，還...(chúle … yǐwài, hái…)

1.	Tā	chúle	tīng lùyīn	yǐwài, hái	niàn kèwén.
2			xué Yīngwén		xué Zhōngwén.
3.			huì shuō Zhōngwén		huì yòng Zhōngwén xiě xìn.
4.			shì wǒ de lǎoshī		shì wǒ de péngyou.
5.			hē kělè		hē chá.
6.			xǐhuan tīng yīnyuè		xǐhuan tiào wǔ.

1. 他　除了　聽錄音　以外，還　念課文。

2. 　　　　學英文　　　　學中文。

3. 　　　　會說中文　　　　會用中文寫信。

4.   是我的老師   是我的朋友。

5.   喝可樂   喝茶。

6.   喜歡聽音樂   喜歡跳舞。

G. 用 (yòng) + Object + Verb + Object

1.	Wǒmen	yòng	Zhōngwén	xiě rìjì.
2.	Xiǎo Gāo		Yīngwén	gěi tā gēge xiě xìn.
3.	Wǒ de tóngxué		diànnǎo	liànxí fāyīn.
4.	Wǒ bàba		píjiǔbēi	hē chá.

1.   我們   用   中文   寫日記。

2.   小高   英文   給他哥哥寫信。

3.   我的同學   電腦   練習發音。

4.   我爸爸   啤酒杯   喝茶。

English Texts

AN ENTRY FROM LI YOU'S DIARY

August 9, Monday

I got up at seven thirty this morning. After a shower I had breakfast. While I was eating, I listened to the tape recording. I went to the classroom at nine o'clock.

The first period was Chinese. The teacher taught us pronunciation, new vocabulary, and grammar. (He/she) also taught us how to write Chinese characters, and gave us a new text. The text was very interesting. The second period was Computer Science. It was very difficult. At noon I went to the cafeteria with my classmates for lunch. While we were eating, we practiced speaking Chinese. In the afternoon I went to the library to read newspapers.

At four o'clock Wang Peng came looking for me to play ball. I had dinner at a quarter to six. At seven thirty I went to Little Bai's dorm for a chat. When I got there, he was doing his homework. I got home at eight thirty. Before I went to bed, I gave Wang Peng a call. I told him there'd be an exam tomorrow. He said he already knew that.

A LETTER: TALKING ABOUT STUDYING CHINESE

August 10

Dear Miss Zhang,

How are you? Long time no see. How are things recently?

This semester I'm very busy. Besides the classes required for my major, I also need to study Chinese. Our Chinese class is really interesting. Because our Chinese teacher can only speak Chinese and does not know how to speak English, in the class we speak only Chinese, and no English. At the beginning I wasn't used to that. Then I made a Chinese friend. He speaks very clearly, and often speaks Chinese with me. As a result, I have made a lot of progress with my Chinese.

Do you like to listen to music? Next Saturday there will be a concert at our school. I hope you can come. I do not write well in Chinese. Please don't make fun of me.

Best wishes,

Your friend,

Yiwen

LESSON 9 ▲ Shopping
第九課 ▲ 買東西
Dì jiǔ kè ▲ *Mǎi dōngxi*

這件襯衫怎麼樣？

Zhè jiàn chènshān zěnmeyàng?

Dialogue I: Buying Clothes

VOCABULARY

1.	買	mǎi	v	to buy
2.	東西	dōngxi	n	things; objects
3.	#售#貨員	shòuhuòyuán	n	shop assistant; salesclerk
4.	要	yào	av	to want to; to have a desire for [see G1]
5.	衣服	yīfu	n	clothes
6.	件	jiàn	m	(a measure word for shirts, dresses, jackets, coats, etc.)

7.	襯衫	chènshān	n	shirt
8.	顏色	yánsè	n	color
9.	黃 (黄)	huáng	adj	yellow
10.	紅	hóng	adj	red
11.	穿	chuān	v	to wear; to put on
12.	條	tiáo	m	(a measure word for long, thin objects)
13.	褲子	kùzi	n	pants
14.	號	hào	m	number; size
15.	中	zhōng	adj	medium
16.	貴	guì	adj	expensive
17.	便宜	piányi	adj	cheap; inexpensive
18.	付錢	fù qián	vo	to pay money
	錢	qián	n	money
19.	這兒	zhèr	pr	here
20.	一共	yígòng	adv	altogether
21.	多少	duōshao	qw	how much; how many
22.	塊	kuài	m	colloquial term for the basic Chinese monetary unit
23.	毛	máo	m	1/10 of a kuai (similar to the U.S. dime)
24.	分	fēn	m	1/100 of a kuai, cent
25.	百	bǎi	nu	hundred
26.	找 (錢)	zhǎo(qián)	v	to give change [see also L.4 Dialogue II]

DIALOGUE I

(Mǎi dōngxi)

Shòuhuòyuán: Xiǎojie[1], nín <u>yào</u>[G1] mǎi shénme yīfu?

Lǐ Xiǎojie: Wǒ xiǎng mǎi yí <u>jiàn</u>[G2] chènshān.

Shòuhuòyuán: Nín xǐhuan shénme yánsè <u>de</u>[G3], huáng de háishi hóng de?

Lǐ Xiǎojie: Wǒ xǐhuan chuān[2] hóng de. Wǒ hái xiǎng mǎi yì <u>tiáo</u>[3] [G2] kùzi.

Shòuhuòyuán: <u>Duō</u>[G4] dà de? Dà hào, zhōng hào háishi xiǎo hào de?

Lǐ Xiǎojie: Zhōng hào de. Bú yào tài guì de, yě bú yào tài piányi[4] de.

Shòuhuòyuán: Zhè tiáo kùzi hé zhè jiàn chènshān zěnmeyàng?

Lǐ Xiǎojie: Hěn hǎo, zài nǎr fù qián?

Shòuhuòyuán: Zài zhèr.

Lǐ Xiǎojie: Yígòng duōshao qián?

Shòuhuòyuán: Chènshān èrshí <u>kuài</u> wǔ, kùzi sānshí'èr <u>kuài</u> jiǔ <u>máo</u> jiǔ, yígòng shì wǔshísān <u>kuài</u> sì <u>máo</u> jiǔ <u>fēn</u>[G5].

Lǐ Xiǎojie: Hǎo, zhè shì yìbǎi kuài qián.

Shòuhuòyuán: Zhǎo nín sìshíliù kuài wǔ máo yī. Xièxie.

No Taxes and No Tipping in China

There is no sales tax in mainland China. It is also not customary to tip in a restaurant, although fancier restaurants often charge a service fee.

DIALOGUE I

(買東西)

售貨員： 小姐[1]，您<u>要</u>[G1]買什麼衣服？

李小姐： 我想買一<u>件</u>[G2]襯衫。

售貨員： 您喜歡什麼顏色<u>的</u>[G3]，黃的還是紅的？

李小姐： 我喜歡穿[2]紅的。我還想買一<u>條</u>[3] [G2]褲子。

售貨員： <u>多</u>[G4]大的？大號、中號還是小號的？

李小姐： 中號的。不要太貴的，也不要太便宜⁽⁴⁾的。

售貨員： 這條褲子和這件襯衫怎麼樣？

李小姐： 很好，在哪兒付錢？

售貨員： 在這兒。

李小姐： 一共多少錢？

售貨員： 襯衫二十塊五，褲子三十二塊九毛九，一共
　　　　 是五十三塊四毛九分⁽ᴳ⁵⁾。

李小姐： 好，這是一百塊錢。

售貨員： 找您四十六塊五毛一。謝謝。

Notes

▲**1**▲ In mainland China a salesperson in a department store or a server in a restaurant is usually addressed as 服務員 (fúwùyuán, "Service Person") or, for speakers who like to be more "modern," 小姐 (xiǎojie, Miss) or 先生 (xiānsheng, Mr.). In speaking to bus drivers and ticket sellers, as well as taxi drivers, the most common form of address (for women as well as men) is 師傅 (shīfu, an old term of respect for a master craftsman or skilled worker). However, these terms vary according to age and preference of the speaker as well as the status or function of the person spoken to, and usage is very much in flux now at the beginning of the twenty-first century. As in so many matters of language usage, students should carefully observe actual usage and follow suit. In Taiwan the terms 小姐 (xiǎojie, Miss) and 先生 (xiānsheng, Mr.) have very broad usage, including the contexts mentioned above.

▲**2**▲ Note that the verb 穿 (chuān) can mean both "to wear" and "to put on." However, for most accessories, especially those for the upper part of the body, 戴 (dài) is used instead of 穿 (chuān). Compare: 穿衣服 (chuān yīfu, to wear clothes); 穿褲子 (chuān kùzi, to wear pants); 穿裙子 (chuān

▽▽▽▽▽▽▽▽▽▽▽▽▽▽▽▽▽▽▽▽▽▽▽▽▽▽▽▽▽▽▽▽▽▽▽▽

qúnzi, to wear a skirt); 穿西裝 (chuān xīzhuāng, to wear a suit); 穿鞋 (chuān xié, to wear shoes); 穿襪子 (chuān wàzi, to wear socks); but 戴帽子 (dài màozi, to wear a hat); 戴眼鏡 (dài yǎnjìng, to wear eyeglasses); 戴手套 (dài shǒutào, to wear gloves); and 戴手錶 (dài shǒubiǎo, to wear a wristwatch).

▲**3**▲ In Chinese, a pair of pants is just one single piece of clothing. Hence 一條褲子 (yì tiáo kùzi, lit. a trouser) instead of *一雙褲子 (*yì shuāng kùzi, lit. a pair of trousers).

▲**4**▲ The character 便 in 便宜 (piányi) is pronounced "pián." However, in 方便 (fāngbiàn) the same character is pronounced "biàn." It is not uncommon in Chinese for the same character to be pronounced differently and carry different meanings. Other examples include 樂 (yuè/lè) in 音樂 (yīnyuè, music) and 可樂 (kělè, cola); and 覺 (jué/jiào) in 覺得 (juéde, to feel) and 睡覺 (shuìjiào, to sleep).

Using this picture as a guide, talk about Miss Li's shopping experience.

▼ ▼

Dialogue II: Exchanging Shoes

VOCABULARY

1.	雙	shuāng	m	a pair of
2.	#鞋	xié	n	shoes
3.	#換	huàn	v	to change; to exchange
4.	一樣	yíyàng	adj	same; alike
5.	雖然	suīrán	conj	although
6.	大小	dàxiǎo	n	size
7.	合#適	héshì	adj	suitable
8.	咖啡色	kāfēisè	n	coffee color; brown
9.	黑	hēi	adj	black
10.	不用	bú yòng	ce	need not

DIALOGUE II

Lǐ Xiǎojie:	Duìbuqǐ, zhè shuāng xié tài xiǎo le. Néng bu néng huàn yì shuāng?
Shòuhuòyuán:	Méi wèntí. Nín kàn, zhè shuāng zěnmeyàng?
Lǐ Xiǎojie:	Yě bù xíng, zhè shuāng <u>gēn</u> nà shuāng <u>yíyàng</u>(G6) dà.
Shòuhuòyuán:	Nà zhè shuāng hēi de ne?
Lǐ Xiǎojie:	Zhè shuāng xié <u>suīrán</u> dàxiǎo héshì, <u>kěshì</u>(G7) yánsè bù hǎo. Yǒu méiyǒu kāfēisè de?
Shòuhuòyuán:	Duìbuqǐ, zhǐ yǒu hēi de.
Lǐ Xiǎojie:	Nà hǎo ba. Wǒ hái yào fù qián ma?
Shòuhuòyuán:	Bú yòng, zhè shuāng de qián gēn nà shuāng yíyàng.

DIALOGUE II

李小姐： 對不起，這雙鞋太小了。能不能
換一雙？

售貨員： 沒問題。您看，這雙怎麼樣？

李小姐： 也不行，這雙<u>跟</u>那雙<u>一樣</u>(G6)大。

售貨員： 那這雙黑的呢？

李小姐： 這雙鞋<u>雖然</u>大小合適，<u>可是</u>(G7)顏
色不好。有沒有咖啡色的？

售貨員： 對不起，只有黑的。

李小姐： 那好吧。我還要付錢嗎？

售貨員： 不用，這雙的錢跟那雙一樣。

Culture Notes

The traditional dress-up attire for Chinese men was a long robe called 長袍 (chángpáo, long gown) and a short jacket called 馬褂 (mǎguà, Mandarin jacket), while women (in the cities) wore a modified Manchu-style dress called 旗袍 (qípáo, close-fitting woman's dress with a high neck and a slit skirt) until 1949 in China and into the 1960s and 70s in Taiwan. Through the early decades of the People's Republic men wore the 中山裝 (Zhōngshānzhuāng, "Sun Yatsen suit") the top part of which came to be called in the West a "Mao jacket." Nowadays Chinese men and women dress in about the same way as Westerners, wearing suits and ties, or dresses on formal occasions and jeans and shirts, or T-shirts, for more casual purposes.

What is Miss Li trying to tell the salesclerk?

What does Miss Li say about the shoes the salesclerk recommends?

What does the salesclerk tell Miss Li about the cost of the shoes?

SUPPLEMENTARY VOCABULARY

1.	賣	mài	v	to sell
2.	裙子	qúnzi	n	skirt
3.	大衣	dàyī	n	overcoat
4.	夾克	jiákè	n	jacket
5.	外套	wàitào	n	coat; jacket
6.	西裝	xīzhuāng	n	suit
7.	毛衣	máoyī	n	sweater

8. T-恤衫	T-xùshān	n	T-shirt
9. 戴	dài	v	to wear (hat, eyeglasses, etc.)
10. 帽子	màozi	n	hat
11. 頂	dǐng	m	(a measure word for hat)
12. 襪子	wàzi	n	socks
13. 長	cháng	adj	long
14. 短	duǎn	adj	short
15. 藍	lán	adj	blue
16. 綠	lǜ	adj	green
17. 紫	zǐ	adj	purple
18. 粉紅色	fěnhóngsè	n	pink
19. 橘紅色	júhóngsè	n	orange
20. 灰	huī	adj	grey

Name the clothing items in the picture.
Don't forget to use the appropriate measure words.

▼▼▼

Yangshuo, Guangxi, China.

Grammar

1. The Auxiliary Verb 要 (yào) (II) [See also L.6 G2]

One of the meanings of 要 (yào) is "to desire to do something."

(1) 明天是週末，你要做什麼？

Míngtiān shì zhōumò, nǐ yào zuò shénme?

(Tomorrow is the weekend. What do you want to do?)

(2) 我要去圖書館看書，你去不去？

Wǒ yào qù túshūguǎn kàn shū, nǐ qù bu qù?

(I want to go to the library to read. Are you going?)

(3) 我要喝可樂，他要喝水。

Wǒ yào hē kělè, tā yào hē shuǐ.

(I want to have a cola. He wants water.)

To negate it, use 不想 (bù xiǎng).

(4) 我不想去圖書館。

Wǒ bù xiǎng qù túshūguǎn.

(I don't feel like going to the library.)

(5) 今天我不想做功課。

Jīntiān wǒ bù xiǎng zuò gōngkè.

(I don't feel like doing my homework today.)

For (4), however, some Chinese, particularly in the South, would say:

"我不要去圖書館" (Wǒ bú yào qù túshūguǎn).

Note: Both modal verbs 想 (xiǎng) and 要 (yào) can express a desire or an intention, but 要 (yào) carries a stronger tone.

2. Measure Words (II) [See also L.2 G1]

The following are the "measure word + noun" combinations that we have covered so far.

一杯茶	yì bēi chá	a cup of tea
一封信	yì fēng xìn	a letter
一個人	yí ge rén	a person
一節課	yì jié kè	a class period
一件襯衫	yí jiàn chènshān	a shirt
一篇日記	yì piān rìjì	a diary entry
一瓶啤酒	yì píng píjiǔ	a bottle of beer
一雙鞋	yì shuāng xié	a pair of shoes
一條褲子	yì tiáo kùzi	a pair of pants
一位先生	yí wèi xiānsheng	a gentleman
一張照片	yì zhāng zhàopiàn	a picture

▼▼▼

SUPPLEMENTARY EXPRESSIONS

一本書	yì běn shū	a book
一張紙	yì zhāng zhǐ	a piece of paper
一枝筆	yì zhī bǐ	a pen
一隻鞋	yì zhī xié	a shoe (one of a pair) [see also "a pair of shoes" above]

3. 的 (de) Structure

We have a 的 (de) structure when a noun, a pronoun, or an adjective is followed by the structural particle 的 (de). Grammatically, a 的 (de) structure is equivalent to a noun, e.g., 老師的 (lǎoshī de, the teacher's), 我的 (wǒ de, mine), 大的 (dà de, the big one), etc. Also see G3 in Lesson 3.

4. 多 (duō) Used Interrogatively

(1) 你今年多大？[see L.3, Dialogue I, Note 2]

Nǐ jīnnián duō dà?

(How old are you this year?)

(2) 你穿多大的衣服？

Nǐ chuān duō dà de yīfu?

(What size clothes do you wear?)

(3) 你弟弟多高？

Nǐ dìdi duō gāo?

(How tall is your younger brother?)

5. Amounts of Money

Chinese monetary units are 元 (yuán, the Chinese dollar), 角 (jiǎo, ¹⁄₁₀ of a *yuan*), and 分 (fēn, one cent or ¹⁄₁₀₀ of a *yuan*). In colloquial speech, alternative terms 塊 (kuài) and 毛 (máo) are usually used instead of 元 (yuán) and 角 (jiǎo), but price markings in stores are likely to be in 元 (yuán) and 角 (jiǎo), and many store clerks also use 元 (yuán) in their speech. Using the colloquial terms, ¥5.99 is 五塊九毛九分錢 (wǔ kuài jiǔ máo jiǔ fēn qián). However, in casual conversation abbreviated forms are often used.

Renminbi: from top to bottom

五元, 二角, 一元 *(wǔ yuán, èr jiǎo, yī yuán).*

The rules for abbreviation of monetary terms are as follows: begin by omitting the last element 錢 (qián) in the expression and then the second to the last element: 五塊九毛九分 (wǔ kuài jiǔ máo jiǔ fēn) omitting 錢 (qián), or 五塊九毛九 (wǔ kuài jiǔ máo jiǔ) omitting both 錢 (qián) and 分 (fēn). Note that if 錢 is included the preceding measure (e.g., 分) must also be included; one doesn't say *五塊九毛九錢 (*wǔ kuài jiǔ máo jiǔ qián). One or more zeros occurring internally in a complex number are read as 零 (líng, zero).

(1) $8.55   八塊五毛五(分)(錢)

                bā kuài wǔ máo wǔ (fēn) (qián)

(2) $15.30   十五塊三(毛)(錢)

                shíwǔ kuài sān (máo) (qián)

(3) $103   一百零三塊(錢)

                yì bǎi líng sān kuài (qián)

(4) $100.30   一百塊零三毛(錢)

                yì bǎi kuài líng sān máo (qián)

(5) $100.03   一百塊零三分(錢)

                yìbǎi kuài líng sān fēn (qián)

Note: To avoid ambiguity, 毛 (máo) and 分 (fēn) cannot be omitted in (4) or (5) above.

▼▼▼▼▼▼▼▼▼▼▼▼▼▼▼▼▼▼▼▼▼▼▼▼▼▼▼▼▼▼▼▼▼▼▼▼

6. 跟/和...(不) 一樣 **(gēn/hé...{bù} yíyàng, {not the} same as...)**

To express similarity or dissimilarity between two objects or people, we use the structure 跟/和...(不) 一樣 (gēn/hé...{bù} yíyàng).

(1) 你的襯衫跟我的一樣。

   Nǐ de chènshān gēn wǒ de yíyàng.

   (Your shirt is the same as mine.)

(2) 貴的衣服和便宜的衣服不一樣。

   Guì de yīfu hé piányi de yīfu bù yíyàng.

   (Expensive clothes are different from cheap ones.)

Following 一樣 (yíyàng), an adjective can be used:

(3) 弟弟跟哥哥一樣高。

   Dìdi gēn gēge yíyàng gāo.

   (The younger brother is as tall as the older one.)

7. 雖然... ，可是/但是... **(suīrán..., kěshì/dànshì..., although...yet...)**

This pair of conjunctions links the two clauses of a complex sentence. Note, however, that 雖然 (suīrán) is often optional.

(1) 雖然這雙鞋很便宜，可是大小不合適。

   Suīrán zhè shuāng xié hěn piányi, kěshì dàxiǎo bù héshì.

   (Although this pair of shoes is inexpensive, it's not the right size.)

(2) 這本書很有意思，可是太貴了。

   Zhè běn shū hěn yǒu yìsi, kěshì tài guì le.

   (This book is very interesting, but it's too expensive.)

(3) 中文不容易，但是很有意思。

Zhōngwén bù róngyì, dànshì hěn yǒu yìsi.

(Chinese is not easy, but it's very interesting.)

Whether or not 雖然 (suīrán) is used in the first clause, 可是 (kěshì) cannot be omitted in the second. The following sentence is, therefore, **incorrect**:

(2a) *雖然這本書很有意思，太貴了。

*Suīrán zhè běn shū hěn yǒu yìsi, tài guì le.

PATTERN DRILLS

A. 要 (yào, to want to; to desire to do {something})

1.	Tā de péngyou	<u>yào</u>	mǎi yì tiáo hóng qúnzi.
2.	Lǐ Yǒu		chuān kāfēisè de yīfu qù tiào wǔ.
3.	Dìdi zhège zhōumò		kàn wàiguó diànyǐng.
4.	Jiějie xǐle zǎo yǐhòu		qù túshūguǎn kàn shū.
5.	Wǒ xué Zhōngwén de shíhou		yòng diànnǎo liànxí fāyīn.
6.	Wǒ mèimei xīngqītiān		qù tóngxué jiā wánr.
7.	Nǐ gēge		mǎi shénme yīfu?

1.	她的朋友	要	買一條紅裙子。
2.	李友		穿咖啡色的衣服去跳舞。
3.	弟弟這個週末		看外國電影。
4.	姐姐洗了澡以後		去圖書館看書。
5.	我學中文的時候		用電腦練習發音。
6.	我妹妹星期天		去同學家玩兒。
7.	你哥哥		買什麼衣服？

A shopping district in Shanghai.

B. 想 (xiǎng, to want to; to feel like; would like to)

1.	Tā	xiǎng	xué Zhōngwén.
2.	Wǒ		kàn Zhōngguó diànyǐng.
3.	Wǒ wǎnshang		yùxí shēngcí.
4.	Xiǎo Gāo		qǐng péngyou chī fàn.
5.	Lǐ Yǒu wǎnfàn yǐhòu		qù Xiǎo Gāo jiā kàn diànshì.
6.	Wáng Péng jīntiān bù		qù kàn diànyǐng.
7.	Zhè jiàn yīfu wǒ bù		mǎi.
8.	Míngtiān yǒu kǎoshì, Xiǎo Bái		gēn péngyou fùxí yǔfǎ.

1. 他　　　　　想　　學中文。

2. 我　　　　　　　　看中國電影。

3. 我晚上　　　　　　預習生詞。

4. 小高　　　　　　　請朋友吃飯。

5. 李友晚飯以後　　　去小高家看電視。

6. 王朋今天不　　　　去看電影。

7. 這件衣服我不　　　　買。

8. 明天有考試，小白　　跟朋友復習語法。

A fruit shop in Taipei.

C. 的 (de) Structure

Complete the sentences with 的.

Example: Zhè jiàn yīfu / wǒ

     → Zhè jiàn yīfu shì wǒ de.

這件衣服 / 我

→ 這件衣服是我的。

1. Nà běn shū / lǎoshī
2. Zhè tiáo qúnzi hé zhè jiàn yīfu / mèimei
3. Tā yào mǎi / qī hào
4. Tā xǐhuan chuān / kāfēisè

1. 那本書 / 老師

2. 這條裙子和這件衣服 / 妹妹

3. 她要買 / 七號

4. 他喜歡穿 / 咖啡色

▼▼▼▼▼▼▼▼▼▼▼▼▼▼▼▼▼▼▼▼▼▼▼▼▼▼▼▼▼▼▼▼▼▼▼

A traditional market in Taipei.

D. 多 (duō)

1.	Nǐ de dìdi jīnnián	<u>duō</u>	dà?
2.	Tā de kùzi		guì?
3.	Tā chuān de yīfu		dà?
4.	Nǐ de péngyou		gāo?
5.	Nà jiàn chènshān		guì?

1. 你的弟弟今年　<u>多</u>　大？

2. 他的褲子　　　　貴？

3. 她穿的衣服　　　大？

4. 你的朋友　　　　高？

5. 那件襯衫　　　　貴？

E. 跟...一樣 (gēn...yíyàng; the same as...)

1.	Zhè jiàn yīfu	<u>gēn</u>	nà jiàn	<u>yíyàng</u>	piàoliang.
2.	Tā		wǒ gēge		gāo.
3.	Měiguó fàn		Zhōngguó fàn		hǎochī.
4.	Tā de chènshān		wǒ de		guì.
5.	Zhōngwén		Rìwén		nán.
6.	Zhè shuāng xié		nà shuāng		héshì.
7.	Jīntiān de shēngcí		zuótiān de		duō.
8.	Zhège xuéxiào		nàge		hǎo.

1.	這件衣服	<u>跟</u>	那件	<u>一樣</u>	漂亮。
2.	他		我哥哥		高。
3.	美國飯		中國飯		好吃。
4.	他的襯衫		我的		貴。
5.	中文		日文		難。
6.	這雙鞋		那雙		合適。
7.	今天的生詞		昨天的		多。
8.	這個學校		那個		好。

F. 雖然...可是/但是 (suīrán...kěshì/dànshì; although...yet)

1.	Suīrán	Zhōngwén hěn nán,	kěshì	wǒ juéde hěn yǒu yìsi.
2.		tā de yīfu hěn duō,		méiyǒu héshì de.
3.		dì bā kè de yǔfǎ hěn nán,		wǒ dōu dǒng le.
4.		jīntiān de gōngkè hěn duō,		tā dōu zuò le.
5.		zhè jiàn yīfu de yánsè hěn hǎokàn,		tài xiǎo le.
6.		wǎnshang de diànshì hěn búcuò,		wǒ méiyǒu shíjiān kàn.
7.		Lǐ Yǒu hěn xǐhuan tiào wǔ,		tā jīntiān méiyǒu kòngr.

1.	雖然	中文很難，	可是	我覺得很有意思。
2.		她的衣服很多，		沒有合適的。
3.		第八課的語法很難，		我都懂了。
4.		今天的功課很多，		他都做了。
5.		這件衣服的顏色很好看，		太小了。
6.		晚上的電視很不錯，		我沒有時間看。
7.		李友很喜歡跳舞，		她今天沒有空兒。

English Texts

DIALOGUE I

(Shopping for clothes.)

Salesperson: Miss, what are you looking for?

Miss Li: I'd like to buy a shirt.

Salesperson: What color do you like, yellow or red?

Miss Li: I like red. I'd also like to get a pair of pants.

Salesperon: What size, large, medium or small?

Miss Li: Medium. Something not too expensive, but not too cheap, either.

Salesperson: How about these pants and this shirt?

Miss Li:	Great. Where do I pay?
Salesperson:	Here.
Miss Li:	How much altogether?
Salesperson:	Twenty dollars and fifty cents for the shirt, and thirty-two ninety-nine for the pants. Fifty-three dollars and forty-nine cents altogether.
Miss Li:	O.K. Here's one hundred.
Salesperson:	Forty-six fifty-one is your change. Thank you.

DIALOGUE II

Miss Li:	Excuse me, this pair of shoes is too small. Can I exchange them for another pair?
Salesperson:	No problem. How about this pair?
Miss Li:	No, that won't do. This pair is the same size as the other pair.
Salesperson:	What about this pair in black?
Miss Li:	Although this pair is the right size, it's not a good color. Do you have any in brown?
Salesperson:	I'm sorry. We have only black ones.
Miss Li:	All right then. Do I have to pay any more money?
Salesperson:	No, that won't be necessary. This pair is the same price as the other one.

LESSON 10 ▲ Talking about the Weather

第十課 ▲ 談天氣

Dì shí kè ▲ *Tán tiānqì*

今天天氣怎麼樣？

Jīntiān tiānqì zěnmeyàng?

Dialogue I: The Weather Is Getting Better

VOCABULARY

1.	天氣	tiānqì	n	weather
2.	比	bǐ	prep	comparison marker [see G1]
3.	下雨	xià yǔ	vo	to rain
4.	報上	bàoshang		in the newspaper
5.	預報	yùbào	n	forecast
6.	更	gèng	adv	even more

7.	不但...而且	búdàn..., érqiě	conj	not only..., but also
8.	會	huì	av	will [see G3]
9.	#暖和	nuǎnhuo	adj	warm
10.	一點兒	yìdiǎnr		a bit
11.	約	yuē	v	to make an appointment
12.	公#園	gōngyuán	n	park
13.	紅#葉	hóngyè	n	red autumn leaves
14.	怎麼辦	zěnme bàn	qw	what to do
15.	錄#像	lùxiàng	n	video recording

Proper Nouns

16.	謝	xiè	n/v	(a surname); thanks
17.	上海	Shànghǎi	pn	Shanghai
	海	hǎi	n	sea; ocean

DIALOGUE I

Xiè Xiǎojie:	Jīntiān tiānqì <u>bǐ</u>(G1) zuótiān hǎo, bú xià yǔ <u>le</u>(G2).
Gāo Xiānsheng:	Míngtiān tiānqì zěnmeyàng? Xīwàng míngtiān yě bú xià yǔ.
Xiè Xiǎojie:	Wǒ kànle bàoshang de tiānqì yùbào, míngtiān tiānqì bǐ jīntiān gèng hǎo. Búdàn bú <u>huì</u>(G3) xià yǔ, érqiě huì nuǎnhuo yìdiǎnr.
Gāo Xiānsheng:	Tài hǎo le! Wǒ yuēle Lǐ Xiǎojie míngtiān qù gōngyuán kàn hóngyè.
Xiè Xiǎojie:	Shì ma? Kěshì Lǐ Xiǎojie jīntiān zǎoshang gēn Wáng Xiānsheng qù Shànghǎi le.
Gāo Xiānsheng:	Zhēn de a? Nà wǒ míngtiān zěnme bàn?
Xiè Xiǎojie:	Nǐ zài jiā kàn lùxiàng ba!

今日大陸天氣

海口	蘭州	瀋陽	西安	開封	北京	肯島	南京	上海	杭州	漢口	重慶	昆明	福州	廣州	城市
雨天	晴天	晴天	晴天	晴天	晴天	晴天	陰天	陰天	雨或雪	多雲	多雲	多雲	雨天	雨天	天氣
22	-8	-3	0	4	2	2	3	5	4	8	9	15	16		高溫
17	-15	-14	-10	-5	-7	-3	-2	0	-1	-2	2	-2	6	11	低溫

What is the weather like in Shanghai today?

DIALOGUE I

謝小姐： 今天天氣比(G1)昨天好，不下雨了(G2)。

高先生： 明天天氣怎麼樣？希望明天也不下雨。

謝小姐： 我看了報上的天氣預報，明天天氣比今天更好。不但不會(G3)下雨，而且會暖和一點兒。

高先生： 太好了！我約了李小姐明天去公園看紅葉。

謝小姐： 是嗎？可是李小姐今天早上跟王先生去上海了。

高先生： 真的啊？那我明天怎麼辦？

謝小姐： 你在家看錄像吧!

What is Miss Xie telling Mr. Gao?

What is Mr. Gao telling Miss Xie?

Tell what is happening in this picture.

*What is Miss Xie suggesting
to Mr. Gao, and why?*

Culture Notes

In China the climatic conditions differ drastically from one part of the country to another. Generally speaking, just as in America, the north is cold and snowy in winter; the south, hot and wet in summer. Three cities, 重慶 (Chóngqìng), 武漢 (Wǔhàn), and 南京 (Nánjīng), are nicknamed "furnaces" for their notoriously hot temperatures in summer. Other cities, such as 昆明 (Kūnmíng), are known for their year-round balmy weather. In the lower 長江 (Chángjiāng, the longest river in China, also known as the Yangtze) valley, there is a 黃梅 (huángméi, lit. yellow plum) season in May and June characterized by copious rain and high humidity. But the major rainy season for most of southern China is in July and August, when almost all the rivers swell to flood level. In winter, the island of 海南 (Hǎinán) provides warmth and appealing resorts for tourists from the north, while many southerners brave the cold and pour into the northern city of 哈爾濱 (Hā'ěrbīn) for its annual exhibition of ice sculptures.

Dialogue II: Complaining about the Weather

VOCABULARY

1.	糟糕	zāogāo	adj	in a terrible mess; too bad
2.	又	yòu	adv	again
3.	剛才	gāngcái	t	just now; a short moment ago
4.	出去	chūqu	vc	to go out
5.	熱	rè	adj	hot
6.	舒服	shūfu	adj	comfortable
7.	夏天	xiàtiān	n	summer
8.	這樣	zhèyàng	pr	so; like this
9.	涼快	liángkuai	adj	pleasantly cool (weather)
10.	春天	chūntiān	n	spring
11.	冬天	dōngtiān	n	winter
12.	又...又...	yòu...yòu		both...and...
13.	冷	lěng	adj	cold
14.	悶	mēn	adj	stuffy
15.	下次	xià cì		next time
	次	cì	m	time; (a measure word for occurrence)
16.	最好	zuìhǎo	adv	had better
17.	秋天	qiūtiān	n	autumn; fall

Proper Nouns

18.	台北	Táiběi	n	Taipei
19.	台灣	Táiwān	n	Taiwan

DIALOGUE II

Xiǎo Yè:	Zhēn zāogāo, yòu(G4) xià dà yǔ le.
Xiǎo Xià:	Gāngcái wǒ kàn bào le, bàoshang shuō, zhège xīngqī tiānqì dōu bù hǎo, xiàge xīngqī tiānqì cái huì(G3) hǎo.
Xiǎo Yè:	Zhēn de a? Nà zhège zhōumò bù néng chūqu wán le. Zuìjìn tiānqì tài rè, zhēn bù shūfu.
Xiǎo Xià:	Táiběi xiàtiān de tiānqì jiù shi zhèyàng. Liǎng ge yuè yǐhòu, tiānqì jiù huì bǐ xiànzài liángkuai yìdiǎnr le.
Xiǎo Yè:	Liǎng ge yuè yǐhòu? Xiàge yuè, wǒ jiù huí Měiguó qu le.
Xiǎo Xià:	Táiwān chūntiān chángcháng xià yǔ, dōngtiān hěn lěng, xiàtiān yòu mēn yòu rè(G5). Nǐ xià cì zuìhǎo qiūtiān lái.

DIALOGUE II

小葉：　真糟糕，又(G4)下大雨了。

小夏：　剛才我看報了，報上說，這個星期天氣都不好，下個星期天氣才會(G3)好。

小葉：　真的啊？那這個週末不能出去玩了。最近天氣太熱，真不舒服。

小夏：　台北夏天的天氣就是這樣。兩個月以後，天氣就會比現在涼快一點兒了。

小葉：　兩個月以後？下個月我就回美國去了。

小夏：　台灣春天常常下雨，冬天很冷，夏天又悶又熱(G5)。你下次最好秋天來。

Using the information in Dialogue I, tell a story about the pictures above.

Do the pictures above accurately depict Dialogue II? Explain each picture separately.

Describe what the weather is like in each of the four seasons.

SUPPLEMENTARY VOCABULARY

1.	潮濕	cháoshī	adj	wet; humid
2.	雲	yún	n	cloud
3.	雪	xuě	n	snow
4.	晴	qíng	adj	sunny; clear
5.	陰	yīn	adj	overcast
6.	台中	Táizhōng	n	Taichung (name of a city in Taiwan)
7.	加拿大	Jiānádà	n	Canada
8.	溫哥華	Wēngēhuá	n	Vancouver
9.	香港	Xiānggǎng	n	Hong Kong
10.	北京	Běijīng	n	Beijing

▼▼▼

Grammar

1. Comparative Sentences with 比 (bǐ)

Specific comparison of two entities is usually expressed with the basic pattern A 比 (bǐ) B + Adj.

(1) 李友比她姐姐高。

Lǐ Yǒu bǐ tā jiějie gāo.

(Li You is taller than her older sister.)

(2) 今天比昨天冷。

Jīntiān bǐ zuótiān lěng.

(It's colder today than yesterday.)

(3) 這本書比那本書有意思。

Zhè běn shū bǐ nà běn shū yǒu yìsi.

(This book is more interesting than that one.)

There are two ways in which the basic comparative construction may be further modified: (a) by adding a modifying term or construction after the adjective (see 4 and 5 below); and (b) by inserting the adverbs 更 (gèng) or 還 (hái) in front of the adjective (see 6 below).

(4) 今天比昨天冷<u>一點兒</u>。

Jīntiān bǐ zuótiān lěng <u>yìdiǎnr</u>.

(It's <u>a bit</u> colder today than yesterday.)

Note that the modifying term must be placed after the adjective (see 4 above), not before it (see 4a below).

(4a) *今天比昨天<u>一點兒</u>冷。

*Jīntiān bǐ zuótiān <u>yìdiǎnr</u> lěng.

(5) 明天會比今天冷<u>得多</u>。

Míngtiān huì bǐ jīntiān lěng <u>de duō</u>.

(It will be <u>much</u> colder tomorrow than today.)

(6) 昨天冷，今天比昨天<u>更</u>冷。

Zuótiān lěng, jīntiān bǐ zuótiān <u>gèng</u> lěng.

(It was cold yesterday. Today is <u>even</u> colder than yesterday.)

To express "much colder" in a comparative construction, 冷多了 (lěng duō le) or 冷得多 (lěng de duō) is used (see 7 below), not 很冷 (hěn lěng, very cold) (see 7a).

(7) 今天比昨天<u>冷多了</u>(or 冷得多)。

Jīntiān bǐ zuótiān lěng <u>duō le</u> (or lěng <u>de duō</u>).

(Today is much colder than yesterday.)

The following sentences are **incorrect**:

(7a) *今天比昨天很冷。

*Jīntiān bǐ zuótiān hěn lěng.

(*Today is very cold than yesterday.)

Note: While 跟 (gēn) and 和 (hé) are also used in sentences of comparison, they only denote that two things are the same or different without indicating the specific disparity as does 比 (bǐ). Compare the following two sentences:

(8a) 這個教室和那個教室一樣大。

Zhège jiàoshì hé nàge jiàoshì yíyàng dà.

(This classroom and that one are the same size.)

The Bund in Shanghai.

(8b) 這個教室跟那個教室不一樣大。

Zhège jiàoshì gēn nàge jiàoshì bù yíyàng dà.

(This classroom and that one are not the same size.)

(8c) 這個教室比那個教室大。

Zhège jiàoshì bǐ nàge jiàoshì dà.

(This classroom is larger than that one.)

(8d) 這個教室比那個教室大得多。

Zhège jiàoshì bǐ nàge jiàoshì dà de duō.

(This classroom is much larger than that one.)

2. The Particle 了 (le) (III): 了 (le) as a Sentence-Final Particle [See also L.5 G5 and L.8 G6]

When 了 (le) occurs at the end of a sentence, it usually indicates a change of status or the realization of a new situation.

(1) 下雨了。

Xià yǔ le.

(It's raining now.)

At 1,667 feet, Taipei 101 towers above the city.

(2) 妹妹的衣服小了。

Mèimei de yīfu xiǎo le.

(My sister's clothes have become small [i.e., too small for her].)

(3) 我昨天沒有空兒，今天有空兒了。

Wǒ zuótiān méiyǒu kòngr, jīntiān yǒu kòngr le.

(I didn't have time yesterday, but I do today.)

(4) 你看，老師來了。

Nǐ kàn, lǎoshī lái le.

(Look, the teacher has come.)

When used in this sense, 了 (le) can still be used at the end of a sentence even if the sentence is in the negative.

(5) 我沒有錢了，不買了。

Wǒ méiyǒu qián le, bù mǎi le.

(I don't have any money [left]. I won't buy it anymore.)

[Indicating that I intended to buy it originally, but I changed my mind.]

Note: Remember that to negate 有 (yǒu, to have), one uses 沒 (méi), not 不 (bù).

A Shanghai street scene.

3. The Auxiliary Verb 會 (huì, will) (II) [See also L.8 G9]

會 (huì) indicates an anticipated event or action in the future.

(1) 白老師現在不在辦公室，可是他明
天會在。

Bái Lǎoshī xiànzài bú zài bàngōngshì, kěshì tā míngtiān huì zài.

(Teacher Bai is not in the office now, but he will be tomorrow.)

(2) A: 你明年做什麼？

Nǐ míngnián zuò shénme?

(What will you do next year?)

B: 我明年會去中國學中文。

Wǒ míngnián huì qù Zhōngguó xué Zhōngwén.

(I'll go to China to learn Chinese next year.)

(3) 他說他晚上會給你打電話。

Tā shuō tā wǎnshang huì gěi nǐ dǎ diànhuà.

(He said he will call you this evening.)

The negative form of 會 (huì) is 不會 (bú huì):

(4) 小王覺得不舒服，今天不會來上
課。

Xiǎo Wáng juéde bù shūfu, jīntiān bú huì lái shàngkè.

(Xiao Wang is not feeling well. She won't come to class today.)

(5) 她很忙，晚上不會去看電影。

Tā hěn máng, wǎnshang bú huì qù kàn diànyǐng.

(She is very busy. She won't be going to see the movie tonight.)

4. The Adverb 又 (yòu, again)

又 (yòu, again) indicates repetition of an action.

(1) 他昨天看電影了，今天又看電影了。

Tā zuótiān kàn diànyǐng le, jīntiān yòu kàn diànyǐng le.

(He saw a movie yesterday, and saw another one today.)

(2) 前天下雨，昨天又下雨了。

Qiántiān xià yǔ, zuótiān yòu xià yǔ le.

(It rained the day before yesterday. Yesterday it rained again.)

(3) 媽媽昨天又給我打電話了。

Māma zuótiān yòu gěi wǒ dǎ diànhuà le.

(My mom called me again yesterday.)

Note: Both 又 (yòu, again) and 再 (zài, again) indicate repetition of an action, but in a sentence with 又 (yòu, again), both the original action and the repetition usually have occurred in the past, whereas 再 (zài, again) indicates an anticipated repetition of an action.

Compare:

(4) 我上個週末跳舞了，昨天我又去跳舞了。

Wǒ shàngge zhōumò tiào wǔ le, zuótiān wǒ yòu qù tiào wǔ le.

(I danced last weekend. Yesterday I went dancing again.)

(5) 我昨天跳舞了，我想明天晚上再去跳舞。

Wǒ zuótiān tiào wǔ le, wǒ xiǎng míngtiān wǎnshang zài qù tiào wǔ.

(I danced yesterday. I'm thinking of going dancing again tomorrow night.)

5. 又…又… (yòu…yòu…, both…and…)

The two adjectives used in this structure are either both commendatory or both derogatory, e.g., 又悶又熱 (yòu mēn yòu rè, both stuffy and humid) [both adjectives are perceived to be derogatory], 又便宜又好 (yòu piányi yòu hǎo, both inexpensive and good) [both adjectives are commendatory].

PATTERN DRILLS

A. Comparative Sentences with 比 (bǐ)

1.	Yīngwén	bǐ	Zhōngwén	róngyì.
2.	Dì liù kè		dì wǔ kè	nán.
3.	Tiào wǔ		tīng yīnyuè	yǒu yìsi.
4.	Lǐ Xiǎojie		Wáng Xiānsheng	máng.
5.	Tā gēge		tā dìdi	gāo.
6.	Tā dìdi		tā gēge	shuài.
7.	Zhè jiàn yīfu		nà jiàn yīfu	piányi.
8.	Nà běn shū		zhè běn shū	guì.
9.	Tā de qián		wǒ de qián	duō.
10.	Jīntiān de tiānqì		zuótiān de tiānqì	nuǎnhuo.
11.	Shànghǎi		Táiběi	lěng.

1.	英文	比	中文	容易。
2.	第六課		第五課	難。
3.	跳舞		聽音樂	有意思。
4.	李小姐		王先生	忙。
5.	她哥哥		她弟弟	高。

6. 他弟弟   他哥哥   帥。

7. 這件衣服   那件衣服   便宜。

8. 那本書   這本書   貴。

9. 她的錢   我的錢   多。

10. 今天的天氣   昨天的天氣   暖和。

11. 上海   台北   冷。

B. 了 (le) as Sentence-final Particle

Example: Zuótiān xià yǔ. (jīntiān, bú xià yǔ)

→ Jīntiān bú xià yǔ le.

昨天下雨。(今天，不下雨)

→ 今天不下雨了。

1. Wǒ qùnián xué Yīngwén.   (jīnnián   xué Zhōngwén)
2. Tā zǎoshang xǐ zǎo le.   (wǎnshang   bù xǐ zǎo)
3. Wǒ zuótiān chī Zhōngguó fàn le.   (jīntiān   bù chī Zhōngguó fàn)
4. Lǐ Yǒu yǐqián xǐhuan chàng gē.   (xiànzài   xǐhuan tiào wǔ)
5. Tā yǐqián xǐhuan Zhōngguó yīnyuè.   (xiànzài   xǐhuān Měiguó yīnyuè)
6. Wǒ yǐqián bú huì yòng Zhōngwén xiě xìn.   (xiànzài   huì yòng Zhōngwén xiě xìn)
7. Wǒ mèimei yǐqián chuān báisè de xié.   (xiànzài   chuān hēisè de xié)
8. Shàngge xīngqī zhèr hěn rè.   (xiànzài   liángkuai)

1. 我去年學英文。   (今年   學中文)

2. 他早上洗澡了。   (晚上   不洗澡)

3. 我昨天吃中國飯了。   (今天   不吃中國飯)

4. 李友以前喜歡唱歌。   (現在   喜歡跳舞)

A Taipei street scene.

5. 他以前喜歡中國音樂。　　　(現在　　喜歡美國音樂)

6. 我以前不會用中文寫信。　　　(現在　　會用中文寫信)

7. 我妹妹以前穿白色的鞋。　　　(現在　　穿黑色的鞋)

8. 上個星期這兒很熱。　　　　　(現在　　涼快)

C. 不但...而且 (búdàn…érqiě)

C1:

1. <u>Tā búdàn</u>	huì shuō Zhōngwén,	<u>érqiě</u>	huì shuō Yīngwén.
2.	xǐhuan chàng gē,		xǐhuan tiào wǔ.
3.	huì zuò Měiguó fàn,		huì zuò Zhōngguó fàn.
4.	xiǎng kàn diànyǐng,		xiǎng kàn diànshì.
5.	xǐhuan bái yánsè,		xǐhuan hóng yánsè.
6.	liànxí le fāyīn,		tīng le kèwén lùyīn.
7.	fùxí le dì qī kè,		yùxí le dì bā kè.

C1:

1. <u>他不但</u>　會說中文，　　<u>而且</u>　　會說英文。

2. 　　　　喜歡唱歌，　　　　　　喜歡跳舞。

3. 　　　會做美國飯，　　　　　　會做中國飯。

4. 　　　想看電影，　　　　　　　想看電視。

5. 　　　喜歡白顏色，　　　　　　喜歡紅顏色。

6. 　　　練習了發音，　　　　　　聽了課文錄音。

7. 　　　復習了第七課，　　　　　預習了第八課。

C2:

1.	Tāde dìdi	<u>búdàn</u>	hěn gāo,	<u>érqiě</u>	hěn shuài.
2.	Zhè jiàn yīfu		tài dà,		yánsè yě bù hǎo.
3.	Jīntiān de tiānqì		hěn mēn,		hěn rè.
4.	Táiwān de dōngtiān		hěn lěng,		hěn cháoshī.
5.	Dì shí kè de shēngcí		hěn duō,		hěn nán.
6.	Zhè shuāng xié		hěn guì,		hěn bù shūfu.
7.	Tā xiě zì		hěn hǎo,		hěn kuài.
8.	Xiǎo Gāo de jiā		hěn dà,		hěn piàoliang.

C2:

1. 他的弟弟　　　<u>不但</u>　很高，　<u>而且</u>　很帥。

2. 這件衣服　　　　　　太大，　　　　顏色也不好。

3. 今天的天氣　　　　　很悶，　　　　很熱。

4. 台灣的冬天　　　　　很冷，　　　　很潮濕。

5. 第十課的生詞　　　　很多，　　　　很難。

6. 這雙鞋　　　　　　　很貴，　　　　很不舒服。

7. 他寫字　　　　　　　很好，　　　　很快。

8. 小高的家　　　　　　很大，　　　　很漂亮。

D. 會 (huì)

For each group of words below, write both a positive and a negative sentence using 會.

Example: Tiānqì yùbào shūo   míngtiān   xià yǔ

→ Tiānqì yùbào shūo míngtiān huì xià yǔ.

→ Tiānqì yùbào shūo míngtiān bú huì xià yǔ.

天氣預報說　明天　下雨

→ 天氣預報說明天會下雨。

→ 天氣預報說明天不會下雨。

1.	Xiǎo Wáng	míngnián	qù Táiwān.
2.	Wáng Péng	jīntiān wǎnshang	jiāo Lǐ Yǒu xiě zì.
3.	Wǒmen	zhōumò	liànxí Zhōngwén.
4.	Lǐ Lǎoshī	xiàwǔ	qù kāi huì.
5.	Wáng Lǎoshī	míngtiān	qù kàn hóngyè.
6.	Xiǎo Gāo	xīngqíliù	qù tiào wǔ.
7.	Xiǎo Bái	xīngqītiān	qǐng wǒmen chī fàn.
8.	Lǐ Xiǎojie	míngtiān xiàwǔ	qù mǎi yīfu.

1.	小王	明年	去台灣。
2.	王朋	今天晚上	教李友寫字。
3.	我們	週末	練習中文。
4.	李老師	下午	去開會。
5.	王老師	明天	去看紅葉。
6.	小高	星期六	去跳舞。
7.	小白	星期天	請我們吃飯。
8.	李小姐	明天下午	去買衣服。

E. 又 (yòu)

For each group of words below, write a sentence using the 又 *structure.*

Example: xīngqīyī/xīngqī'èr   yǒu Zhōngwénkè

→ Wǒ xīngqīyī yǒu Zhōngwénkè, xīngqī'èr yòu yǒu Zhōngwénkè.

星期一/星期二   有中文課

→ 我星期一有中文課，星期二又有中文課。

1.	zuótiān shàngwǔ/jīntiān xiàwǔ	dǎle yí ge diànhuà
2.	zuótiān/jīntiān	mǎile yí jiàn yīfu
3.	shàng kè yǐqián/xià kè yǐhòu	tīngle yí cì lùyīn
4.	qùnián/jīnnián chūntiān	qùle yí cì Táiwān
5.	zuótiān/jīntiān	qù kàn hóngyè le
6.	zuótiān wǎnshang/jīntiān wǎnshang	tiào wǔ le
7.	shàngge xīngqī/zhège xīngqī	kàn le yí ge Rìběn diànyǐng

1. 昨天上午/今天下午   打了一個電話

2. 昨天/今天   買了一件衣服

3. 上課以前/下課以後   聽了一次錄音

4. 去年/今年春天   去了一次台灣

5. 昨天/今天   去看紅葉了

▼▼▼▼▼▼▼▼▼▼▼▼▼▼▼▼▼▼▼▼▼▼▼▼▼▼▼▼▼▼

6. 昨天晚上/今天晚上　　　　跳舞了

7. 上個星期/這個星期　　　　看了一個日本電影

F. 又...又... (yòu…yòu…)

1. Zhè shuāng xié	<u>yòu</u>	piányi	<u>yòu</u>	hǎokàn.
2. Zhè jiàn yīfu		guì		nánkàn.
3. Zhège diànnǎo		hǎo		piányi.
4. Shànghǎi de xiàtiān		rè		mēn.
5. Táiwān de dōngtiān		lěng		cháoshī.
6. Tā de dìdi		gāo		shuài.
7. Zhè běn shū		guì		méi yìsi.
8. Dì bā kè		róngyì		yǒu yìsi.
9. Xiǎo Gāo de jiā		shūfu		piàoliang.

1. 這雙鞋　　　　<u>又</u>　　便宜　　<u>又</u>　　好看。

2. 這件衣服　　　　　　貴　　　　　　難看。

3. 這個電腦　　　　　　好　　　　　　便宜。

4. 上海的夏天　　　　　熱　　　　　　悶。

5. 台灣的冬天　　　　　冷　　　　　　潮濕。

6. 他的弟弟　　　　　　高　　　　　　帥。

7.	這本書	貴	沒意思。
8.	第八課	容易	有意思。
9.	小高的家	舒服	漂亮。

English Texts

DIALOGUE I

Miss Xie:	The weather is better today than yesterday. It's no longer raining.
Mr. Gao:	What's the weather going to be like tomorrow? I hope it won't rain tomorrow, either.
Miss Xie:	I read the weather forecast in today's paper. The weather will be even better tomorrow than today. Not only will it not rain, but it will also be a bit warmer.
Mr. Gao:	That's great. I asked Miss Li to go to the park with me to see the red autumn leaves tomorrow.
Miss Xie:	Really? But Miss Li went to Shanghai this morning with Mr. Wang.
Mr. Gao:	You don't say! What shall I do tomorrow?
Miss Xie:	You can watch a video at home!

DIALOGUE II

Xiao Ye:	Too bad. It's pouring again.
Xiao Xia:	I just read the newspaper. The paper says the weather is going to be bad all week. It won't get better until next week.
Xiao Ye:	Really? Then we can't go out this weekend. It's been too hot lately. It's really uncomfortable.
Xiao Xia:	The weather is like this in the summer in Taipei. In two months the weather will be a bit cooler than it is now.
Xiao Ye:	In two months? I'm going back to the United States next month.
Xiao Xia:	In Taiwan it rains often in spring, and it's cold in winter. In summer it's hot and muggy. Next time you'd better come in the fall.

LESSON 11 ▲ Transportation
第十一課 ▲ 交通
Dì shíyī kè ▲ *Jiāotōng*

坐公共汽車

Zuò gōnggòng qìchē

Dialogue: Going Home for the Winter Vacation

VOCABULARY

1.	#寒假	hánjià	n	winter vacation
2.	飛機	fēijī	n	airplane
	飛	fēi	v	to fly
	機	jī	n	machine
3.	票	piào	n	ticket
4.	(飛)機場	(fēi)jīchǎng	n	airport

5.	坐	zuò	v	to travel by [see also L.5]
6.	公共汽車	gōnggòng qìchē	n	bus
	公共	gōnggòng	adj	public
	汽車	qìchē	n	automobile
	車	chē	n	vehicle; car
7.	或者	huòzhě	conj	or [see G2]
8.	地#鐵	dìtiě	n	subway
9.	走	zǒu	v	to walk; to go by way of
10.	先	xiān	adv	first; before
11.	(車)站	(chē)zhàn	n	(bus, train, etc.) stop; station
12.	下車	xià chē	vo	to get off (a bus, train, etc.)
13.	然後	ránhòu	adv	then
14.	#綠	lǜ	adj	green
15.	#線	xiàn	n	line
16.	最後	zuìhòu	adv	finally
17.	#藍	lán	adj	blue
18.	#麻#煩	máfan	adj	troublesome
19.	還是	háishi	conj	had better [see G4]
20.	出#租汽車	chūzū qìchē	n	taxi
	出租	chūzū	v	to rent out; to let
	租	zū	v	to rent
21.	開車	kāi chē	vo	to drive a car
	開	kāi	v	to drive; to operate
22.	送	sòng	v	to see off or out; to take someone (somewhere)

DIALOGUE

Wáng Péng: Hánjià nǐ huí jiā ma?

Lǐ Yǒu: Wǒ yào huí jiā.

Wáng Péng: <u>Fēijī piào nǐ mǎi le ma</u> (G1)?

Lǐ Yǒu: Yǐjīng mǎi le. Shì èrshíyī hào de.

Wáng Péng: Fēijī shì jǐ diǎn de?

Lǐ Yǒu: Wǎnshang bā diǎn de.

Wáng Péng: Nǐ zěnme qù jīchǎng?

Lǐ Yǒu: Wǒ xiǎng zuò gōnggòng qìchē <u>huòzhě</u>(G2) zuò dìtiě. Nǐ zhīdao zěnme zǒu ma?

Wáng Péng: Nǐ xiān zuò yí hào(1) qìchē, zuò sān zhàn xià chē, ránhòu huàn dìtiě. <u>Xiān</u> zuò hóngxiàn, <u>zài</u>(G3) huàn lǜ xiàn, zuìhòu huàn lán xiàn.

Lǐ Yǒu: Bù xíng, bù xíng, tài máfan le. Wǒ <u>háishi</u>(G4) zuò chūzū qìchē(2) ba.

Wáng Péng: Zuò chūzū qìchē tài guì, wǒ kěyǐ kāi chē sòng nǐ qù.

Lǐ Yǒu: Xièxie nǐ.

Wáng Péng: Bú yòng kèqi.

DIALOGUE

王朋：　寒假你回家嗎？

李友：　我要回家。

王朋：　<u>飛機票你買了嗎</u>(G1)？

李友：　已經買了。是二十一號的。

王朋：　飛機是幾點的？

李友：　晚上八點的。

王朋：　你怎麼去機場？

李友：　我想坐公共汽車<u>或者</u>(G2)坐地鐵。你知道怎麼走嗎？

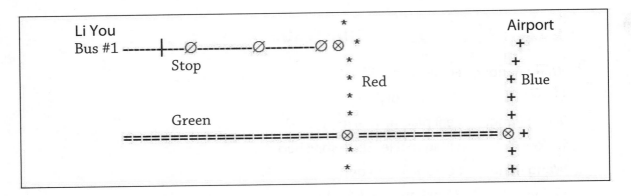

The route from Li You's home to the airport.

王朋： 你先坐一號⑴汽車，坐三站下車，
　　　然後換地鐵。<u>先</u>坐紅線，<u>再</u>(G3)換綠
　　　線，最後換藍線。

李友： 不行，不行，太麻煩了。我<u>還是</u>
　　　(G4)坐出租汽車⑵吧。

王朋： 坐出租汽車太貴，我可以開車送你
　　　去。

李友： 謝謝你。

王朋： 不用客氣。

Notes

▲**1**▲ Both 號 (hào) and 路 (lù) are used to refer to bus routes. Therefore, 一路車 (yí lù chē) also refers to bus route #1.

▲**2**▲ In Taiwan taxis are called 計程車 (jìchéngchē) or 出租車 (chū-zūchē).

A Letter: Thanking Someone for a Ride

VOCABULARY

1. 不過	búguò	conj	however; but
2. 讓	ràng	v	to allow or cause (somebody to do something)
3. 花	huā	v	to spend
4. 不好意思	bù hǎoyìsi	ce	to feel embarrassed
5. 這幾天	zhè jǐ tiān	np	the past few days
6. 每天	měitiān		every day
每	měi	prep	every; each (usually followed by a measure word)
7. 高速公路	gāosù gōnglù		super highway; highway
高速	gāosù	adj	high speed
公路	gōnglù	n	highway; road
路	lù	n	road; path
8. 緊張	jǐnzhāng	adj	nervous, anxious
9. 自己	zìjǐ	pr	oneself
10. 新年	xīnnián	n	new year
11. 快	kuài	adv	soon; be about to; before long (usually takes 了 {le} at the end of the sentence)
12. 快樂	kuàilè	adj	happy

A LETTER

Wáng Péng:

Xièxie nǐ nà tiān kāi chē sòng wǒ dào jīchǎng. Búguò, ràng nǐ huā nàme duō shíjiān, zhēn bù hǎoyìsi. Wǒ zhè jǐ tiān <u>měi</u> tiān <u>dōu</u>(G5) kāi chē chūqu kàn lǎo péngyou. Zhèr de rén kāi chē kāi de hěn kuài. Wǒ zài gāosù gōnglù shang kāi chē, zhēn yǒu diǎnr jǐnzhāng. Kěshì zhèr méiyǒu gōnggòng qìchē, yě méiyǒu dìtiě, hěn bù fāngbiàn, zhǐ néng zìjǐ kāi chē.

Xīnnián kuài dào le, zhù(F) nǐ xīnnián kuàilè!

Lǐ Yǒu

Shí'èryuè èrshíliù rì

A LETTER

王朋：

　謝謝你那天開車送我到機場。不過，讓你花那麼多時間，真不好意思。我這幾天每天都(G5)開車出去看老朋友。這兒的人開車開得很快。我在高速公路上開車，真有點兒緊張。可是這兒沒有公共汽車，也沒有地鐵，很不方便，只能自己開車。

　新年快到了，祝(F)你新年快樂！

李友

十二月二十六日

FUNCTIONAL EXPRESSIONS

祝 (zhù, to offer good wishes)

祝你新年快樂！(I wish you a happy New Year!)

Zhù nǐ xīnnián kuàilè!

祝你生日快樂！(Happy Birthday to you!)

Zhù nǐ shēngrì kuàilè!

祝你考試考得好！(I wish you success with the exam!)

Zhù nǐ kǎoshì kǎo de hǎo!

祝寒假快樂！(Have a happy winter break!)

Zhù hánjià kuàilè!

祝聖誕快樂！(Merry Christmas!)

Zhù Shèngdàn kuàilè!

祝春節快樂！(Happy Chinese New Year!)

Zhù Chūnjié kuàilè!

Culture Notes

▲1▲ In China the railroad system has long constituted the principal means of travel as well as transport in general. However, in recent years both the highway system and airline travel have expanded very rapidly. China now ranks second only to the United States in total roadway miles covered by the highway system.

▲2▲ Chinese New Year, which is determined by the lunar calendar and usually falls in late January or early February, is the most important annual holiday in China and Taiwan. However, nowadays the January 1 international New Year is also recognized. The most common New Year greetings are "新年好" (xīnnián hǎo) and "新年快樂" (xīnnián kuàilè), which can be used for both New Years, but for the Chinese New Year many people prefer the traditional greeting: 恭喜發財 (gōngxǐ fācái). The phrase, which literally means "Congratulations and may you make a fortune," can be translated as "May you be happy and prosperous!"

SUPPLEMENTARY VOCABULARY

1.	走路	zǒu lù	vo	to walk
2	火車	huǒchē	n	train
3.	計程車	jìchéngchē	n	taxi (in Taiwan)
4.	電車	diànchē	n	cable car; trolley bus; tram
5.	船	chuán	n	boat; ship

| 6. | 輛 | liàng | m | (a measure for vehicles) |
| 7. | 暑假 | shǔjià | n | summer vacation |

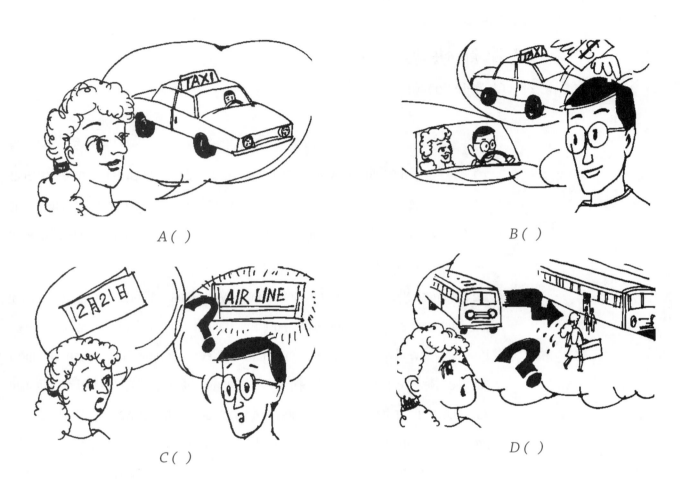

A ( )

B ( )

C ( )

D ( )

Review Dialogue I and put the above pictures in the correct sequence by using the numbers 1–4.

Grammar

1. Topic-Comment Sentences

When a noun or noun phrase has become established as a known element in a conversation, it can occur at the beginning of the sentence, serving as the "topic," with the rest of the sentence functioning as a "comment" on it. This forms what is known as a "topic-comment sentence." In such a sentence the object of the verb can be brought forward to serve as the topic of the sentence.

(1) A: 我昨天買了一本書。

Wǒ zuótiān mǎile yì běn shū.

(I bought a book yesterday.)

B: <u>那本書</u>你看了嗎？

<u>Nà běn shū</u> nǐ kànle ma?

(Have you read that book?)

(2) A: 你知道<u>我的襯衫</u>在哪兒嗎？

Nǐ zhīdao <u>wǒ de chènshān</u> zài nǎr ma?

(Do you know where my shirt is?)

B: <u>你的襯衫</u>我給你媽媽了。

<u>Nǐ de chènshān</u> wǒ gěi nǐ māma le.

(I have given your shirt to your mother.)

(3) A: 你有<u>朋友</u>嗎？

Nǐ yǒu <u>péngyou</u> ma?

(Do you have friends?)

B: <u>朋友</u>我有很多，可是都不在這兒。

<u>Péngyou</u> wǒ yǒu hěn duō, kěshì dōu bú zài zhèr.

(I have many friends, but none of them are here.)

(4) 她不想去日本，可是<u>飛機票</u>她媽媽
已經買好了。

Tā bù xiǎng qù Rìběn, kěshì <u>fēijīpiào</u> tā māma yǐjīng mǎi hǎo le.

(She does not want to go to Japan, but her mother has already booked the airplane ticket.)

2. 或者 (huòzhě, or) and 還是 (háishi, or)

While both 或者 (huòzhě, or) and 還是 (háishi, or) link up two words or phrases that indicate different alternatives, the former usually appears in statements and the latter in questions.

A subway entrance in Beijing.

(1) A: 你今天晚上做什麼？

Nǐ jīntiān wǎnshang zuò shénme?

(What are you going to do tonight?)

B: 聽音樂或者看錄像。

Tīng yīnyuè huòzhě kàn lùxiàng.

(Listen to music or watch a video tape.)

(2) A: 你喜歡學中文還是喜歡學日文？

Nǐ xǐhuan xué Zhōngwén háishi xǐhuan xué Rìwén?

(Do you like studying Chinese or Japanese?)

B: 中文或者日文我都喜歡學。

Zhōngwén huòzhě Rìwén wǒ dōu xǐhuan xué.

(Whether it's Chinese or Japanese, I like studying both [equally].)

(3) A: 你喜歡什麼顏色的鞋？黑的還是
咖啡色的？

Nǐ xǐhuan shénme yánsè de xié? Hēi de háishi kāfēisè de?

(What color shoes do you like, black or brown?)

▼▼▼▼▼▼▼▼▼▼▼▼▼▼▼▼▼▼▼▼▼▼▼▼▼▼▼▼▼▼

Taking a taxi.

B: 黑的或者咖啡色的我都不喜歡，
我喜歡白的。

Hēi de huòzhě kāfēisè de wǒ dōu bù xǐhuan, wǒ xǐhuan bái de.

(I don't like either black or brown; I like white ones.)

(4) A: 你晚上看電影還是看電視？

Nǐ wǎnshang kàn diànyǐng háishi kàn diànshì?

(Are you going to see a movie or watch TV this evening?)

B: 看電影或者看電視都可以。

Kàn diànyǐng huòzhě kàn diànshì dōu kěyǐ.

(Either going to a movie or watching TV would be fine with me.)

(5) 明天你去開會或者他去開會都可以。

Míngtiān nǐ qù kāi huì huòzhě tā qù kāi huì dōu kěyǐ.

(Either you or he may attend tomorrow's meeting.)

3. 先...再...(xiān...zài..., first..., then...)

Sometimes 再 (zài) indicates a sequence of actions rather than a repetition. "先看電影再吃飯" (Xiān kàn diànyǐng zài chī fàn; First go to the movie, then eat) means "看電影以後吃飯" (Kàn diànyǐng yǐhòu chī fàn; Eat after seeing the movie). More examples:

China-based Air China.

(1) A: 你什麼時候給媽媽打電話？

Nǐ shénme shíhou gěi māma dǎ diànhuà?

(When are you going to call Mom?)

B: 下課以後再打。

Xiàkè yǐhòu zài dǎ.

(I'll call after class.)

(2) 我想先打球再去圖書館。

Wǒ xiǎng xiān dǎ qiú zài qù túshūguǎn.

(I'm thinking of going to the library after playing ball.)

(3) 你先做功課再看電視。

Nǐ xiān zuò gōngkè zài kàn diànshì.

(You'd better finish doing the homework before you watch TV.)

Note: As adverbs, 先 (xiān) and 再 (zài) must come immediately before a verb. They cannot be placed in front of the subject.

(3a) *先你做功課再你看電視。

*Xiān nǐ zuò gōngkè zài nǐ kàn diànshì.

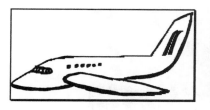  

Name the three forms of transportation above.

4. 還是 (háishi, had better)

還是 (háishi, had better) can be used to signify making a selection after considering two or more options. Sometimes in making such a decision one is forced to give up one's preference.

(1)   A: 高先生：下雨了。怎麼辦？

     Gāo Xiānsheng: Xià yǔ le. Zěnme bàn?

     (Mr. Gao: It's raining. What shall we do?)

  B: 白小姐：我們還是在家看錄像吧。

     Bái Xiǎojie: Wǒmen háishi zài jiā kàn lùxiàng ba.

     (Miss Bai: We had better stay home and watch a video.)

(2)   A: 你說，明天看電影還是看打球？

     Nǐ shuō, míngtiān kàn diànyǐng háishi kàn dǎ qiú?

     (What do you think we should watch tomorrow, a movie or a ball game?)

  B: 還是看電影吧。

     Háishi kàn diànyǐng ba.

     (Let's go see a movie.)

5. 每...都...(měi...dōu..., every...)

In a sentence that contains the term 每 (měi, every), usually 都 (dōu, all) has to be inserted further along in the sentence, immediately in front of the verb.

(1) 他每天晚上都看電視。

     Tā měi tiān wǎnshang dōu kàn diànshì.

     (He watches TV every evening.)

Taiwan-based China Airlines.

(2) 我每節課都來。

Wǒ měi jié kè dōu lái.

(I come to every class.)

(3) 這兒每個人我都認識。

Zhèr měi gè rén wǒ dōu rènshi.

(I know everyone here.)

(4) 王老師寫的字每個都好看。

Wáng Lǎoshī xiě de zì měi gè dōu hǎokàn.

(Every character written by Teacher Wang looks nice.)

PATTERN DRILLS

A. Topic-comment Sentences

Write a topic-comment sentence based on each sentence given below.

Example: Nǐ yǒu hěn duō <u>péngyou</u> ma?

→ <u>Péngyou</u> wǒ yǒu hěn duō.

你有很多<u>朋友</u>嗎？

→ <u>朋友</u>我有很多。

1.   Nǐ chángcháng qù <u>Xiǎo Bái jiā</u> ma?

2.   Tā dìdi huì bu huì xiě <u>Zhōngwén xìn</u>?

3. Nǐ yǐjīng mǎile <u>diànnǎo</u> ma?

4. Nǐ xiǎng kàn <u>nàge diànyǐng</u> ma?

5. Tā chángcháng hē <u>píjiǔ</u> ma?

6. Nǐ mǎi méi mǎi <u>fēijīpiào</u>?

7. Nǐ dìdi xǐhuan bù xǐhuan kàn <u>Zhōngwén shū</u>?

8. Tā chángcháng tīng <u>Méiguó yīnyuè</u> ma?

1. 你常常去<u>小白家</u>嗎？

2. 她弟弟會不會寫<u>中文信</u>？

3. 你已經買了<u>電腦</u>嗎？

4. 你想看<u>那個電影</u>嗎？

5. 他常常喝<u>啤酒</u>嗎？

6. 你買沒買<u>飛機票</u>？

7. 你弟弟喜歡不喜歡看<u>中文書</u>？

8. 她常常聽<u>美國音樂</u>嗎？

B. 或者 (huòzhě)

For each group of words below, write a sentence containing 或者.

Example: (jīntiān wǎnshang, kàn diànshì/kàn diànyǐng)

→ Jīntiān wǎnshang wǒ xiǎng kàn diànshì huòzhě kàn diànyǐng.

(今天晚上，看電視/看電影)

→ 今天晚上我想看電視或者看電影。

1. míngtiān shàngwǔ   zhǎo Wáng Lǎoshī/zhǎo Lǐ Lǎoshī wèn wèntí
2. míngtiān xiàwǔ   qù dǎ qiú/qù tiào wǔ
3. jīntiān wǎnshang   chī Zhōngguó fàn/chī Rìběn fàn

北京的公共汽車

Běijīng de gōnggòng qìchē

4.	xiàge xuéqí	xué Zhōngwén/xué Rìwén
5.	xīngqīliù/xīngqītiān	kàn lùxiàng
6.	zuò dìtiě/zuò gōnggòng qìchē	qù Wáng Lǎoshī jiā
7.	jīnnián/míngnián	qù Táiwān
8.	xiàwǔ sān diǎn/sì diǎn	qù Xiǎo Bái jiā
9.	jīntiān xiàwǔ/wǎnshang	zuò gōngkè

1.	明天上午	找王老師/找李老師問問題
2.	明天下午	去打球/去跳舞
3.	今天晚上	吃中國飯/吃日本飯
4.	下個學期	學中文/學日文
5.	星期六/星期天	看錄像
6.	坐地鐵/坐公共汽車	去王老師家
7.	今年/明年	去台灣
8.	下午三點/四點	去小白家
9.	今天下午/晚上	做功課

▼▼▼

Shanghai Railway Station.

C. 先...再... (xiān...zài...)

For each group of words below, create a sentence containing the 先...再... *pattern.*

Example: (chī zǎofàn, qù túshūguǎn)

        → Wǒ xiān chī zǎofàn, zài qù túshūguǎn.

(吃早飯，去圖書館)

→ 我先吃早飯，再去圖書館。

1.	qù túshūguǎn	shàng Zhōngwénkè
2.	shàng Zhōngwénkè	shàng diànnǎokè
3.	chī wǎnfàn	qù kàn diànyǐng
4.	zuò gōngkè	qù dǎ qiú
5.	liànxí fāyīn	xiě Hànzì
6.	hē píjiǔ	chī fàn
7.	kàn lùxiàng	tiào wǔ
8.	tīng Měiguó yīnyuè	tīng Zhōngguó yīnyuè

1. 去圖書館   上中文課

2. 上中文課   上電腦課

3. 吃晚飯   去看電影

Entering Shanghai Railway Station.

4. 做功課   去打球

5. 練習發音   寫漢字

6. 喝啤酒   吃飯

7. 看錄像   跳舞

8. 聽美國音樂   聽中國音樂

D. 還是 (háishi)

For each group of words below, write a question with 還是, and then answer the question using 還是. Use the underlined words in your answer.

Example: kàn hóngyè   <u>kàn lùxiàng</u>

→ A: Wǒmen qù gōngyuán kàn hóngyè háishi zài jiā kàn lùxiàng?

→ B: Wǒmen háishi zài jiā kàn lùxiàng ba.

看紅葉   <u>看錄像</u>

→ A: 我們去公園看紅葉還是在家看錄像？

→ B: 我們還是在家看錄像吧。

Taipei Rapid Transit Station.

1.	kàn diànyǐng	<u>kàn diànshì</u>
2.	<u>xué Zhōngwén</u>	xué Fǎwén
3.	qù Táiběi wánr	<u>qù Shànghǎi wánr</u>
4.	shàng Zhōngwénkè	<u>shàng diànnǎokè</u>
5.	xiān dǎ qiú	<u>xiān zuò gōngkè</u>
6.	<u>qù chī Zhōngguó fàn</u>	qù chī Měiguó fàn
7.	jīnnián qù Táiwān	<u>míngnián qù Táiwān</u>
8.	<u>qù túshūguǎn zuò gōngkè</u>	zài sùshè zuò gōngkè

1. 看電影 　　　　　<u>看電視</u>

2. <u>學中文</u> 　　　　學法文

3. 去台北玩兒 　　　<u>去上海玩兒</u>

4. 上中文課 　　　　<u>上電腦課</u>

5. 先打球 　　　　　<u>先做功課</u>

6. <u>去吃中國飯</u> 　　去吃美國飯

7. 今年去台灣 　　　<u>明年去台灣</u>

8. <u>去圖書館做功課</u> 　在宿舍做功課

中國的高速公路

Zhōngguó de gāosù gōnglù

E. 每...都... (měi...dōu...)

For each group of words below, create a sentence containing the 每...都...
pattern.

Example: (wǎnshang, kàn diànshì)

→ Tā měitiān wǎnshang dōu kàn diànshì.

(晚上   看電視)

→ 他每天晚上都看電視。

1.	xiàwǔ	liànxí Zhōngwén
2.	zǎoshang	tīng Zhōngwén lùyīn
3.	zì	xiě de hěn hǎo
4.	yīfu	shì xīn de
5.	rén	rènshi
6.	wǎnshang	shí diǎnzhōng shuì jiào
7.	xīngqīliù	gěi māma dǎ diànhuà
8.	chènshān	shì báisè de
9.	shū	hěn yǒuyìsi

1. 下午   練習中文

2. 早上   聽中文錄音

▼▼▼

3. 字 　　　寫得很好

4. 衣服 　　是新的

5. 人 　　　認識

6. 晚上 　　十點鐘睡覺

7. 星期六 　給媽媽打電話

8. 襯衫 　　是白色的

9. 書 　　　很有意思

English Texts

DIALOGUE

Wang Peng:	Are you going home during the winter break?
Li You:	Yes, I am.
Wang Peng:	Have you booked a plane ticket?
Li You:	Yes. It's for the twenty-first.
Wang Peng:	When is the plane leaving?
Li You:	8 p.m.
Wang Peng:	How are you going to the airport?
Li You:	I'm thinking of taking the bus or the subway. Do you know how to get there?
Wang Peng:	You first take bus No. 1. Get off after three stops. Then take the subway. First take the red line, then change to the green line, and finally change to the blue line.
Li You:	Oh no, oh no. That's too much trouble. I'd better take a cab.
Wang Peng:	It's too expensive to take a cab. I can take you to the airport.
Li You:	Thank you very much.
Wang Peng:	Don't mention it.

A sleeper car in a Chinese train.

A LETTER

December 26

Wang Peng:

Thank you for driving me to the airport the other day. But I'm really embarrassed about having had you spend so much time. The past few days I've been going out by car to see old friends. People here drive fast. I was really nervous driving on the highway. But there are no public buses or subway. It's very inconvenient. I have to drive.

New Year is almost here. Happy New Year!

Li You

Taxi Drivers in China

Many taxi drivers in China, especially those in Beijing, are known to be very outgoing and talkative. If you go to China and your taxi driver happens to be a chatty one, it may be a good opportunity for you to learn about ordinary Chinese people's lives, and about their opinions on current affairs.

Describe the modes of transportation above.

新疆維吾爾自治區

烏魯木齊

黑龍江

哈爾濱

長春

吉林

內蒙古自治區

瀋陽

遼寧

甘肅

呼和浩特

北京☆
天津

河北

寧夏回族自治區

銀川

太原

山西

濟南

山東

青海

西寧

蘭州

西安

陝西

鄭州

河南

江蘇

合肥

南京

上海

西藏自治區

拉薩

成都

四川

湖北

武漢

安徽

杭州

浙江

貴州

長沙

南昌

江西

貴陽

湖南

福州

福建

台北

昆明

云南

廣西壯族
自治區

南寧

廣州

廣東

香港

台灣

海南

海口

中國地圖

Map of China

APPENDIX: PLACE NAMES IN CHINA

Provinces and Their Capital Cities

Province Name		Capital City	
1. 安徽	Ānhuī	合肥	Héféi
2. 福建	Fújiàn	福州	Fúzhōu
3. 甘肅	Gānsù	蘭州	Lánzhōu
4. 廣東	Guǎngdōng	廣州	Guǎngzhōu
5. 貴州	Guìzhōu	貴陽	Guìyáng
6. 海南	Hǎinán	海口	Hǎikǒu
7. 河北	Héběi	石家莊	Shíjiāzhuāng
8. 河南	Hénán	鄭州	Zhèngzhōu
9. 黑龍江	Hēilóngjiāng	哈爾濱	Hā'ěrbīn
10. 湖北	Húběi	武漢	Wǔhàn
11. 湖南	Húnán	長沙	Chángshā
12. 吉林	Jílín	長春	Chángchūn
13. 江蘇	Jiāngsū	南京	Nánjīng
14. 江西	Jiāngxī	南昌	Nánchāng
15. 遼寧	Liáoníng	瀋陽	Shěnyáng
16. 青海	Qīnghǎi	西寧	Xīníng
17. 山東	Shāndōng	濟南	Jǐnán
18. 山西	Shānxī	太原	Tàiyuán
19. 陝西	Shǎnxī	西安	Xī'ān
20. 四川	Sìchuān	成都	Chéngdū
21. 云南	Yúnnán	昆明	Kūnmíng
22. 浙江	Zhèjiāng	杭州	Hángzhōu
23. 台灣	Táiwān		

Municipalities Directly under the Central Government and the Provinces in Which They Are Located

Municipality		Province	
1. 北京	Běijīng	河北	Héběi
2. 上海	Shànghǎi	江蘇	Jiāngsū
3. 天津	Tiānjīn	河北	Héběi
4. 重慶	Chóngqìng	四川	Sìchuān

Autonomous Regions and Their Capital Cities

Autonomous Region			Capital City
1. 內蒙古自治區	Nèi Ménggǔ Zìzhìqū	呼和浩特	Hūhéhàotè (Huhhot)
2. 廣西壯族自治區	Guǎngxī Zhuàngzú Zìzhìqū	南寧	Nánníng
3. 寧夏回族自治區	Níngxià Huízú Zìzhìqū	銀川	Yínchuān
4. 新疆維吾爾自治區	Xīnjiāng Wéiwǔ'ěr (Uygur) Zìzhìqū	烏魯木齊	Wūlǔmùqí (Urumqi)
5. 西藏自治區	Xīzàng Zìzhìqū	拉薩	Lāsà (Lhasa)

Special Administrative Regions

1. 香港特別行政區	Xiānggǎng tèbié xíngzhèng qū	Hong Kong	Xiānggǎng
2. 澳門特別行政區	Aòmén tèbié xíngzhèng qū	Macau/Macao	Aòmén

Other Major Cities in China and the Provinces in Which They Are Located

City		Province	
1. 重慶	Chóngqìng	四川	Sìchuān
2. 青島	Qīngdǎo	山東	Shāndōng
3. 大連	Dàlián	遼寧	Liáoníng
4. 桂林	Guìlín	廣西壯族自治區	Guǎngxī Zhuàngzú Zìzhìqū

Major Cities in Taiwan

1. 台北	Táiběi	Taipei
2. 高雄	Gāoxióng	Kaohsiung
3. 台中	Táizhōng	Taichung
4. 台南	Táinán	Tainan
5. 台東	Táidōng	Taitung
6. 花蓮	Huālián	Hualien

VOCABULARY INDEX (CHINESE-ENGLISH): LESSONS 1–11

Key: c=Culture Notes; f=Functional Expressions; g=Grammar; n=Notes; s=Supplementary Vocabulary

The Chinese-English index is arranged in syllable-by-syllable alphabetic order except that entries with the same first Chinese characters are kept together.

Pinyin	Characters	Grammar	English	Lesson
▲**A**▲				
a	啊	P	(a sentence-final particle of exclamation, interrogation, etc.)	6
▲**B**▲				
ba	吧	P	(a "suggestion" particle; softens the tone of the sentence to which it is appended)	5
bā	八	Nu	eight	Intro.
bāyuè	八月	N	August	3g
bàba	爸爸	N	dad; father	2
bái	白	Adj	white; (a surname)	3
bǎi	百	Nu	hundred	9
Bǎishìkělè	百事可樂	N	Pepsi	5s
bàn	半	Nu	half; half an hour	3
bànyè	半夜	T	midnight	7
bàngōngshì	辦公室	N	office	6
bāng	幫	V	to help	6
bāng máng	幫忙	VO	to help; to do someone a favor	6
bāngzhù	幫助	V	to help	7
bàngqiú	棒球	N	baseball	4s
bào	報	N	newspaper	8
bàoshang	報上		in the newspaper	10
bēi	杯	M	cup; glass	5
Běijīng	北京	PN	Beijing	10s
běnzi	本子	N	notebook	7s
bǐ	筆	N	pen	7
bǐ	比	Prep	(a comparison marker)	10
biǎo	錶	N	watch	3s
bié	別		don't	6
bié (de)	別(的)	Adv	other	4
bié kèqi	別客氣	CE	Don't be so polite!	6
biérén	別人	N	others; other people; another person	4
bù	不	Adv	not; no	1
búcuò	不錯	Adj	not bad; pretty good	4
búdàn..., érqiě	不但...而且	Conj	not only..., but also	10
búguò	不過	Conj	however; but	11
bú kèqi	不客氣	CE	You are welcome. Don't be (so) polite.	6

▼▼▼▼▼▼▼▼▼▼▼▼▼▼▼▼▼▼▼▼▼▼▼▼▼▼▼▼▼▼▼▼

Pinyin	Characters	Grammar	English	Lesson
bú xiè	不謝	CE	Don't mention it. Not at all. You're welcome.	7
bú yòng	不用	CE	need not	6g, 9
bù hǎoyìsi	不好意思	CE	to feel embarrassed	11
bùshǒu	部首	N	radical	Intro.

▲C▲

Pinyin	Characters	Grammar	English	Lesson
cái	才	Adv	not until; only then	5
cāntīng	餐廳	N	dining room; cafeteria	8
chá	茶	N	tea	5
chà	差	V	to be short of; to be lacking	3s
cháng	長	Adj	long	9s
Chángjiāng	長江	PN	Yangtze river	10c
chángpáo	長袍	N	long gown	9c
chángshòu	長壽	N	longevity	3c
chángshòu miàn	長壽麵	N	longevity noodles	3c
chángcháng	常常	Adv	often	4
chàng	唱	V	to sing	4
chàng gē	唱歌	VO	to sing (a song)	4
cháoshī	潮濕	Adj	wet; humid	10s
chē	車	N	vehicle; car	11
(chē)zhàn	車站	N	(bus, train, etc.) stop; station	11
chén	陳	N	(a surname)	1n
chènshān	襯衫	N	shirt	9
chī	吃	V	to eat	3
chī fàn	吃飯	VO	to eat (a meal)	3
Chóngqìng	重慶	PN	Chongqing	10c
chūqu	出去	VC	to go out	10
chūzū	出租	V	to rent out; to let	11
chūzū qìchē	出租汽車	N	taxi	11
chūzhōng	初中	N	junior high (grades 7–9)	2c
chúle...yǐwài	除了...以外	Conj	in addition to; besides	8
chūntiān	春天	N	spring	10
chuān	穿	V	to wear; to put on	9
chuán	船	N	boat; ship	11s
chuáng	床	N	bed	2g, 8
cì	次	M	time; (a measure word for occurrence)	10
cuò	錯	Adj	wrong	4

▲D▲

Pinyin	Characters	Grammar	English	Lesson
dǎ	打	V	to hit; to strike	4
dǎ diànhuà	打電話	VO	to make a phone call	6
dǎ gōng	打工	VO	to work part-time; to do manual work	5s
dǎ qiú	打球	VO	to play ball	4
dà	大	Adj	big; old	3
dàgē	大哥	N	oldest brother	7g
dàjiā	大家	Pr	everybody	7
dàjiě	大姐	N	oldest sister	7g

▼▼

Pinyin	Characters	Grammar	English	Lesson
dàxiǎo	大小	N	size	9
dàxué	大學	N	university; college	2c
dàxuéshēng	大學生	N	college student	2
dàyī	大衣	N	overcoat	9s
dài	戴	V	to wear (hat, glasses, etc.)	9s
dànshì	但是	Conj	but	6
dào	到	V	to arrive	8
dào…qù	到…去		to go to (a place)	6
de	得	P	(a structural particle)	7
de	的	P	(a possessive, modifying, or descriptive particle)	2
de shíhou	的時候		when…; at the time of…	8
Déguó	德國	PN	Germany	1s
Déguórén	德國人	N	German people/person	1s
Déwén	德文	N	the German language	6s
děi	得	AV	must; to have to	6
děng	等	V	to wait; to wait for	6
dì	第	prefix	(a prefix for ordinal numbers)	7
dìdi	弟弟	N	younger brother	2
dìtiě	地鐵	N	subway	11
diǎn	點	M	o'clock	3
diǎn(r)	點(兒)	M	a little; a bit; some	5
diǎnzhōng	點鐘	M	o'clock	3
diàn	電	N	electricity	4
diànchē	電車	N	cable car; trolley bus; tram	11s
diànhuà	電話	N	telephone	6
diànnǎo	電腦	N	computer	8
diànshì	電視	N	TV	4
diànyǐng	電影	N	movie	4
diànzǐ jìsuànjī	電子計算機	N	computer	8n
dǐng	頂	M	(a measure word for hat)	9s
dōngtiān	冬天	N	winter	10
dōngxi	東西	N	things; objects	9
dǒng	懂	V	to understand	7
dōu	都	Adv	both; all	2
duǎn	短	Adj	short	9s
duì	對	Adj	right; correct	4
duì bu qǐ	對不起	CE	I'm sorry.	5
duì le	對了	CE	That's right!	4s
duō	多	Adv	how many/much; to what extent	3
duō	多	Adj	many; much	7
duō dà	多大	CE	how old	3
duōshao	多少	QW	how much; how many	9

▲E▲

Éguó	俄國	PN	Russia	6s
Éwén	俄文	N	the Russian language	6s
érzi	兒子	N	son	2

Pinyin	Characters	Grammar	English	Lesson
èr	二	Nu	two	Intro.
èrgē	二哥	N	second oldest brother	7g
èrjiě	二姐	N	second oldest sister	7g
èryuè	二月	N	February	3g
▲F▲				
fācái	發財	V	to make a fortune	11c
fāyīn	發音	N	pronunciation	8
Fǎguó	法國	PN	France	1s
Fǎguórén	法國人	N	French people/person	1s
Fǎwén	法文	N	the French language	6s
fántǐzì	繁體字	N	traditional character	7c
fàn	飯	N	meal; (cooked) rice	3
fāngbiàn	方便	Adj	convenient	6
fēi	飛	V	to fly	11
fēijī	飛機	N	airplane	11
fēijīchǎng	飛機場	N	airport	11
Fēilǜbīn	菲律賓	PN	the Philippines	6s
fēn	分	M	minute	3s
fēn	分	M	¹⁄₁₀₀ of a kuai; cent	9
fěnhóngsè	粉紅色	N	pink	9s
fēng	封	M	(measure word for letters)	8
fúwùyuán	服務員	N	service person; waiter; waitress	9n
fù qián	付錢	VO	to pay money	9
fùxí	復習	V	to review	7
▲G▲				
gǎnlǎn	橄欖	N	olive	4s
gǎnlǎnqiú	橄欖球	N	American style football (used in Taiwan)	4s
gāngbǐ	鋼筆	N	fountain pen	7s
gāngcái	剛才	T	just now; a moment ago	10
gāo	高		(a surname); tall	2
gāosù	高速	Adj	high speed	11
gāosù gōnglù	高速公路	N	super highway; highway	11
gāoxìng	高興	Adj	happy; pleased	5
gāozhōng	高中	N	senior high (grades 10–12)	2c
gàosu	告訴	V	to tell	8
gē	歌	N	song	4
gēge	哥哥	N	older brother	2
gè	個	M	(a common measure word)	2
gěi	給	V	to give	5
gěi	給	Prep	to; for	6
gēn	跟	Conj	and	7
gèng	更	Adv	even more	10
gōnggòng	公共	Adj	public	11
gōnggòng qìchē	公共汽車	N	bus	11
gōnglù	公路	N	highway; road	11
gōngyuán	公園	N	park	10

Pinyin	Characters	Grammar	English	Lesson
gōngkè	功課	N	schoolwork; homework	7
gōngxǐ	恭喜	V	to congratulate	11c
gōngxǐ fācái	恭喜發財	CE	Congratulations and may you make a fortune!	11n
gōngzuò	工作	V/N	to work; work; job	5
guì	貴	Adj	honorable	1
guì	貴	Adj	expensive	9
guì xìng	貴姓	CE	What is your honorable surname?	1
▲H▲				
Hā'ěrbīn	哈爾濱	PN	Harbin	10c
hái	還	Adv	also; too; as well	3
háishi	還是	Conj	or	3
háishi	還是	Conj	had better	11
hái yǒu	還有		also there are	3
háizi	孩子	N	child	2
Hǎinán	海南	PN	Hainan	10c
Hánguó	韓國	PN	Korea	6s
Hánguórén	韓國人	N	Korean people/person	1s
Hánwén	韓文	N	the Korean language	6s
hánjià	寒假	N	winter vacation	11
Hànyǔ	漢語	N	Chinese language	6n
Hànzì	漢字	N	Chinese character	7
hǎo	好	Adj	fine; good; nice; O.K.	1, 3
hǎochī	好吃	Adj	good to eat; delicious	5s
hǎohē	好喝	Adj	good to drink; tasty	5s
hǎojiǔ	好久	CE	a long time	4
hǎokàn	好看	Adj	good-looking	5s, 7n
hǎowán(r)	好玩(兒)	Adj	fun	5s
hào	號	M	number in a series; day of the month	3
hào	號	M	number; size	9
hào	號	N	number (bus route)	11n
hē	喝	V	to drink	5
hé	和	Conj	and	2
héshì	合適	Adj	suitable	9
hēi	黑	Adj	black	9
hěn	很	Adv	very	3
hóng	紅	Adj	red	9
hóngyè	紅葉	N	red autumn leaves	10
hòulái	後來	T	later	8
hòunián	後年	T	the year after next	3s
hòutiān	後天	T	the day after tomorrow	3s
huā	花	V	to spend	11
huà	話	N	speech; talk; words	6
huàn	換	V	to change; to exchange	9
huáng	黃	Adj	yellow	9
huángméi	黃梅	N	rainy season	10c
huī	灰	Adj	gray	9s

▼▼▼▼▼▼▼▼▼▼▼▼▼▼▼▼▼▼▼▼▼▼▼▼▼▼▼▼▼▼▼▼▼▼▼

Pinyin	Characters	Grammar	English	Lesson
huí	回	V	to return	5
huí jiā	回家	VO	to go home	5
huílai	回來	VC	to come back	6
huì	會	AV	can; to know how to	8
huì	會	AV	will	10
huǒchē	火車	N	train	11s
huòzhě	或者	Conj	or	11

▲ J ▲

Pinyin	Characters	Grammar	English	Lesson
jī	機	N	machine	11
jīchǎng	機場	N	airport	11
jǐ	幾	QW	how many	2
jǐ	幾	Nu	some; a few (an indefinite number, usually less than ten)	6
jìchéngchē	計程車	N	taxi (in Taiwan)	11s
jìsuànjī	計算機	N	calculator; computer	8n
jiā	家	N	family; home	2
Jiānádà	加拿大	PN	Canada	10s
jiákè	夾克	N	jacket	9s
jiǎntǐzì	簡體字	N	simplified character	7c
jiàn	見	V	to see	3
jiàn	件	M	(a measure word for shirts, dresses, jackets, coats, etc.)	9
jiāo	教	V	to teach	7
jiǎo	角	M	dime	9g
jiào	叫	V	to be called; to call	1
jiàoshì	教室	N	classroom	8
jié	節	M	(a measure word for class periods)	6, 6n
jiějie	姐姐	N	older sister	2
jièshào	介紹	V	to introduce	5
jīnnián	今年	T	this year	3
jīntiān	今天	T	today	3
jǐnzhāng	緊張	Adj	nervous; anxious	11
jìn	近	Adj	near	8
jìn	進	V	to enter	5
jìnbù	進步	V/N	to make progress; progress	8
jìnlai	進來	VC	to come in	5
jìnqu	進去	VC	to go in	6g
jiǔ	久	Adj	a long time; for a long time	4
jiǔ	酒	N	wine; any alcoholic beverage	5
jiǔ	九	Nu	nine	Intro.
jiǔyuè	九月	N	September	3
jiù	就	Adv	the very one (indicating verification of something mentioned before)	6
jiù	就	Adv	(indicates that something takes place sooner than expected)	7
júhóngsè	橘紅色	N	orange	9s
juéde	覺得	V	to feel	4

▼▼▼

Pinyin	Characters	Grammar	English	Lesson
▲K▲				
kāfēi	咖啡	N	coffee	5
kāfēisè	咖啡色	N	coffee color; brown	9
kāi	開	V	to hold (a meeting, party, etc.)	6
kāi	開	V	to drive; to operate	11
kāi chē	開車	VO	to drive a car	11
kāi huì	開會	VO	to have a meeting	6
kāishǐ	開始	N/V	in the beginning; to begin; to start	7, 8
kàn	看	V	to watch; to look	4
kàn shū	看書	VO	to read books; to read	4
Kāngxī Zìdiǎn	康熙字典	N	*Kangxi Dictionary*	Intro.
kǎo	考	V	to give or take a test	6
kǎoshì	考試	V/N	to give or take a test; test	6
Kěkǒukělè	可口可樂	N	Coke	5s
kělè	可樂	N	cola	5
kěshì	可是	Conj	but	3
kěyǐ	可以	AV	can; may	5
kè	課	N	class; lesson	6
kèwén	課文	N	text of a lesson	7
kè	刻	M	quarter (hour); 15 minutes	3
kèqi	客氣	Adj	polite	6
kòng(r)	空(兒)	N	free time	6
kǒu	口	N/M	mouth; (a measure for people)	2n
kùzi	褲子	N	pants	9
kuài	塊	M	colloquial term for the basic Chinese monetary unit	9
kuài	快	Adv	fast; quickly	5
kuài	快	Adj	quick; fast	7
kuài	快	Adv	soon; be about to; before long	11
kuàilè	快樂	Adj	happy	11
kuàngquánshuǐ	礦泉水	N	mineral water	5s
Kūnmíng	昆明	PN	Kunming	10c
▲L▲				
Lādīngwén	拉丁文	N	Latin	6s
lái	來	V	to come	5
lán	藍	Adj	blue	9s, 11
lánqiú	籃球	N	basketball	4s
lǎoshī	老師	N	teacher	1
le	了	P	(a particle indicating superlative degree)	3
le (I)	了	P	(a dynamic particle)	5g
le (II)	了	P	(a dynamic particle)	8g
le (III)	了	P	(a sentence particle)	10g
lěng	冷	Adj	cold	10
lǐ	李	N	(a surname); plum	1
Lǐ Yǒu	李友	PN	(a personal name)	1
lǐbài	禮拜	N	week	3g
lǐbàisì	禮拜四	N	Thursday	3g

Pinyin	Characters	Grammar	English	Lesson
liànxí	練習	V	to practice	6
liángkuai	涼快	Adj	pleasantly cool (weather)	10
liǎng	兩	Nu	two; a couple of	2
liàng	輛	M	(measure for vehicles)	11s
liáo tiān(r)	聊天(兒)	VO	to chat	5
líng	零	Nu	zero	3g
liú	劉	N	(a surname)	1n
liù	六	Nu	six	Intro.
liùyuè	六月	N	June	3g
lù	路	N	road; path	11
lù	路	N	number (bus route)	11n
lùxiàng	錄像	N	video recording	10
lùyīn	錄音	N/VO	sound recording; to record	7
lǜ	綠	Adj	green	9s, 11
lǜshī	律師	N	lawyer	2

▲M▲

Pinyin	Characters	Grammar	English	Lesson
ma	嗎	QP	(an interrogative particle)	1
māma	媽媽	N	mom; mother	2
máfan	麻煩	Adj	troublesome	11
mǎguà	馬褂	N	Mandarin jacket	9c
Mǎláixīyà	馬來西亞	PN	Malaysia	6s
mǎi	買	V	to buy	9
mài	賣	V	to sell	9s
màn	慢	Adj	slow	7
máng	忙	Adj	busy	3
máo	毛	M	¹⁄₁₀ of a kuai (similar to the U.S. dime)	9
máobǐ	毛筆	N	writing brush	7s
máoyī	毛衣	N	sweater	9s
Máotái	茅台	PN	Maotai (name of a liquor)	5c
màozi	帽子	N	hat	9s
méi	沒	Adv	not	2
méi shìr	沒事兒	CE	no problem; it's O.K.	8f
méi wèntí	沒問題	CE	no problem	6, 6f
měi	每	Prep	every; each (usually followed by a measure word)	11
měitiān	每天	T	every day	11
Měiguó	美國	PN	America	1
Měiguórén	美國人	N	American people/person	1
Měishì zúqiú	美式足球	N	American style football (used in mainland China)	4s
mèimei	妹妹	N	younger sister	2
mēn	悶	Adj	stuffy	10
mén	門	M	(a measure for academic courses)	6n
miàn	麵	N	noodles	3c
míngnián	明年	T	next year	3s
míngtiān	明天	T	tomorrow	3
míngzi	名字	N	name	1

▼▼▼

Pinyin	Characters	Grammar	English	Lesson
▲N▲				
nǎ/něi	哪	QPr	which	6
nǎli	哪裏	CE	You flatter me. Not at all. (a polite reply to a compliment)	7, 7f
nǎr	哪兒	QPr	where	5
nà	那	Conj	in that case; then	4
nà/nèi	那	Pr	that	2
nàr	那兒	Pr	there	8
nán	男	N	male	2
nán de	男的		male	7
nánháizi	男孩子	N	boy	2
nán	難	Adj	difficult	7
Nánjīng	南京	PN	Nanjing	10c
nǎo	腦	N	brain	8
ne	呢	QP	(an interrogative particle)	1
néng	能	AV	can; to be able to	8
nǐ	你	Pr	you	1
nǐ hǎo	你好	CE	How do you do? Hello!	1
nián	年	N	year	3
niánjí	年級	N	grade in school	6
niánjì	年紀	N	age	3n
niàn	念	V	to read aloud	7
nín	您	Pr	you (singular; polite)	1
nuǎnhuo	暖和	Adj	warm	10
nǚ	女	N	female	2
nǚ'ér	女兒	N	daughter	2
nǚháizi	女孩子	N	girl	2
▲P▲				
páiqiú	排球	N	volleyball	4s
péngyou	朋友	N	friend	1s, 7
piān	篇	M	(a measure for essays, articles, etc.)	8
piányi	便宜	Adj	cheap; inexpensive	9
piào	票	N	ticket	11
piàoliang	漂亮	Adj	pretty	5
píjiǔ	啤酒	N	beer	5
píng	瓶	M	bottle	5
píngcháng	平常	T	usually	7
Pútáoyá	葡萄牙	PN	Portugal	6s
Pútáoyáwén	葡萄牙文	N	the Portuguese language	6s
▲Q▲				
qī	七	Nu	seven	Intro.
qīyuè	七月	N	July	3g
qípáo	旗袍	N	Manchu-style dress	9c
qǐ chuáng	起床	VO	to get up	8
qìchē	汽車	N	automobile	11
qìshuǐ(r)	汽水(兒)	N	soft drink; soda pop	5s
qiānbǐ	鉛筆	N	pencil	7s

Pinyin	Characters	Grammar	English	Lesson
qián	錢	N	money	9
qiánnián	前年	T	the year before last	3s
qiántiān	前天	T	the day before yesterday	3s
qiāo mén	敲門	VO	to knock at the door	5f
qīngchu	清楚	Adj	clear	8
qíng	晴	Adj	sunny; clear	10s
qǐng	請	V	please (a polite form of request)	1, 6n
qǐng	請	V	to treat (somebody); to invite	3, 6n
qǐng kè	請客	VO	to invite someone to dinner; to be the host	4
qǐng wèn	請問	CE	May I ask...	1
qiūtiān	秋天	N	autumn; fall	10
qiú	球	N	ball	4
qù	去	V	to go	4
qùnián	去年	T	last year	3s, 6n
qúnzi	裙子	N	skirt	9s
▲R▲				
ránhòu	然後	Adv	then	11
ràng	讓	V	to allow or cause (somebody to do something)	11
rè	熱	Adj	hot	10
rén	人	N	people; person	1
rènshi	認識	V	to know (someone); to recognize	3
rì	日	N	day; the sun	3
Rìběn	日本	PN	Japan	1s
Rìběnrén	日本人	N	Japanese people/person	1s
rìjì	日記	N	diary	8
Rìwén	日文	N	the Japanese language	6s
róngyì	容易	Adj	easy	7
▲S▲				
sān	三	Nu	three	Intro.
sāngē	三哥	N	third oldest brother	7g
sānjiě	三姐	N	third oldest sister	7g
sānyuè	三月	N	March	3g
shàngge xīngqī	上個星期	T	last week	6n, 7
shàngge yuè	上個月	T	last month	6n
Shànghǎi	上海	PN	Shanghai	10
shàng kè	上課	VO	to go to class; to start a class	7
shàngwǔ	上午	T	morning	6
shéi	誰	QPr	who	2
shéi ya	誰呀?	CE	Who is it?	5f
shénme	什麼	QPr	what	1
shēng	生	V	to give birth to; to be born	3
shēngcí	生詞	N	new words	7
shēngrì	生日	N	birthday	3
shīfu	師傅	N	master craftsman; skilled worker	9n
shí	十	Nu	ten	Intro.
shíbā	十八	Nu	eighteen	3

Pinyin	Characters	Grammar	English	Lesson
shí'èr	十二	Nu	twelve	3
shí'èryuè	十二月	N	December	3g
shíyīyuè	十一月	N	November	3g
shíyuè	十月	N	October	3g
shíhou	時候	N	(a point in) time; moment; (a duration of) time	4
shíjiān	時間	T	time	6
shì	事	N	matter; affair; business	3
shì	是	V	to be	1
shì ma	是嗎	CE	Really?	5f, 5n
shì	視	N	vision	4
shǒubiǎo	手錶	N	wristwatch	9n
shǒutào	手套	N	gloves	9n
shòuhuòyuán	售貨員	N	shop assistant; salesclerk	9
shū	書	N	book	4
shūfu	舒服	Adj	comfortable	10
shuài	帥	Adj	handsome	7
shuāng	雙	M	a pair of	9
shuǐ	水	N	water	5
shuì	睡	V	to sleep	4
shuì jiào	睡覺	VO	to sleep	4
shǔjià	暑假	N	summer vacation	11s
shuō	說	V	to say; to speak	6
shuō huà	說話	VO	to talk	7
sì	四	Nu	four	Intro.
sìyuè	四月	N	April	3g
sòng	送	V	to take someone (somewhere)	11
sùshè	宿舍	N	dormitory	8
suàn le	算了	CE	Forget it. Never mind.	4, 4f
suīrán	雖然	Conj	although	9
suì	歲	N	year of age	3
suìshù	歲數	N	year of age	3n
suǒyǐ	所以	Conj	so	4

▲ T ▲

Pinyin	Characters	Grammar	English	Lesson
T-xùshān	T-恤衫	N	T-shirt	9s
tā	他	Pr	he; him	2
tā	她	Pr	she	2
Táiběi	台北	PN	Taipei	10
Táiwān	台灣	PN	Taiwan	10
Táizhōng	台中	PN	Taichung	10s
Tàiguó	泰國	PN	Thailand	6s
tài...(le)	太...(了)	Adv	too; extremely	3
tàitai	太太	N	wife; Mrs.	1s
tèbié	特別	Adj/Adv	special; especially	7g
tiān	天	N	day	3
tiānqì	天氣	N	weather	10
tiáo	條	M	(a measure word for long, thin objects)	9

Pinyin	Characters	Grammar	English	Lesson
tiào	跳	V	to jump	4
tiào wǔ	跳舞	VO	to dance	4
tīng	聽	V	to listen	4
tóngxué	同學	N	classmate	3
túshūguǎn	圖書館	N	library	5
▲W▲				
wàzi	襪子	N	socks	9s
wàiguó	外國	N	foreign country	4
wàitào	外套	N	coat; jacket	9s
wán(r)	玩(兒)	V	to have fun; to play	5
wǎn	晚	N/Adj	evening; night; late	3
wǎnfàn	晚飯	N	dinner; supper	3
wǎnshang	晚上	T	evening; night	3
wáng	王	N	(a surname); king	1
Wáng Péng	王朋	PN	(a personal name)	1
wǎngqiú	網球	N	tennis	4s
wéi	喂	Interj	(on telephone) Hello!; Hey!	6, 6f, 6n
wèi	喂	Interj	(on telephone) Hello!; Hey!	6, 6f, 6n
wèi	位	M	(a polite measure for people)	6
wèi	為(爲)	Prep	for	3
wèishénme	為什麼	QPr	why	3
Wēngēhuá	溫哥華	PN	Vancouver	10s
wén	文	N	language; script; written language	6
wèn	問	V	to ask (a question)	1, 6n
wèntí	問題	N	question; problem	6
wǒ	我	Pr	I; me	1
wǒmen	我們	Pr	we	3
wǔ	五	Nu	five	Intro.
wǔyuè	五月	N	May	3g
wǔ	舞	N	dance	4
wǔfàn	午飯	N	lunch; midday meal	8
wǔjiào	午覺	N	nap	7s
Wǔhàn	武漢	PN	Wuhan	10c
▲X▲				
Xīlà	希臘	PN	Greece	6s
Xīlàwén	希臘文	N	the Greek language	6s
xīwàng	希望	V/N	to hope; hope	8
Xībānyá	西班牙	PN	Spain	6s
Xībānyáwén	西班牙文	N	the Spanish language	6s
xīzhuāng	西裝	N	suit	9s
xíguàn	習慣	V/N	to be accustomed to; habit	8
xǐhuan	喜歡	V	to like; to prefer	3
xǐ zǎo	洗澡	VO	to take a bath/shower	8
xià	下		below; next	6
xià chē	下車	VO	to get off (a bus, train, etc.)	11
xià cì	下次		next time	10

Pinyin	Characters	Grammar	English	Lesson
xiàge xīngqī	下個星期	T	next week	6
xià(ge)yuè	下(個)月	T	next month	3s
xiàwǔ	下午	T	afternoon	6
xià yǔ	下雨	VO	to rain	10
xiàtiān	夏天	N	summer	10
Xiàwēiyí	夏威夷	PN	Hawaii	6s
xiān	先	Adv	first; before	11
xiānsheng	先生	N	Mr.; husband; teacher	1
xiàn	線	N	line	11
xiànzài	現在	T	now	3
Xiānggǎng	香港	PN	Hong Kong	10s
xiǎng	想	AV	to want to; to think	4
xiǎo	小	Adj	small; little	2
Xiǎo Bái	小白	PN	Little Bai	3
Xiǎo Gāo	小高	PN	Little Gao	2
xiǎojie	小姐	N	Miss; young lady	1
Xiǎo Lǐ	小李	PN	Little Li	3
xiǎoxué	小學	N	elementary school; grade school	2c
Xiǎo Zhāng	小張	PN	Little Zhang	2
xiào	笑	V	to laugh; to laugh at	8
xié	鞋	N	shoes	9
xiě	寫	V	to write	7
xiè	謝	N/V	(a surname); thanks	10
xièxie	謝謝	CE	thank you	3, 6f
xīn	新	Adj	new	8
xīnnián	新年	N	new year	11
xìn	信	N	letter (mail)	8
Xīngbākè	星巴克	PN	Starbucks	5c
xīngqī	星期	N	week	3
xīngqī'èr	星期二	N	Tuesday	3g
xīngqīliù	星期六	N	Saturday	3g
xīngqīrì	星期日	N	Sunday	3g
xīngqīsān	星期三	N	Wednesday	3g
xīngqīsì	星期四	N	Thursday	3
xīngqītiān	星期天	N	Sunday	3g
xīngqīwǔ	星期五	N	Friday	3g
xīngqīyī	星期一	N	Monday	3g
xíng	行	Adj	all right; O.K.	6
xìng	姓	V/N	(one's) surname is...; to be surnamed; surname	1
xué	學	V	to study	7
xuéqī	學期	N	school term; semester/quarter	8
xuésheng	學生	N	student	1
xuéxiào	學校	N	school	5
xuéyuàn	學院	N	college	2c
xuě	雪	N	snow	10s
Xuěbì	雪碧	N	Sprite	5s

Pinyin	Characters	Grammar	English	Lesson
▲Y▲				
ya	呀	P	(an interjectory particle used to soften a question)	5
yánsè	顏色	N	color	9
yǎnjìng	眼鏡	N	eyeglasses; glasses	9n
yào	要	V/AV	to want to; to have a desire for	5, 9
yào	要	AV	will; to be going to	6
yàoshi	要是	Conj	if	6
yě	也	Adv	too; also	1
yè	夜	N	night	7
yī	一	Nu	one	Intro.
yīyuè	一月	N	January	3g
yīfu	衣服	N	clothes	9
yīshēng	醫生	N	doctor; physician	2
yígòng	一共	Adv	altogether	9
yí xià	一下	M	(a measure word used after a verb indicating short duration)	5
yíyàng	一樣	Adj	same; alike	9
yǐhòu	以後	T	after	6, 6n
yǐjīng	已經	Adv	already	8
yǐqián	以前	T	before; ago; previously	7g, 8
yìbiān...yìbiān	一邊...一邊		(a parallel construction indicating two simultaneous actions)	8
yìdiǎnr	一點兒		a bit	5g, 10
yìqǐ	一起	Adv	together	5
Yìdàlì	意大利	PN	Italy	6s
Yìdàlìwén	意大利文	N	the Italian language	6s
yìsi	意思	N	meaning	4
Yìwén	意文	PN	(a given name)	8
yīn	陰	Adj	overcast	10s
yīnwei	因為	Conj	because	3
yīnyuè	音樂	N	music	4
yīnyuèhuì	音樂會	N	concert	8
Yīngguó	英國	PN	Britain; England	1s
Yīngguórén	英國人	N	British people/person	1s
Yīngwén	英文	N	the English language	2
yǐng	影	N	shadow	4
yòng	用	V/N	to use; use	8
yǒu	有	V	to have; to exist	2
yǒu kòng(r)	有空(兒)	VO	to have free time	6
yǒu shíhou	有時候	CE	sometimes	4
yǒu yìdiǎnr	有一點兒	CE	a little; somewhat	7
yǒu yìsi	有意思	CE	interesting	4
yòu	又	Adv	again	10
yòu...yòu	又...又...		both...and...	10
yǔ	語	N	speech	6n
yǔfǎ	語法	N	grammar	7

Pinyin	Characters	Grammar	English	Lesson
yùbào	預報	N	forecast	10
yùxí	預習	V	to preview	7
yuán	元	M	Chinese dollar	9g
yuánzhūbǐ	圓珠筆	N	ballpoint pen	7c
yuánzǐbǐ	原子筆	N	ballpoint pen	7c
yuē	約	V	to make an appointment	10
yuè	月	N	month	3
Yuènán	越南	PN	Vietnam	6s
Yuènánrén	越南人	N	Vietnamese people/person	1s
yún	雲	N	cloud	10s

▲**Z**▲

Pinyin	Characters	Grammar	English	Lesson
zài	在	Prep	at; in; on	5
zài	在	V	to be present; to be at (a place)	6
zài	再	Adv	again	3
zàijiàn	再見	CE	goodbye; see you again	3
zāogāo	糟糕	Adj	in a terrible mess; too bad	10
zǎo	早	Adj	Good morning!; early	7
zǎo ān	早安	CE	Good morning!	7n
zǎofàn	早飯	N	breakfast	3s, 8
zǎoshang	早上	T	morning	8
zěnme	怎麼	QPr	how; how come (used to inquire about the cause of something, implying a degree of surprise or disapproval)	7
zěnme bàn	怎麼辦	QW	what to do	10
zěnmeyàng	怎麼樣	QPr	Is it O.K.? What is it like? How does that sound?	3
zhàn	站	N	(of bus, train, etc.) stop; station	11
zhāng	張	PN/M	(a surname); (a measure word for flat objects)	1n, 2
zhǎo	找	V	to look for	4
zhǎo(qián)	找(錢)	V	to give change	9
zhàopiàn	照片	N	picture; photo	2
zhè	這	Pr	this	2
zhège	這個	Pr	this	12
zhèi	這	Pr	this	2
zhè jǐ tiān	這幾天	NP	the past few days	11
zhème	這麼	Pr	so; such	7
zhèr	這兒	Pr	here	9
zhèyàng	這樣	Pr	so; like this	10
zhēn	真	Adv	really	7
zhèngzài	正在	Adv	in the middle of (doing something)	8
zhī	枝	M	(a measure for pen and long items)	9g
zhī	隻	M	(a measure for bird, shoe, etc.)	9g
zhīdao	知道	V	to know	6
zhǐ	只	Adv	only	4
zhǐ	紙	N	paper	2g, 7s
zhōng	鐘	N	clock	3

Pinyin	Characters	Grammar	English	Lesson
zhōng	中	Adj	medium	9
zhōngfàn	中飯	N	lunch	3s
Zhōngguó	中國	PN	China	1
Zhōngguórén	中國人	N	Chinese people/person	1
Zhōngguózì	中國字	N	Chinese character	Intro.
Zhōngshānzhuāng	中山裝	N	Sun Yatsen suit	9c
Zhōngwén	中文	N	the Chinese language	6
zhōngwǔ	中午	T	noon	6s; 8
zhōngxué	中學	N	middle school	2c
zhōu	週	N	week	3g
zhōu'èr	週二	N	Tuesday	3g
zhōumò	週末	T	weekend	4
zhōurì	週日	N	Sunday	3g
zhōuyī	週一	N	Monday	3g
zhù	祝	V	to express good wishes	8, 11f
zhuānyè	專業	N	major (in college); specialty	8
zǐ	紫	Adj	purple	9s
zì	字	N	character	7
zìjǐ	自己	Pr	oneself	11
zǒu	走	V	to walk; to go by way of	11
zǒu lù	走路	VO	to walk	11s
zū	租	V	to rent	11
zúqiú	足球	N	soccer	4s
zuì	最	Adv	(an adverb of superlative degree; most, -est)	8
zuìhǎo	最好	Adv	had better	10
zuìhòu	最後	Adv	finally	11
zuìjìn	最近	T	recently	8
zuótiān	昨天	T	yesterday	3s, 4
zuò	做	V	to do	2
zuò	坐	V	to sit	5
zuò	坐	V	to travel by	11

VOCABULARY INDEX (ENGLISH-CHINESE): LESSONS 1–11

Key: c=Culture Notes; f=Functional Expressions; g=Grammar; n=Notes;
s=Supplementary Vocabulary

English	Pinyin	Characters	Grammar	Lesson
▲A▲				
a bit	yìdiǎnr	一點兒		10
a bit; a little; some	diǎn(r)	點(兒)	M	5
a couple of; two	liǎng	兩	Nu	2
a little; a bit; some	diǎn(r)	點(兒)	M	5
a little; somewhat	yǒu yìdiǎnr	有一點兒	CE	7
able to; can	néng	能	AV	8
affair; matter; business	shì	事	N	3
after	yǐhòu	以後	T	6, 6n
afternoon	xiàwǔ	下午	T	6
again	yòu	又	Adv	10
again	zài	再	Adv	3
age	niánjì	年紀	N	3n
ago; before; previously	yǐqián	以前	T	8
airplane	fēijī	飛機	N	11
airport	fēijīchǎng	飛機場	N	11
airport	jīchǎng	機場	N	11
alike; same	yíyàng	一樣	Adj	9
all; both	dōu	都	Adv	2
allow or cause (somebody to do something)	ràng	讓	V	11
already	yǐjīng	已經	Adv	8
also; too	yě	也	Adv	1
also; too; as well	hái	還	Adv	3
although	suīrán	雖然	Conj	9
altogether	yígòng	一共	Adv	9
America	Měiguó	美國	PN	1
American people/person	Měiguórén	美國人	N	1
American style football (used in mainland China)	Měishì zúqiú	美式足球	N	4s
American style football (used in Taiwan)	gǎnlǎnqiú	橄欖球	N	4s
and	gēn	跟	Conj	7
and	hé	和	Conj	2
another person; other people; others	biérén	別人	Adv	4
anxious; nervous	jǐnzhāng	緊張	Adj	11
arrive	dào	到	V	8
ask (a question)	wèn	問	V	1, 6n
at; in; on	zài	在	Prep	5
at the time of...; when...	de shíhou	的時候		8

English	Pinyin	Characters	Grammar	Lesson
August	bāyuè	八月	N	3g
automobile	qìchē	汽車	N	11
autumn; fall	qiūtiān	秋天	N	10
▲B▲				
ball	qiú	球	N	4
ballpoint pen	yuánzhūbǐ	圓珠筆	N	7c
ballpoint pen	yuánzǐbǐ	原子筆	N	7c
baseball	bàngqiú	棒球	N	4s
basketball	lánqiú	籃球	N	4s
be	shì	是	V	1
be about to; soon; before long	kuài	快	Adv	11
be accustomed to	xíguàn	習慣	V	8
be all right; O.K.	xíng	行	Adj	6
be at; be there	zài	在	V	6
be born; give birth to	shēng	生	V	3
be called	jiào	叫	V	1
be going to; will	yào	要	AV	6
be host; invite someone to dinner	qǐng kè	請客	VO	4
be present; be at (a place)	zài	在	V	6
because	yīnwei	因為	Conj	3
bed	chuáng	床	N	2g, 8
beer	píjiǔ	啤酒	N	5
before; ago; previously	yǐqián	以前	T	8
before; first	xiān	先	Adv	11
begin; in the beginning; start	kāishǐ	開始	N/V	8
Beijing	Běijīng	北京	PN	10s
besides; in addition to	chúle...yǐwài	除了...以外	Conj	8
big; old	dà	大	Adj	3
birthday	shēngrì	生日	N	3
black	hēi	黑	Adj	9
blue	lán	藍	Adj	9s, 11
boat; ship	chuán	船	N	11s
book	shū	書	N	4
both...and...	yòu...yòu	又...又...		10
both; all	dōu	都	Adv	2
bottle	píng	瓶	M	5
boy	nánháizi	男孩子	N	2
brain	nǎo	腦	N	8
breakfast	zǎofàn	早飯	N	3s, 8
Britain; England	Yīngguó	英國	PN	1s
British people/person	Yīngguórén	英國人	N	1s
brown; coffee color	kāfēisè	咖啡色	N	9
bus	gōnggòng qìchē	公共汽車	N	11
business; matter; affair	shì	事	N	3
busy	máng	忙	Adj	3
but	dànshì	但是	Conj	6
but	kěshì	可是	Conj	3

English	Pinyin	Characters	Grammar	Lesson
but; however	búguò	不過	Conj	11
buy	mǎi	買	V	9
▲C▲				
cable car; trolley bus; tram	diànchē	電車	N	11s
cafeteria; dining room	cāntīng	餐廳	N	8
calculator; computer	jìsuànjī	計算機	N	8n
can; able to	néng	能	AV	8
can; know how to	huì	會	AV	8
can; may	kěyǐ	可以	AV	5
Canada	Jiānádà	加拿大	PN	10s
car, vehicle	chē	車	N	11
cause or allow (somebody to do something)	ràng	讓	V	11
cent; 1/100 of a kuai	fēn	分	M	9
change; exchange	huàn	換	V	9
character; word	zì	字	N	7
chat	liáo tiān(r)	聊天(兒)	VO	5
cheap; inexpensive	piányi	便宜	Adj	9
child	háizi	孩子	N	2
China	Zhōngguó	中國	PN	1
Chinese character	Hànzì	漢字	N	7
Chinese character	Zhōngguózì	中國字	N	Intro.
Chinese dollar	yuán	元	M	9g
Chinese language	Hànyǔ	漢語	N	6n
Chinese language	Zhōngwén	中文	N	6
Chinese people/person	Zhōngguórén	中國人	N	1
Chongqing	Chóngqìng	重慶	PN	10c
class; lesson	kè	課	N	6
classmate	tóngxué	同學	N	3
classroom	jiàoshì	教室	N	8
clear	qīngchu	清楚	Adj	8
clear; sunny	qíng	晴	Adj	10s
clock	zhōng	鐘	N	3
clothes	yīfu	衣服	N	9
cloud	yún	雲	N	10s
coat; jacket	wàitào	外套	N	9s
coffee	kāfēi	咖啡	N	5
coffee color; brown	kāfēisè	咖啡色	N	9
Coke	Kěkǒukělè	可口可樂	N	5s
cola	kělè	可樂	N	5
cold	lěng	冷	Adj	10
college	xuéyuàn	學院	N	2c
college student	dàxuéshēng	大學生	N	2
college; university	dàxué	大學	N	2c
color	yánsè	顏色	N	9
come	lái	來	V	5
come back	huílai	回來	VC	6

▼▼

English	Pinyin	Characters	Grammar	Lesson
come in	jìnlai	進來	VC	5
comfortable	shūfu	舒服	Adj	10
computer	diànnǎo	電腦	N	8
computer	diànzǐ jìsuànjī	電子計算機	N	8n
computer; calculator	jìsuànjī	計算機	N	8n
concert	yīnyuèhuì	音樂會	N	8
congratulate	gōngxǐ	恭喜	V	11c
Congratulations and may you make a fortune!	gōngxǐ fācái	恭喜發財	CE	11n
convenient	fāngbiàn	方便	Adj	6
correct; right	duì	對	Adj	4
cup; glass	bēi	杯	M	5
▲**D**▲				
dad; father	bàba	爸爸	N	2
dance	tiào wǔ	跳舞	VO	4
dance	wǔ	舞	N	4
daughter	nǚ'ér	女兒	N	2
day	tiān	天	N	3
day after tomorrow	hòutiān	後天	T	3s
day before yesterday	qiántiān	前天	T	3s
day of the month; number in a series; size	hào	號	M	3, 9
day; the sun	rì	日	N	3
December	shí'èryuè	十二月	N	3g
delicious; good to eat	hǎochī	好吃	Adj	5s
diary	rìjì	日記	N	8
difficult	nán	難	Adj	7
dime; 1/10 of a kuai	jiǎo	角	M	9g
dime; 1/10 of a kuai	máo	毛	M	9
dining room; cafeteria	cāntīng	餐廳	N	8
dinner; supper	wǎnfàn	晚飯	N	3
do	zuò	做	V	2
do manual work; work part-time	dǎ gōng	打工	VO	5s
doctor; physician	yīshēng	醫生	N	2
dollar	kuài	塊	M	9
don't	bié	別		6
Don't be so polite!	bié kèqi	別客氣	CE	6
Don't be (so) polite. You are welcome.	bú kèqi	不客氣	CE	6
Don't mention it. Not at all. You're welcome.	bú xiè	不謝	CE	7
door; (a measure for academic courses)	mén	門	N	6n
dormitory	sùshè	宿舍	N	8
drink	hē	喝	V	5
drive a car	kāi chē	開車	VO	11
drive; operate	kāi	開	V	11
▲**E**▲				
each; every	měi	每	Prep	11
early; Good morning!	zǎo	早	Adj	7

English	Pinyin	Characters	Grammar	Lesson
easy	róngyì	容易	Adj	7
eat	chī	吃	V	3
eat (a meal)	chī fàn	吃飯	VO	3
eight	bā	八	Nu	Intro.
eighteen	shíbā	十八	Nu	3
electricity	diàn	電	N	4
elementary school; grade school	xiǎoxué	小學	N	2c
embarrassed	bù hǎoyìsi	不好意思	CE	11
England; Britain	Yīngguó	英國	PN	1s
English language	Yīngwén	英文	N	2
enter	jìn	進	V	5
especially; special	tèbié	特別	Adv/Adj	7g
even more	gèng	更	Adv	10
evening; night	wǎnshang	晚上	T	3
evening; night; late	wǎn	晚	N/Adj	3
every day	měitiān	每天	T	11
every; each	měi	每	Prep	11
everybody	dàjiā	大家	Pr	7
exchange; change	huàn	換	V	9
exist; have	yǒu	有	V	2
expensive	guì	貴	Adj	9
extremely; too	tài	太	Adv	3
eyeglasses; glasses	yǎnjìng	眼鏡	N	9n

▲**F**▲

English	Pinyin	Characters	Grammar	Lesson
fall; autumn	qiūtiān	秋天	N	10
family; home	jiā	家	N	2
fast; quick; quickly	kuài	快	Adj/Adv	5, 7
father; dad	bàba	爸爸	N	2
February	Èryuè	二月	N	3g
feel embarrassed	bù hǎoyìsi	不好意思	CE	11
feel/think that	juéde	覺得	V	4
female	nǚ	女	N	2
fifteen minutes; quarter (hour)	kè	刻	M	3
finally	zuìhòu	最後	Adv	11
fine; good; nice; O.K.	hǎo	好	Adj	1, 3
first; before	xiān	先	Adv	11
five	wǔ	五	Nu	Intro.
fly	fēi	飛	V	11
for	wèi	為(爲)	Prep	3
for; to	gěi	給	Prep	6
forecast	yùbào	預報	N	10
foreign country	wàiguó	外國	N	4
Forget it. Never mind.	suàn le	算了	CE	4
fountain pen	gāngbǐ	鋼筆	N	7s
four	sì	四	Nu	Intro.
France	Fǎguó	法國	PN	1s
free time	kòng(r)	空(兒)	N	6

English	Pinyin	Characters	Grammar	Lesson
French language	Fǎwén	法文	N	6s
French people/person	Fǎguórén	法國人	N	1s
Friday	xīngqīwǔ	星期五	N	3g
friend	péngyou	朋友	N	1s, 7
fun	hǎowán(r)	好玩(兒)	Adj	5s
▲G▲				
German language	Déwén	德文	N	6s
German people/person	Déguórén	德國人	N	1s
Germany	Déguó	德國	PN	1s
get off (a bus, train, etc.)	xià chē	下車	VO	11
get up	qǐ chuáng	起床	VO	8
girl	nǚháizi	女孩子	N	2
give	gěi	給	V	5
give birth to; be born	shēng	生	V	3
give change	zhǎo(qián)	找(錢)	V	9
give or take a test	kǎo	考	V	6
give or take a test; test	kǎoshì	考試	V/N	6
give (someone a gift)	sòng	送	V	11
glass; cup	bēi	杯	M	5
glasses; eyeglasses	yǎnjìng	眼鏡	N	9n
gloves	shǒutào	手套	N	9n
go	qù	去	V	4
go by way of; walk	zǒu	走	V	11
go home	huí jiā	回家	VO	5
go in	jìnqu	進去	VC	6g
go out	chūqu	出去	VC	10
go to (a place)	dào…qù	到…去		6
go to class; start a class	shàng kè	上課	VO	7
good; fine; nice; O.K.	hǎo	好	Adj	1, 3
Good morning!	zǎo ān	早安	CE	7n
Good morning!; early	zǎo	早	Adj	7
good to drink; tasty	hǎohē	好喝	Adj	5s
good to eat; delicious	hǎochī	好吃	Adj	5s
good-looking	hǎokàn	好看	Adj	5s
goodbye; see you again	zàijiàn	再見	CE	3
grade in school	niánjí	年級	N	6
grade school; elementary school	xiǎoxué	小學	N	2c
grammar	yǔfǎ	語法	N	7
gray	huī	灰	Adj	9s
Greece	Xīlà	希臘	PN	6s
Greek language	Xīlàwén	希臘文	N	6s
green	lǜ	綠	Adj	9s, 11
▲H▲				
habit	xíguàn	習慣	N	8
had better	háishi	還是	Conj	11
had better	zuìhǎo	最好	Adv	10
Hainan	Hǎinán	海南	PN	10c

English	Pinyin	Characters	Grammar	Lesson
half; half an hour	bàn	半	Nu	3
handsome	shuài	帥	Adj	7
happy	kuàilè	快樂	Adj	11
happy; pleased	gāoxìng	高興	Adj	5
Harbin	Hā'ěrbīn	哈爾濱	PN	10c
hat	màozi	帽子	N	9s
have; exist	yǒu	有	V	2
have a desire for; want to	yào	要	V/AV	5, 9
have a meeting	kāi huì	開會	VO	6
have free time	yǒu kòng(r)	有空(兒)	VO	6
have fun; play	wán(r)	玩(兒)	V	5
have to; must	děi	得	AV	6
Hawaii	Xiàwēiyí	夏威夷	PN	6s
he	tā	他	Pr	2
Hello! Hey! (on telephone)	wèi	喂	Interj	6, 6f, 6n
Hello! How do you do?	nǐ hǎo	你好	CE	1
help	bāng	幫	V	6
help	bāngzhù	幫助	V	7
help; to do someone a favor	bāng máng	幫忙	VO	6
here	zhèr	這兒	Pr	9
Hey! Hello! (on telephone)	wèi/wéi	喂	Interj	6, 6f, 6n
high speed	gāosù	高速	Adj	11
highway; road	gōnglù	公路	N	11
highway; super highway	gāosù gōnglù	高速公路	N	11
hit; strike	dǎ	打	V	4
hold (a meeting, party, etc.)	kāi	開	V	6
home; family	jiā	家	N	2
homework; schoolwork	gōngkè	功課	N	7
Hong Kong	Xiānggǎng	香港	PN	10s
honorable	guì	貴	Adj	1
hope	xīwàng	希望	V	8
hot	rè	熱	Adj	10
how; how come	zěnme	怎麼	QPr	7
How do you do? Hello!	nǐ hǎo	你好	CE	1
How does it sound?	zěnmeyàng	怎麼樣	QPr	3
how many	jǐ	幾	QW	2
how many/much; to what extent	duō	多	Adv	3
how many; how much	duōshao	多少	QW	9
how much; how many	duōshao	多少	QW	9
how old	duō dà	多大	CE	3
however; but	búguò	不過	Conj	11
humid; wet	cháoshī	潮濕	Adj	10s
hundred	bǎi	百	Nu	9

▲ I ▲

English	Pinyin	Characters	Grammar	Lesson
I; me	wǒ	我	Pr	1
I'm sorry.	duì bu qǐ	對不起	CE	5
if	yàoshi	要是	Conj	6

English	Pinyin	Characters	Grammar	Lesson
in; at; on	zài	在	Prep	5
in a terrible mess	zāogāo	糟糕	Adj	10
in addition to; besides	chúle...yǐwài	除了...以外	Conj	8
in that case; then	nà	那	Conj	4
in the beginning; begin; start	kāishǐ	開始	N/V	8
in the middle of (doing something)	zhèngzài	正在	Adv	8
in the newspaper	bàoshang	報上		10
inexpensive; cheap	piányi	便宜	Adj	9
interesting	yǒu yìsi	有意思	CE	4
introduce	jièshào	介紹	V	5
invite; treat (somebody)	qǐng	請	V	3, 6n
invite someone to dinner; be the host	qǐng kè	請客	VO	4
Italian language	Yìdàlìwén	意大利文	N	6s
Italy	Yìdàlì	意大利	PN	6s

▲J▲

jacket	jiákè	夾克	N	9s
jacket; coat	wàitào	外套	N	9s
January	yīyuè	一月	N	3g
Japan	Rìběn	日本	PN	1s
Japanese language	Rìwén	日文	N	6s
Japanese people/person	Rìběnrén	日本人	N	1s
job; to work	gōngzuò	工作	N/V	5
July	qīyuè	七月	N	3g
jump	tiào	跳	V	4
June	liùyuè	六月	N	3g
junior high (grades 7–9)	chūzhōng	初中	N	2c
just now; a short moment ago	gāngcái	剛才	T	10

▲K▲

Kangxi Dictionary	*Kāngxī Zìdiǎn*	康熙字典	N	Intro.
king; a surname	wáng	王	N	1
knock at the door	qiāo mén	敲門	VO	5f
know	zhīdao	知道	V	6
know (someone); recognize	rènshi	認識	V	3
know how to; can	huì	會	AV	8
Korea	Hánguó	韓國	PN	6s
Korean language	Hánwén	韓文	N	6s
Korean people/person	Hánguórén	韓國人	N	1s
Kunming	Kūnmíng	昆明	PN	10c

▲L▲

lacking; short of	chà	差	V	3s
language; written language	wén	文	N	6
last month	shàngge yuè	上個月	T	6n
last week	shàngge xīngqī	上個星期	T	7
last year	qùnián	去年	T	3s
late; night; evening	wǎn	晚	Adj/N	3
later	hòulái	後來	T	8

English	Pinyin	Characters	Grammar	Lesson
Latin	Lādīngwén	拉丁文	N	6s
laugh; laugh at	xiào	笑	V	8
laugh at; laugh	xiào	笑	V	8
lawyer	lǜshī	律師	N	2
lesson; class	kè	課	N	6
letter	xìn	信	N	8
library	túshūguǎn	圖書館	N	5
like; prefer	xǐhuan	喜歡	V	3
like this; so	zhèyàng	這樣	Pr	10
line	xiàn	線	N	11
listen	tīng	聽	V	4
little; small	xiǎo	小	Adj	2
Little Bai	Xiǎo Bái	小白	PN	3
Little Gao	Xiǎo Gāo	小高	PN	2
Little Li	Xiǎo Lǐ	小李	PN	3
Little Zhang	Xiǎo Zhāng	小張	PN	2
long	cháng	長	Adj	9s
long gown	chángpáo	長袍	N	9c
long time	hǎojiǔ	好久	CE	4
long time; for a long time	jiǔ	久	Adj	4
longevity	chángshòu	長壽	N	3c
longevity noodles	chángshòu miàn	長壽麵	N	3c
look; watch	kàn	看	V	4
look for	zhǎo	找	V	4
lunch	wǔfàn	午飯	N	8
lunch	zǎofàn	中飯	N	3s

▲**M**▲

machine	jī	機	N	11
major; specialty	zhuānyè	專業	N	8
make a fortune	fācái	發財	V	11c
make a phone call	dǎ diànhuà	打電話	VO	6
make an appointment	yuē	約	V	10
make progress	jìnbù	進步	V	8
Malaysia	Mǎláixīyà	馬來西亞	PN	6s
male	nán	男	N	2
male	nán de	男的		7
Manchu-style dress	qípáo	旗袍	N	9c
Mandarin jacket	mǎguà	馬褂	N	9c
many; much	duō	多	Adj	7
Maotai (name of a liquor)	Máotái	茅台	PN	5c
March	Sānyuè	三月	N	3g
master craftsman; skilled worker	shīfu	師傅	N	9n
matter; affair; business	shì	事	N	3
May	wǔyuè	五月	N	3g
may; can	kěyǐ	可以	AV	5
May I ask...	qǐng wèn	請問	CE	1
me; I	wǒ	我	Pr	1

▼▼▼▼▼▼▼▼▼▼▼▼▼▼▼▼▼▼▼▼▼▼▼▼▼▼▼▼▼▼▼▼▼

English	Pinyin	Characters	Grammar	Lesson
meal; (cooked) rice	fàn	飯	N	3
meaning	yìsi	意思	N	4
medium	zhōng	中	Adj	9
middle school	zhōngxué	中學	N	2c
midnight	bànyè	半夜	T	7
mineral water	kuàngquánshuǐ	礦泉水	N	5s
minute	fēn	分	M	3s
Miss; young lady	xiǎojie	小姐	N	1
mom; mother	māma	媽媽	N	2
moment; (a point in) time; (a duration of) time	shíhou	時候	N	4
moment ago; just now	gāngcái	剛才	T	10
Monday	xīngqīyī	星期一	N	3g
Monday	zhōuyī	週一	N	3g
money	qián	錢	N	9
month	yuè	月	N	3
morning	shàngwǔ	上午	T	6
morning	zǎoshang	早上	T	8
mother; mom	māma	媽媽	N	2
mouth; (measure for people)	kǒu	口	N/M	2n
movie	diànyǐng	電影	N	4
Mr.; husband; teacher	xiānsheng	先生	N	1
Mrs.; wife	tàitai	太太	N	1s
much; many	duō	多	Adj	7
music	yīnyuè	音樂	N	4
must; have to	děi	得	AV	6

▲N▲

name	míngzi	名字	N	1
Nanjing	Nánjīng	南京	PN	10c
nap	wǔjiào	午覺	N	7s
near	jìn	近	Adj	8
need not	bú yòng	不用	CE	9
nervous; anxious	jǐnzhāng	緊張	Adj	11
Never mind. Forget it.	suàn le	算了	CE	4
new	xīn	新	Adj	8
new words	shēngcí	生詞	N	7
new year	xīnnián	新年	N	11
newspaper	bào	報	N	8
next; under	xià	下		6
next month	xià(ge)yuè	下(個)月	T	3s
next time	xià cì	下次		10
next week	xiàge xīngqī	下個星期	T	6
next year	míngnián	明年	T	3s
nice; good; fine; O.K.	hǎo	好	Adj	1, 3
night	yè	夜	N	7
night; evening	wǎnshang	晚上	T	3
night; evening; late	wǎn	晚	N/Adj	3

English	Pinyin	Characters	Grammar	Lesson
nine	jiǔ	九	Nu	Intro.
no; not	bù	不	Adv	1
no problem	méi shìr	沒事兒	CE	8f
no problem	méi wèntí	沒問題	CE	6, 6f
noodles	miàn	麵	N	3c
noon	zhōngwǔ	中午	T	6s; 8
not; no	bù	不	Adv	1
not	méi	沒	Adv	2
not bad; pretty good	búcuò	不錯	Adj	4
not only..., but also	búdàn..., érqiě	不但...而且	Conj	10
not until; only then	cái	才	Adv	5
notebook	běnzi	本子	N	7s
November	shíyīyuè	十一月	N	3g
now	xiànzài	現在	T	3
number (bus route)	hào	號	N	11n
number (bus route)	lù	路	N	11n
number in a series; day of the month; size	hào	號	M	3, 9

▲**O**▲

English	Pinyin	Characters	Grammar	Lesson
O.K.; all right	xíng	行	Adj	6
O.K.; good; fine; nice	hǎo	好	Adj	1, 3
object; things	dōngxi	東西	N	9
o'clock	diǎn	點	N	3
o'clock	-diǎnzhōng	點鐘	M	3
October	shíyuè	十月	N	3g
office	bàngōngshì	辦公室	N	6
often	chángcháng	常常	Adv	4
old; big	dà	大	Adj	3
older brother	gēge	哥哥	N	2
older sister	jiějie	姐姐	N	2
oldest brother	dàgē	大哥	N	7g
oldest sister	dàjiě	大姐	N	7g
olive	gǎnlǎn	橄欖	N	4s
on; at; in	zài	在	Prep	5
one	yī	一	Nu	Intro.
1/100 of a kuai; cent	fēn	分	M	9
1/10 of a kuai (similar to the U.S. dime)	máo	毛	M	9
oneself	zìjǐ	自己	Pr	11
only	zhǐ	只	Adv	4
only then; not until	cái	才	Adv	5
operate; drive	kāi	開	V	11
or	háishi	還是	Conj	3
or	huòzhě	或者	Conj	11
orange	júhóngsè	橘紅色	N	9s
other	bié (de)	別(的)	Adv	4
others; other people; another person	biérén	別人	Adv	4
overcast	yīn	陰	Adj	10s
overcoat	dàyī	大衣	N	9s

English	Pinyin	Characters	Grammar	Lesson
▲P▲				
pair of	shuāng	雙	M	9
pants	kùzi	褲子	N	9
paper	zhǐ	紙	N	2g, 7s
park	gōngyuán	公園	N	10
past few days	zhè jǐ tiān	這幾天	NP	11
path; road	lù	路	N	11
pay money	fù qián	付錢	VO	9
pen	bǐ	筆	N	7
pencil	qiānbǐ	鉛筆	N	7s
people; person	rén	人	N	1
Pepsi	Bǎishìkělè	百事可樂	N	5s
person; people	rén	人	N	1
Philippines (the)	Fēilǜbīn	菲律賓	PN	6s
photo; picture	zhàopiàn	照片	N	2
physician; doctor	yīshēng	醫生	N	2
picture; photo	zhàopiàn	照片	N	2
pink	fěnhóngsè	粉紅色	N	9s
play; have fun	wán(r)	玩(兒)	V	5
play ball	dǎ qiú	打球	VO	4
pleasantly cool (weather)	liángkuai	涼快	Adj	10
please (polite form of request)	qǐng	請	V	1, 6n
pleased; happy	gāoxìng	高興	Adj	5
plum; a surname	lǐ	李	N	1
polite	kèqi	客氣	Adj	6
Portugal	Pútáoyá	葡萄牙	PN	6s
Portuguese language	Pútáoyáwén	葡萄牙文	N	6s
practice	liànxí	練習	V	6
pretty	piàoliang	漂亮	Adj	5
pretty good; not bad	búcuò	不錯	Adj	4
preview	yùxí	預習	V	7
previously; before; ago	yǐqián	以前	T	8
pronunciation	fāyīn	發音	N	8
public	gōnggòng	公共	Adj	11
purple	zǐ	紫	Adj	9s
put on; wear	chuān	穿	V	9
▲Q▲				
quarter (hour); 15 minutes	kè	刻	M	3
question; problem	wèntí	問題	N	6
quickly; fast;quick	kuài	快	Adv/Adj	5, 7
▲R▲				
radical	bùshǒu	部首	N	Intro.
rain	xià yǔ	下雨	VO	10
rainy season	huángméi	黃梅	N	10c
read	niàn	念	V	7
read; read books	kàn shū	看書	VO	4
read books; read	kàn shū	看書	VO	4

English	Pinyin	Characters	Grammar	Lesson
sit	zuò	坐	V	5
six	liù	六	Nu	Intro.
size	dàxiǎo	大小	N	9
size; number in a series; day of the month	hào	號	M	3, 9
skilled worker; master craftsman	shīfu	師傅	N	9n
skirt	qúnzi	裙子	N	9s
sleep	shuì	睡	V	4
sleep	shuì jiào	睡覺	VO	4
slow	màn	慢	Adj	7
small; little	xiǎo	小	Adj	2
snow	xuě	雪	N	10s
so	suǒyǐ	所以	Conj	4
so; like this	zhèyàng	這樣	Pr	10
so; such	zhème	這麼	Pr	7
soccer	zúqiú	足球	N	4s
socks	wàzi	襪子	N	9s
soda pop; soft drink	qìshuǐ(r)	汽水(兒)	N	5s
soft drink; soda pop	qìshuǐ(r)	汽水(兒)	N	5s
some; a few (an indefinite number, usually less than ten)	jǐ	幾	Nu	6
sometimes	yǒu shíhou	有時候	CE	4
somewhat; a little	yǒu yìdiǎnr	有一點兒	CE	7
son	érzi	兒子	N	2
song	gē	歌	N	4
soon; be about to; before long	kuài	快	Adv	11
sound recording	lùyīn	錄音	N	7
Spain	Xībānyá	西班牙	PN	6s
Spanish language	Xībānyáwén	西班牙文	N	6s
speak; say	shuō	說	V	6
special; especially	tèbié	特別	Adj/Adv	7g
specialty; major	zhuānyè	專業	N	8
speech	yǔ	語	N	6n
speech; talk; words	huà	話	N	6
spend	huā	花	V	11
spring	chūntiān	春天	N	10
Sprite	Xuěbì	雪碧	N	5s
Starbucks	Xīngbākè	星巴克	PN	5c
start	kāishǐ	開始	V	7
start; begin; in the beginning	kāishǐ	開始	N/V	8
start a class; go to class	shàng kè	上課	VO	7
station; stop (of bus, train, etc.)	zhàn	站	N	11
station; stop (of bus, train, etc.)	chēzhàn	車站	N	11
stop; station (of bus, train, etc.)	zhàn	站	N	11
stop; station (of bus, train, etc.)	chēzhàn	車站	N	11
strike, hit	dǎ	打	V	4
student	xuésheng	學生	N	1
study	xué	學	V	7

English	Pinyin	Characters	Grammar	Lesson
stuffy	mēn	悶	Adj	10
subway	dìtiě	地鐵	N	11
such; so	zhème	這麼	Pr	7
suit	xīzhuāng	西裝	N	9s
suitable	héshì	合適	Adj	9
summer	xiàtiān	夏天	N	10
summer vacation	shǔjià	暑假	N	11s
sun; day	rì	日	N	3
Sun Yatsen suit	Zhōngshānzhuāng	中山裝	N	9c
Sunday	xīngqīrì	星期日	N	3g
Sunday	xīngqītiān	星期天	N	3g
Sunday	zhōurì	週日	N	3g
sunny; clear	qíng	晴	Adj	10s
super highway; highway	gāosù gōnglù	高速公路	N	11
supper; dinner	wǎnfàn	晚飯	N	3
surname; (one's) surname is...; to be surnamed	xìng	姓	N/V	1
sweater	máoyī	毛衣	N	9s

▲**T**▲

English	Pinyin	Characters	Grammar	Lesson
Taichung	Táizhōng	台中	PN	10s
Taipei	Táiběi	台北	PN	10
Taiwan	Táiwān	台灣	PN	10
take a bath/shower	xǐ zǎo	洗澡	VO	8
take someone (somewhere)	sòng	送	V	11
talk	shuō huà	說話	VO	7
talk; speech; words	huà	話	N	6
tall; (a surname)	gāo	高	Adj/N	2
tasty; good to drink	hǎohē	好喝	Adj	5s
taxi	chūzū qìchē	出租汽車	N	11
taxi (in Taiwan)	jìchéngchē	計程車	N	11s
tea	chá	茶	N	5
teach	jiāo	教	V	7
teacher	lǎoshī	老師	N	1
telephone	diànhuà	電話	N	6
tell	gàosu	告訴	V	8
ten	shí	十	Nu	Intro.
tennis	wǎngqiú	網球	N	4s
test; give or take a test	kǎoshì	考試	V/N	6
text	kèwén	課文	N	7
Thailand	Tàiguó	泰國	PN	6s
thank you	xièxie	謝謝	CE	3
thanks; (a surname)	xiè	謝	V/N	10
that	nà/nèi	那	Pr	2
That's right!	duì le	對了	CE	4s
then	ránhòu	然後	Adv	11
then; in that case	nà	那	Conj	4
there	nàr	那兒	Pr	8

English	Pinyin	Characters	Grammar	Lesson
things; objects	dōngxi	東西	N	9
think; feel that	juéde	覺得	V	4
think; want to	xiǎng	想	AV	4
third oldest brother	sāngē	三哥	N	7g
third oldest sister	sānjiě	三姐	N	7g
this	zhè/zhèi	這	Pr	2
this	zhège	這個	Pr	12
this year	jīnnián	今年	T	3
three	sān	三	Nu	Intro.
Thursday	lǐbàisì	禮拜四	N	3g
Thursday	xīngqīsì	星期四	N	3
ticket	piào	票	N	11
time	shíjiān	時間	T	6
time (a point in); moment; time (a duration of)	shíhou	時候	N	4
to; for	gěi	給	Prep	6
to what extent; how many/much	duō	多	Adv	3
today	jīntiān	今天	T	3
together	yìqǐ	一起	Adv	5
tomorrow	míngtiān	明天	T	3
too; also	yě	也	Adv	1
too; also; as well	hái	還	Adv	3
too; extremely	tài…(le)	太…(了)	Adv	3
traditional character	fántǐzì	繁體字	N	7c
train	huǒchē	火車	N	11s
travel by	zuò	坐	V	11
treat (somebody); invite	qǐng	請	V	3, 6n
trolley bus; cable car; tram	diànchē	電車	N	11s
troublesome	máfan	麻煩	Adj	11
T-shirt	T-xùshān	T-恤衫	N	9s
Tuesday	xīngqí'èr	星期二	N	3g
Tuesday	zhōu'èr	週二	N	3g
TV	diànshì	電視	N	4
twelve	shí'èr	十二	Nu	3
two	èr	二	Nu	Intro.
two; a couple of	liǎng	兩	Nu	2

▲ U ▲

English	Pinyin	Characters	Grammar	Lesson
under; next	xià	下		6
understand	dǒng	懂	V	7
university; college	dàxué	大學	N	2c
use; to use	yòng	用	V/N	8
usually	píngcháng	平常	T	7

▲ V ▲

English	Pinyin	Characters	Grammar	Lesson
Vancouver	Wēngēhuá	溫哥華	PN	10s
vehicle; car	chē	車	N	11
very	hěn	很	Adv	3
video recording	lùxiàng	錄像	N	10

English	Pinyin	Characters	Grammar	Lesson
Vietnam	Yuènán	越南	PN	6s
Vietnamese people/person	Yuènánrén	越南人	N	1s
vision	shì	視	N	4
volleyball	páiqiú	排球	N	4s
▲W▲				
wait	děng	等	V	6
waiter; waitress; service person	fúwùyuán	服務員	N	9n
waitress; waiter; service person	fúwùyuán	服務員	N	9n
walk	zǒu lù	走路	VO	11s
walk; go by way of	zǒu	走	V	11
want to; have a desire for	yào	要	V/AV	5, 9
want to; think	xiǎng	想	AV	4
warm (weather)	nuǎnhuo	暖和	Adj	10
watch	biǎo	錶	N	3s
watch; look	kàn	看	V	4
water	shuǐ	水	N	5
we	wǒmen	我們	Pr	3
wear (hat, glasses, etc.)	dài	戴	V	9s
wear; put on	chuān	穿	V	9
weather	tiānqì	天氣	N	10
week	lǐbài	禮拜	N	3g
week	xīngqī	星期	N	3
weekend	zhōumò	週末	T	4
wet; humid	cháoshī	潮濕	Adj	10s
what	shénme	什麼	QPr	
What is your honorable surname?	guì xìng	貴姓	CE	1
what to do	zěnme bàn	怎麼辦	QW	10
when...; at the time of...	de shíhou	的時候		8
where	nǎr	哪兒	QPr	5
which	nǎ/něi	哪	QPr	6
white; (a surname)	bái	白	Adj	3
who	shéi	誰	QPr	2
Who is it?	shéi ya	誰呀?	CE	5f
why	wèishénme	為什麼	QPr	3
wife; Mrs.	tàitai	太太	N	1s
will	huì	會	AV	10
will; be going to	yào	要	AV	6
wine	jiǔ	酒	N	5
winter	dōngtiān	冬天	N	10
winter vacation	hánjià	寒假	N	11
wish	zhù	祝	V	8, 11f
word; character	zì	字	N	7
words; speech; talk	huà	話	N	6
work; job	gōngzuò	工作	V/N	5
work part-time; do manual work	dǎ gōng	打工	VO	5s
wristwatch	shǒubiǎo	手錶	N	9n
write	xiě	寫	V	7

English	Pinyin	Characters	Grammar	Lesson
writing brush	máobǐ	毛筆	N	7s
wrong	cuò	錯	Adj	4
Wuhan	Wǔhàn	武漢	PN	10c
▲Y▲				
Yangtze river	Chángjiāng	長江	PN	10c
year	nián	年	N	3
year after next	hòunián	後年	T	3s
year before last	qiánnián	前年	T	3s
year of age	suìshù	歲數	N	3n
year of age	suì	歲	N	3
yellow	huáng	黃	Adj	9
yesterday	zuótiān	昨天	T	3s, 4
you	nǐ	你	Pr	1
you (singular; polite)	nín	您	Pr	1
You are welcome. Don't be (so) polite.	bú kèqi	不客氣	CE	6
You flatter me. Not at all.	nǎli	哪裏	CE	7, 7f
young lady; Miss	xiǎojie	小姐	N	1
younger brother	dìdi	弟弟	N	2
younger sister	mèimei	妹妹	N	2

VOCABULARY INDEX (BY GRAMMAR CATEGORY):
LESSONS 1–11

Key: c=Culture Notes; f=Functional Expressions; g=Grammar; n=Notes;
s=Supplementary Vocabulary

Grammar	Pinyin	Characters	English	Lesson
Adjectives				
Adj	bái	白	white	3
Adj	búcuò	不錯	not bad; pretty good	4
Adj	cháng	長	long	9s
Adj	cháoshī	潮濕	wet; humid	10s
Adj	cuò	錯	wrong	4
Adj	dà	大	big; old	3
Adj	duǎn	短	short	9s
Adj	duì	對	right; correct	4
Adj	duō	多	many; much	7
Adj	fāngbiàn	方便	convenient	6
Adj	gāo	高	tall	2
Adj	gāosù	高速	high speed	11
Adj	gāoxìng	高興	happy; pleased	5
Adj	gōnggòng	公共	public	11
Adj	guì	貴	honorable	1
Adj	guì	貴	expensive	9
Adj	hǎo	好	fine; good; nice; O.K.	1, 3
Adj	hǎochī	好吃	good to eat; delicious	5s
Adj	hǎohē	好喝	good to drink; tasty	5s
Adj	hǎokàn	好看	good-looking	5s, 7n
Adj	hǎowán(r)	好玩(兒)	fun	5s
Adj	hēi	黑	black	9
Adj	héshì	合適	suitable	9
Adj	hóng	紅	red	9
Adj	huáng	黃	yellow	9
Adj	huī	灰	gray	9s
Adj	jìn	近	near	8
Adj	jǐnzhāng	緊張	nervous; anxious	11
Adj	jiǔ	久	a long time; for a long time	4
Adj	kèqi	客氣	polite	6
Adj	kuài	快	quick; fast	7
Adj	kuàilè	快樂	happy	11
Adj	lán	藍	blue	9s, 11
Adj	lěng	冷	cold	10
Adj	liángkuai	涼快	pleasantly cool (weather)	10
Adj	lǜ	綠	green	9s, 11
Adj	máfan	麻煩	troublesome	11
Adj	màn	慢	slow	7
Adj	máng	忙	busy	3

▼▼

Grammar	Pinyin	Characters	English	Lesson
Adj	mēn	悶	stuffy	10
Adj	nán	難	difficult	7
Adj	nuǎnhuo	暖和	warm (weather)	10
Adj	piányi	便宜	cheap; inexpensive	9
Adj	piàoliang	漂亮	pretty	5
Adj	qíng	晴	sunny; clear	10s
Adj	qīngchu	清楚	clear	8
Adj	rè	熱	hot	10
Adj	róngyì	容易	easy	7
Adj	shuài	帥	handsome	7
Adj	shūfu	舒服	comfortable	10
Adj	tèbié	特別	special	7g
Adj	wǎn	晚	late	3
Adj	xiǎo	小	small; little	2
Adj	xīn	新	new	8
Adj	xíng	行	all right; O.K.	6
Adj	yīn	陰	overcast	10s
Adj	yíyàng	一樣	same; alike	9
Adj	zǎo	早	Good morning!; early	7
Adj	zāogāo	糟糕	in a terrible mess; too bad	10
Adj	zhōng	中	medium	9
Adj	zǐ	紫	purple	9s
Adverbs				
Adv	bié	別	don't	6
Adv	bié (de)	別(的)	other	4
Adv	bù	不	not; no	1
Adv	cái	才	not until; only then	5
Adv	chángcháng	常常	often	4
Adv	dōu	都	both; all	2
Adv	duō	多	how many/much; to what extent	3
Adv	gèng	更	even more	10
Adv	hái	還	also; too; as well	3
Adv	hěn	很	very	3
Adv	jiù	就	(indicates that something takes place sooner than expected)	7
Adv	jiù	就	the very one (indicating verification of something mentioned before)	6
Adv	kuài	快	soon; be about to; before long	11
Adv	kuài	快	fast; quickly	5
Adv	méi	沒	not	2
Adv	píngcháng	平常	usually	7
Adv	ránhòu	然後	then	11
Adv	tài…(le)	太…(了)	too; extremely	3
Adv	tèbié	特別	especially	7g
Adv	xiān	先	first; before	11
Adv	yě	也	too; also	1
Adv	yígòng	一共	altogether	9

Grammar	Pinyin	Characters	English	Lesson
Adv	yǐjīng	已經	already	8
Adv	yìqǐ	一起	together	5
Adv	yòu	又	again	10
Adv	zài	再	again	3
Adv	zhēn	真	really	7
Adv	zhèngzài	正在	in the middle of (doing something)	8
Adv	zhǐ	只	only	4
Adv	zuì	最	(an adverb of superlative degree; most, -est)	8
Adv	zuìhǎo	最好	had better	10
Adv	zuìhòu	最後	finally	11

Auxiliary Verbs

Grammar	Pinyin	Characters	English	Lesson
AV	děi	得	must; to have to	6
AV	huì	會	can; to know how to	8
AV	huì	會	will	10
AV	kěyǐ	可以	can; may	5
AV	néng	能	can; to be able to	8
AV	xiǎng	想	to want to; to think	4
AV	yào	要	will; to be going to	6
AV	yào	要	to want to; to have a desire for	9

Common Expressions

Grammar	Pinyin	Characters	English	Lesson
CE	bié kèqi	別客氣	Don't be so polite!	6
CE	bù hǎoyìsi	不好意思	to feel embarrassed	11
CE	bú kèqi	不客氣	You are welcome. Don't be (so) polite.	6
CE	bú xiè	不謝	Don't mention it. Not at all. You're welcome.	7
CE	bú yòng	不用	need not	6g, 9
CE	duì bu qǐ	對不起	I'm sorry.	5
CE	duì le	對了	That's right!	4s
CE	duō dà	多大	how old	3
CE	gōngxǐ fācái	恭喜發財	Congratulations and may you make a fortune!	11n
CE	guì xìng	貴姓	What is your honorable surname?	1
CE	hǎojiǔ	好久	a long time	4
CE	méi shìr	沒事兒	no problem; it's O.K.	8f
CE	méi wèntí	沒問題	no problem	6, 6f
CE	nǎli	哪裏	You flatter me. Not at all. (a polite reply to a compliment)	7, 7f
CE	nǐ hǎo	你好	How do you do? Hello!	1
CE	qǐng wèn	請問	May I ask...	1
CE	shéi ya	誰呀?	Who is it?	5f
CE	shì ma	是嗎	Really?	5f, 5n
CE	suàn le	算了	Forget it. Never mind.	4
CE	xièxie	謝謝	thank you	3
CE	yǒu shíhou	有時候	sometimes	4
CE	yǒu yìdiǎnr	有一點兒	a little; somewhat	7

▼ ▼

Grammar	Pinyin	Characters	English	Lesson
CE	yǒu yìsi	有意思	interesting	4
CE	zàijiàn	再見	good-bye; see you again	3
CE	zǎo ān	早安	Good morning!	7n

Conjunctions

Conj	búdàn..., érqiě	不但...而且	not only..., but also	10
Conj	búguò	不過	however; but	11
Conj	chúle...yǐwài	除了...以外	in addition to; besides	8
Conj	dànshì	但是	but	6
Conj	gēn	跟	and	7
Conj	háishi	還是	had better	11
Conj	háishi	還是	or	3
Conj	hé	和	and	2
Conj	huòzhě	或者	or	11
Conj	kěshì	可是	but	3
Conj	nà	那	in that case; then	4
Conj	suīrán	雖然	although	9
Conj	suǒyǐ	所以	so	4
Conj	yàoshi	要是	if	6
Conj	yīnwei	因為	because	3

Interjections

Interj	wèi/wéi	喂	(on telephone) Hello!; Hey!	6, 6f, 6n

Measure Words

M	bēi	杯	cup; glass	5
M	cì	次	time; (a measure word for occurrence)	10
M	diǎn	點	o'clock	3
M	diǎn(r)	點(兒)	a little; a bit; some	5
M	diǎnzhōng	點鐘	o'clock	3
M	dǐng	頂	(a measure word for hat)	9s
M	fēn	分	minute	3s
M	fēn	分	$\frac{1}{100}$ of a kuai; cent	9
M	fēng	封	(a measure word for letters)	8
M	gè	個	(a common measure word)	2
M	hào	號	number in a series; day of the month	3
M	hào	號	number; size	9
M	jiàn	件	(a measure word for shirts, dresses, jackets, coats, etc.)	9
M	jiǎo	角	dime	9g
M	jié	節	(a measure word for class periods)	6, 6n
M	kè	刻	quarter (hour); 15 minutes	3
M	kǒu	口	(a measure for people)	2n
M	kuài	塊	colloquial term for the basic Chinese monetary unit	9
M	liàng	輛	(a measure for vehicles)	11s
M	máo	毛	$\frac{1}{10}$ of a kuai (similar to the U.S. dime)	9
M	mén	門	(a measure for academic courses)	6n

Grammar	Pinyin	Characters	English	Lesson
M	piān	篇	(a measure for essays, articles, etc.)	8
M	píng	瓶	bottle	5
M	shuāng	雙	a pair of	9
M	tiáo	條	(a measure word for long, thin objects)	9
M	wèi	位	(a polite measure for people)	6
M	yí xià	一下	(a measure word used after a verb indicating short duration)	5
M	yuán	元	Chinese dollar	9g
M	zhāng	張	(a measure word for flat objects)	2
M	zhī	枝	(a measure for pens and long items)	9g
M	zhī	隻	(a measure for bird, shoe, etc.)	9g

Nouns

Grammar	Pinyin	Characters	English	Lesson
N	bàba	爸爸	dad; father	2
N	Bǎishìkělè	百事可樂	Pepsi	5s
N	bàngōngshì	辦公室	office	6
N	bàngqiú	棒球	baseball	4s
N	bào	報	newspaper	8
N	bāyuè	八月	August	3g
N	běnzi	本子	notebook	7s
N	bǐ	筆	pen	7
N	biǎo	錶	watch	3s
N	biérén	別人	others; other people; another person	4
N	bùshǒu	部首	radical	Intro.
N	cāntīng	餐廳	dining room; cafeteria	8
N	chá	茶	tea	5
N	chángpáo	長袍	long gown	9c
N	chángshòu	長壽	longevity	3c
N	chángshòu miàn	長壽麵	longevity noodles	3c
N	chē	車	vehicle; car	11
N	chènshān	襯衫	shirt	9
N	chēzhàn	車站	(bus, train, etc.) stop; station	11
N	chuán	船	boat; ship	11s
N	chuáng	床	bed	2g, 8
N	chūntiān	春天	spring	10
N	chūzhōng	初中	junior high (grades 7–9)	2c
N	chūzū qìchē	出租汽車	taxi	11
N	dàgē	大哥	oldest brother	7g
N	dàjiě	大姐	oldest sister	7g
N	dàxiǎo	大小	size	9
N	dàxué	大學	university; college	2c
N	dàxuéshēng	大學生	college student	2
N	dàyī	大衣	overcoat	9s
N	Déguórén	德國人	German people/person	1s
N	Déwén	德文	the German language	6s
N	diàn	電	electricity	4
N	diànchē	電車	cable car; trolley bus; tram	11s

Grammar	Pinyin	Characters	English	Lesson
N	diànhuà	電話	telephone	6
N	diànnǎo	電腦	computer	8
N	diànshì	電視	TV	4
N	diànyǐng	電影	movie	4
N	diànzǐ jìsuànjī	電子計算機	computer	8n
N	dìdi	弟弟	younger brother	2
N	dìtiě	地鐵	subway	11
N	dōngtiān	冬天	winter	10
N	dōngxi	東西	things; objects	9
N	èrgē	二哥	second oldest brother	7g
N	èrjiě	二姐	second oldest sister	7g
N	èryuè	二月	February	3g
N	érzi	兒子	son	2
N	Éwén	俄文	the Russian language	6s
N	Fǎguórén	法國人	French people/person	1s
N	fàn	飯	meal; (cooked) rice	3
N	fántǐzì	繁體字	traditional character	7c
N	Fǎwén	法文	the French language	6s
N	fāyīn	發音	pronunciation	8
N	fēijī	飛機	airplane	11
N	fēijīchǎng	飛機場	airport	11
N	fěnhóngsè	粉紅色	pink	9s
N	fúwùyuán	服務員	service person; waiter; waitress	9n
N	gāngbǐ	鋼筆	fountain pen	7s
N	gǎnlǎn	橄欖	olive	4s
N	gǎnlǎnqiú	橄欖球	American style football (used in Taiwan)	4s
N	gāosù gōnglù	高速公路	super highway; highway	11
N	gāozhōng	高中	senior high (grades 10–12)	2c
N	gē	歌	song	4
N	gēge	哥哥	older brother	2
N	gōnggòng qìchē	公共汽車	bus	11
N	gōngkè	功課	schoolwork; homework	7
N	gōnglù	公路	highway; road	11
N	gōngyuán	公園	park	10
N	gōngzuò	工作	work; job	5
N	háizi	孩子	child	2
N	Hánguórén	韓國人	Korean people/person	1s
N	hánjià	寒假	winter vacation	11
N	Hánwén	韓文	the Korean language	6s
N	Hànyǔ	漢語	the Chinese language	6n
N	Hànzì	漢字	Chinese character	7
N	hào	號	number (bus route)	11n
N	hóngyè	紅葉	red autumn leaves	10
N	huángméi	黃梅	rainy season	10c
N	huà	話	speech; talk; words	6
N	huǒchē	火車	train	11s
N	jī	機	machine	11

Grammar	Pinyin	Characters	English	Lesson
N	jiā	家	family; home	2
N	jiákè	夾克	jacket	9s
N	jiǎntǐzì	簡體字	simplified character	7c
N	jiàoshì	教室	classroom	8
N	jīchǎng	機場	airport	11
N	jìchéngchē	計程車	taxi (in Taiwan)	11s
N	jiějie	姐姐	older sister	2
N	jìnbù	進步	progress	8
N	jìsuànjī	計算機	calculator; computer	8n
N	jiǔ	酒	wine; any alcoholic beverage	5
N	jiǔyuè	九月	September	3
N	júhóngsè	橘紅色	orange	9s
N	kāfēi	咖啡	coffee	5
N	kāfēisè	咖啡色	coffee color; brown	9
N	kāishǐ	開始	in the beginning	7, 8
N	*Kāngxī Zìdiǎn*	康熙字典	*Kangxi Dictionary*	Intro.
N	kǎoshì	考試	test	6
N	kè	課	class; lesson	6
N	Kěkǒukělè	可口可樂	Coke	5s
N	kělè	可樂	cola	5
N	kèwén	課文	text of a lesson	7
N	kòng(r)	空(兒)	free time	6
N	kǒu	口	mouth	2n
N	kuàngquánshuǐ	礦泉水	mineral water	5s
N	kùzi	褲子	pants	9
N	Lādīngwén	拉丁文	Latin	6s
N	lánqiú	籃球	basketball	4s
N	lǎoshī	老師	teacher	1
N	lǐ	李	plum	1
N	lǐbài	禮拜	week	3g
N	lǐbàisì	禮拜四	Thursday	3g
N	liùyuè	六月	June	3g
N	lù	路	road; path	11
N	lù	路	number (bus route)	11n
N	lǜshī	律師	lawyer	2
N	lùxiàng	錄像	video recording	10
N	lùyīn	錄音	sound recording	
N	mǎguà	馬褂	Mandarin jacket	9c
N	māma	媽媽	mom; mother	2
N	máobǐ	毛筆	writing brush	7s
N	máoyī	毛衣	sweater	9s
N	màozi	帽子	hat	9s
N	Měiguórén	美國人	American people/person	1
N	mèimei	妹妹	younger sister	2
N	Měishì zúqiú	美式足球	American style football (used in mainland China)	4s
N	mén	門	door; (a measure for academic courses)	6n
N	miàn	麵	noodles	3c

▼▼▼

Grammar	Pinyin	Characters	English	Lesson
N	míngzi	名字	name	1
N	nán	男	male	2
N	nánháizi	男孩子	boy	2
N	nǎo	腦	brain	8
N	nián	年	year	3
N	niánjì	年紀	age	3n
N	niánjí	年級	grade in school	6
N	nǚ	女	female	2
N	nǚ'ér	女兒	daughter	2
N	nǚháizi	女孩子	girl	2
N	páiqiú	排球	volleyball	4s
N	péngyou	朋友	friend	1s, 7
N	piào	票	ticket	11
N	píjiǔ	啤酒	beer	5
N	Pútáoyáwén	葡萄牙文	the Portuguese language	6s
N	qián	錢	money	9
N	qiānbǐ	鉛筆	pencil	7s
N	qìchē	汽車	automobile	11
N	qípáo	旗袍	Manchu-style dress	9c
N	qìshuǐ(r)	汽水(兒)	soft drink; soda pop	5s
N	qiú	球	ball	4
N	qiūtiān	秋天	autumn; fall	10
N	qīyuè	七月	July	3g
N	qúnzi	裙子	skirt	9s
N	rén	人	people; person	1
N	rì	日	day; the sun	3
N	Rìběnrén	日本人	Japanese people/person	1s
N	rìjì	日記	diary	8
N	Rìwén	日文	the Japanese language	6s
N	sāngē	三哥	third oldest brother	7g
N	sānjiě	三姐	third oldest sister	7g
N	sānyuè	三月	March	3g
N	shēngcí	生詞	new words	7
N	shēngrì	生日	birthday	3
N	shì	事	matter; affair; business	3
N	shì	視	vision	4
N	shí'èryuè	十二月	December	3g
N	shīfu	師傅	master craftsman; skilled worker	9n
N	shíhou	時候	(a point in) time; moment; (a duration of) time	4
N	shíyīyuè	十一月	November	3g
N	shíyuè	十月	October	3g
N	shǒubiǎo	手錶	wristwatch	9n
N	shòuhuòyuán	售貨員	shop assistant; salesclerk	9
N	shǒutào	手套	gloves	9n
N	shū	書	book	4
N	shuǐ	水	water	5
N	shǔjià	暑假	summer vacation	11s

Grammar	Pinyin	Characters	English	Lesson
N	sìyuè	四月	April	3g
N	suì	歲	year of age	3
N	suìshù	歲數	year of age	3n
N	sùshè	宿舍	dormitory	8
N	tàitai	太太	wife; Mrs.	1s
N	tiān	天	day	3
N	tiānqì	天氣	weather	10
N	tóngxué	同學	classmate	3
N	túshūguǎn	圖書館	library	5
N	T-xùshān	T-恤衫	T-shirt	9s
N	wàiguó	外國	foreign country	4
N	wàitào	外套	coat; jacket	9s
N	wǎn	晚	evening; night	3
N	wǎnfàn	晚飯	dinner; supper	3
N	wáng	王	king	1
N	wǎngqiú	網球	tennis	4s
N	wàzi	襪子	socks	9s
N	wén	文	language; script; written language	6
N	wèntí	問題	question; problem	6
N	wǔ	舞	dance	4
N	wǔfàn	午飯	lunch; midday meal	8
N	wǔjiào	午覺	nap	7s
N	wǔyuè	五月	May	3g
N	xiàn	線	line	11
N	xiānsheng	先生	Mr.; husband; teacher	1
N	xiǎojie	小姐	Miss; young lady	1
N	xiǎoxué	小學	elementary school; grade school	2c
N	xiàtiān	夏天	summer	10
N	Xībānyáwén	西班牙文	the Spanish language	6s
N	xié	鞋	shoes	9
N	xíguàn	習慣	habit	8
N	Xīlàwén	希臘文	the Greek language	6s
N	xìn	信	letter (mail)	8
N	xìng	姓	surname	1
N	xīngqī	星期	week	3
N	xīngqī'èr	星期二	Tuesday	3g
N	xīngqīliù	星期六	Saturday	3g
N	xīngqīrì	星期日	Sunday	3g
N	xīngqīsān	星期三	Wednesday	3g
N	xīngqīsì	星期四	Thursday	3
N	xīngqītiān	星期天	Sunday	3g
N	xīngqīwǔ	星期五	Friday	3g
N	xīngqīyī	星期一	Monday	3g
N	xīnnián	新年	new year	11
N	xīwàng	希望	hope	8
N	xīzhuāng	西裝	suit	9s
N	xuě	雪	snow	10s
N	Xuěbì	雪碧	Sprite	5s

▼▼▼

Grammar	Pinyin	Characters	English	Lesson
N	xuéqī	學期	school term; semester/quarter	8
N	xuésheng	學生	student	1
N	xuéxiào	學校	school	5
N	xuéyuàn	學院	college	2c
N	yǎnjìng	眼鏡	eyeglasses; glasses	9n
N	yánsè	顏色	color	9
N	yè	夜	night	7
N	Yìdàlìwén	意大利文	the Italian language	6s
N	yīfu	衣服	clothes	9
N	yǐng	影	shadow	4
N	Yīngguórén	英國人	British people/person	1s
N	Yīngwén	英文	the English language	2
N	yīnyuè	音樂	music	4
N	yīnyuèhuì	音樂會	concert	8
N	yīshēng	醫生	doctor; physician	2
N	yìsi	意思	meaning	4
N	yīyuè	一月	January	3g
N	yòng	用	use	8
N	yǔ	語	speech	6n
N	yuánzhūbǐ	圓珠筆	ballpoint pen	7c
N	yuánzǐbǐ	原子筆	ballpoint pen	7c
N	yùbào	預報	forecast	10
N	yuè	月	month	3
N	Yuènánrén	越南人	Vietnamese people/person	1s
N	yǔfǎ	語法	grammar	7
N	yún	雲	cloud	10s
N	zǎofàn	中飯	lunch	3s
N	zǎofàn	早飯	breakfast	3s, 8
N	zhàn	站	(bus, train, etc.) stop; station	11
N	zhàopiàn	照片	picture; photo	2
N	zhǐ	紙	paper	2g, 7s
N	zhōng	鐘	clock	3
N	Zhōngguórén	中國人	Chinese people/person	1
N	Zhōngguózì	中國字	Chinese character	Intro.
N	Zhōngshānzhuāng	中山裝	Sun Yatsen suit	9c
N	Zhōngwén	中文	the Chinese language	6
N	zhōngxué	中學	middle school	2c
N	zhōu	週	week	3g
N	zhōu'èr	週二	Tuesday	3g
N	zhōurì	週日	Sunday	3g
N	zhōuyī	週一	Monday	3g
N	zhuānyè	專業	major (in college); specialty	8
N	zì	字	character	7
N	zúqiú	足球	soccer	4s

Noun Phrases

NP	zhè jǐ tiān	這幾天	the past few days	11

▼ ▼

Grammar	Pinyin	Characters	English	Lesson
Numerals				
Nu	bā	八	eight	Intro.
Nu	bǎi	百	hundred	9
Nu	bàn	半	half; half an hour	3
Nu	èr	二	two	Intro.
Nu	jǐ	幾	some; a few (an indefinite number, usually less than ten)	6
Nu	jiǔ	九	nine	Intro.
Nu	liǎng	兩	two; a couple of	2
Nu	líng	零	zero	3g
Nu	liù	六	six	Intro.
Nu	qī	七	seven	Intro.
Nu	sān	三	three	Intro.
Nu	shí	十	ten	Intro.
Nu	shí'èr	十二	twelve	3
Nu	shíbā	十八	eighteen	3
Nu	sì	四	four	Intro.
Nu	wǔ	五	five	Intro.
Nu	yī	一	one	Intro.
Particles				
P	a	啊	(a sentence-final particle of exclamation, interrogation, etc.)	6
P	ba	吧	(a "suggestion" particle; softens the tone of the sentence to which it is appended)	5
P	de	的	(a possessive, modifying, or descriptive particle)	2
P	de	得	(a structural particle)	7
P	le	了	(a particle indicating superlative degree)	3
P	le	了	(a dynamic particle; a sentence particle)	5g, 8g, 10g
P	ya	呀	(an interjectory particle used to soften a question)	5
Proper Nouns				
PN	Bái	白	(a surname)	3
PN	Běijīng	北京	Beijing	10s
PN	Chángjiāng	長江	Yangtze river	10c
PN	Chén	陳	(a surname)	1n
PN	Chóngqìng	重慶	Chongqing	10c
PN	Déguó	德國	Germany	1s
PN	Éguó	俄國	Russia	6s
PN	Fǎguó	法國	France	1s
PN	Fēilǜbīn	菲律賓	the Philippines	6s
PN	Gāo	高	(a surname)	2
PN	Hā'ěrbīn	哈爾濱	Harbin	10c

▼▼▼▼▼▼▼▼▼▼▼▼▼▼▼▼▼▼▼▼▼▼▼▼▼▼▼▼▼▼▼▼▼▼▼▼▼▼

Grammar	Pinyin	Characters	English	Lesson
PN	Hǎinán	海南	Hainan	10c
PN	Hánguó	韓國	Korea	6s
PN	Jiānádà	加拿大	Canada	10s
PN	Kūnmíng	昆明	Kunming	10c
PN	Lǐ	李	(a surname)	1
PN	Lǐ Yǒu	李友	(a personal name)	1
PN	Liú	劉	(a surname)	1n
PN	Mǎláixīyà	馬來西亞	Malaysia	6s
PN	Máotái	茅台	Maotai (name of a liquor)	5c
PN	Měiguó	美國	America	1
PN	Nánjīng	南京	Nanjing	10c
PN	Pútáoyá	葡萄牙	Portugal	6s
PN	Rìběn	日本	Japan	1s
PN	Shànghǎi	上海	Shanghai	10
PN	Táiběi	台北	Taipei	10
PN	Tàiguó	泰國	Thailand	6s
PN	Táiwān	台灣	Taiwan	10
PN	Táizhōng	台中	Taichung	10s
PN	Wáng	王	(a surname)	1
PN	Wáng Péng	王朋	(a personal name)	1
PN	Wēngēhuá	溫哥華	Vancouver	10s
PN	Wǔhàn	武漢	Wuhan	10c
PN	Xiānggǎng	香港	Hong Kong	10s
PN	Xiǎo Bái	小白	Little Bai	3
PN	Xiǎo Gāo	小高	Little Gao	2
PN	Xiǎo Lǐ	小李	Little Li	3
PN	Xiǎo Zhāng	小張	Little Zhang	2
PN	Xiàwēiyí	夏威夷	Hawaii	6s
PN	Xībānyá	西班牙	Spain	6s
PN	Xiè	謝	(a surname)	10
PN	Xīlà	希臘	Greece	6s
PN	Xīngbākè	星巴克	Starbucks	5c
PN	Yìdàlì	意大利	Italy	6s
PN	Yīngguó	英國	Britain; England	1s
PN	Yìwén	意文	(a given name)	8
PN	Yuènán	越南	Vietnam	6s
PN	Zhōngguó	中國	China	1
PN	Zhāng	張	(a surname)	1n

Pronouns

Pr	dàjiā	大家	everybody	7
Pr	nà/nèi	那	that	2
Pr	nàr	那兒	there	8
Pr	nǐ	你	you	1
Pr	nín	您	you (singular; polite)	1
Pr	tā	他	he; him	2
Pr	tā	她	she	2
Pr	wǒ	我	I; me	1

▼▼▼▼▼▼▼▼▼▼▼▼▼▼▼▼▼▼▼▼▼▼▼▼▼▼▼▼▼▼▼▼▼▼▼▼▼▼

Grammar	Pinyin	Characters	English	Lesson
Pr	wǒmen	我們	we	3
Pr	zhè/zhèi	這	this	2
Pr	zhège	這個	this	12
Pr	zhème	這麼	so; such	7
Pr	zhèr	這兒	here	9
Pr	zhèyàng	這樣	so; like this	10
Pr	zìjǐ	自己	oneself	11

Prefixes

prefix	dì	第	(a prefix for ordinal numbers)	7

Prepositions

Prep	bǐ	比	(a comparison marker)	10
Prep	gěi	給	to; for	6
Prep	měi	每	every; each (usually followed by a measure word)	11
Prep	wèi	為	for	3
Prep	zài	在	at; in; on	5

Question Particles

QP	ma	嗎	(an interrogative particle)	1
QP	ne	呢	(an interrogative particle)	1

Question Pronouns

QPr	nǎ/něi	哪	which	6
QPr	nǎr	哪兒	where	5
QPr	shéi	誰	who	2
QPr	shénme	什麼	what	1
QPr	wèishénme	為什麼	why	3
QPr	zěnme	怎麼	how; how come (used to inquire about the cause of something, implying a degree of surprise or disapproval)	7
QPr	zěnmeyàng	怎麼樣	Is it O.K.? What is it like? How does that sound?	3

Question Words

QW	duōshao	多少	how much; how many	9
QW	jǐ	幾	how many	2
QW	zěnme bàn	怎麼辦	what to do	10

Time Words

T	bànyè	半夜	midnight	7
T	gāngcái	剛才	just now; a moment ago	10
T	hòulái	後來	later	8
T	hòunián	後年	the year after next	3s
T	hòutiān	後天	the day after tomorrow	3s
T	jīnnián	今年	this year	3
T	jīntiān	今天	today	3
T	měitiān	每天	every day	11
T	míngnián	明年	next year	3s

Grammar	Pinyin	Characters	English	Lesson
T	míngtiān	明天	tomorrow	3
T	qiánnián	前年	the year before last	3s
T	qiántiān	前天	the day before yesterday	3s
T	qùnián	去年	last year	3s, 6n
T	shàngge xīngqī	上個星期	last week	6n, 7
T	shàngge yuè	上個月	last month	6n
T	shàngwǔ	上午	morning	6
T	shíjiān	時間	time	6
T	wǎnshang	晚上	evening; night	3
T	xià(ge)yuè	下(個)月	next month	3s
T	xiàge xīngqī	下個星期	next week	6
T	xiànzài	現在	now	3
T	xiàwǔ	下午	afternoon	6
T	yǐhòu	以後	after	6, 6n
T	yǐqián	以前	before; ago; previously	7g, 8
T	zǎoshang	早上	morning	8
T	zhōngwǔ	中午	noon	6s; 8
T	zhōumò	週末	weekend	4
T	zuìjìn	最近	recently	8
T	zuótiān	昨天	yesterday	3s, 4

Verbs

Grammar	Pinyin	Characters	English	Lesson
V	bāng	幫	to help	6
V	bāngzhù	幫助	to help	7
V	chà	差	to be short of; to be lacking	3s
V	chàng	唱	to sing	4
V	chī	吃	to eat	3
V	chuān	穿	to wear; to put on	9
V	chūzū	出租	to rent out; to let	11
V	dǎ	打	to hit; to strike	4
V	dài	戴	to wear (hat, glasses, etc.)	9s
V	dào	到	to arrive	8
V	děng	等	to wait; to wait for	6
V	dǒng	懂	to understand	7
V	fācái	發財	to make a fortune	11c
V	fēi	飛	to fly	11
V	fùxí	復習	to review	7
V	gàosu	告訴	to tell	8
V	gěi	給	to give	5
V	gōngxǐ	恭喜	to congratulate	11c
V	gōngzuò	工作	to work	5
V	hē	喝	to drink	5
V	huā	花	to spend	11
V	huàn	換	to change; to exchange	9
V	huí	回	to return	5
V	jiàn	見	to see	3
V	jiào	叫	to be called; to call	1
V	jiāo	教	to teach	7

Grammar	Pinyin	Characters	English	Lesson
V	jièshào	介紹	to introduce	5
V	jìn	進	to enter	5
V	jìnbù	進步	to make progress	8
V	juéde	覺得	to feel	4
V	kāi	開	to hold (a meeting, party, etc.)	6
V	kāi	開	to drive; to operate	11
V	kāishǐ	開始	to begin; to start	7, 8
V	kàn	看	to watch; to look	4
V	kǎo	考	to give or take a test	6
V	kǎoshì	考試	to give or take a test	6
V	lái	來	to come	5
V	liànxí	練習	to practice	6
V	mǎi	買	to buy	9
V	mài	賣	to sell	9s
V	niàn	念	to read aloud	7
V	qǐng	請	please (a polite form of request)	1, 6n
V	qǐng	請	to treat (somebody); to invite	3, 6n
V	qù	去	to go	4
V	ràng	讓	to allow or cause (somebody to do something)	11
V	rènshi	認識	to know (someone); to recognize	3
V	shēng	生	to give birth to; to be born	3
V	shì	是	to be	1
V	shuì	睡	to sleep	4
V	shuō	說	to say; to speak	6
V	sòng	送	to take someone (somewhere)	11
V	tiào	跳	to jump	4
V	tīng	聽	to listen	4
V	wán(r)	玩(兒)	to have fun; to play	5
V	wèn	問	to ask (a question)	1, 6n
V	xiào	笑	to laugh; to laugh at	8
V	xiě	寫	to write	7
V	xiè	謝	thanks	10
V	xíguàn	習慣	to be accustomed to	8
V	xǐhuan	喜歡	to like; to prefer	3
V	xìng	姓	(one's) surname is...	1
V	xīwàng	希望	to hope	8
V	xué	學	to study	7
V	yào	要	to want to; to have a desire for	5
V	yòng	用	to use	8
V	yǒu	有	to have; to exist	2
V	yuē	約	to make an appointment	10
V	yùxí	預習	to preview	7
V	zài	在	to be present; to be at (a place)	6
V	zhǎo	找	to look for	4
V	zhǎo(qián)	找(錢)	to give change	9
V	zhīdao	知道	to know	6
V	zhù	祝	to express good wishes	8, 11f

Grammar	Pinyin	Characters	English	Lesson
V	zǒu	走	to walk; to go by way of	11
V	zū	租	to rent	11
V	zuò	做	to do	2
V	zuò	坐	to sit	5
V	zuò	坐	to travel by	11

Verbs plus Complement

VC	chūqu	出去	to go out	10
VC	huílai	回來	to come back	6
VC	jìnlai	進來	to come in	5
VC	jìnqu	進去	to go in	6g

Verbs plus Object

VO	bāng máng	幫忙	to help; to do someone a favor	6
VO	chàng gē	唱歌	to sing (a song)	4
VO	chī fàn	吃飯	to eat (a meal)	3
VO	dǎ diànhuà	打電話	to make a phone call	6
VO	dǎ gōng	打工	to work part-time; to do manual work	5s
VO	dǎ qiú	打球	to play ball	4
VO	fù qián	付錢	to pay money	9
VO	huí jiā	回家	to go home	5
VO	kāi chē	開車	to drive a car	11
VO	kāi huì	開會	to have a meeting	6
VO	kàn shū	看書	to read books; to read	4
VO	liáo tiān(r)	聊天(兒)	to chat	5
VO	lù yīn	錄音	to record	7
VO	qǐ chuáng	起床	to get up	8
VO	qiāo mén	敲門	to knock at the door	5f
VO	qǐng kè	請客	to invite someone to dinner; to be the host	4
VO	shàng kè	上課	to go to class; to start a class	7
VO	shuì jiào	睡覺	to sleep	4
VO	shuō huà	說話	to talk	7
VO	tiào wǔ	跳舞	to dance	4
VO	xǐ zǎo	洗澡	to take a bath/shower	8
VO	xià chē	下車	to get off (a bus, train, etc.)	11
VO	xià yǔ	下雨	to rain	10
VO	yǒu kòng(r)	有空(兒)	to have free time	6
VO	zǒu lù	走路	to walk	11s

LESSON 1 ▲ Greetings

Dialogue I: Exchanging Greetings

DIALOGUE I

王先生(1)：   你好(2)！

李小姐：   你好！

王先生：   请问，您贵姓(3)？

李小姐：   我姓(G1)李。你呢(G2)？

王先生：   我姓王，叫(G3)王朋(4)。你叫
什么名字(5)？

李小姐：   我叫李友。

Dialogue II: Asking One's Status

DIALOGUE II

李小姐： 王先生，你是(G4)老师吗(G5)？

王先生： 不(G6)，我不(1)是老师，我是学
生。李小姐，你呢？

李小姐： 我也(G7)是学生。你是中国人吗？

王先生： 是，我是中国人。你是美国人吗？

李小姐： 我是美国人。

LESSON 2 ▲ Family

Dialogue I: Looking at a Family Photo

DIALOGUE I

(Wang Peng is in Little Gao's room pointing to a picture on the wall.)

王朋： 小高⁽¹⁾，那<u>张</u>⁽ᴳ¹⁾照片是你的吗？

(They both walk toward the picture and then stand in front of it.)

小高： 是。这是我爸爸，这是我妈妈。

王朋： 这个男孩子是<u>谁</u>⁽ᴳ²⁾？

小高： 他是我弟弟。

王朋： 这个女孩子是你妹妹吗？

小高： 不是，她是李先生的⁽²⁾女儿。

王朋： 李先生<u>有</u>⁽ᴳ³⁾儿子吗？

小高： 他没有儿子。

Dialogue II: Asking about Someone's Family

DIALOGUE II

李友： 小张，你家⁽¹⁾<u>有</u>⁽ᴳ⁴⁾几个⁽²⁾人？

小张： 我家有六个人。我爸爸⁽³⁾、我妈妈、
        一⁽⁴⁾<u>个</u>⁽ᴳ¹⁾哥哥、<u>两</u>⁽ᴳ⁵⁾个姐姐和⁽⁵⁾
        我⁽⁶⁾。李小姐，你家有几个人？

李友：　我家有五个人。爸爸、妈妈、两个
　　　　妹妹和我。你爸爸妈妈是做什么
　　　　的(7)？

小张：　我妈妈是英文老师，爸爸是律师，
　　　　哥哥、姐姐都(G6)是大学生。

李友：　我妈妈也是老师，我爸爸是医生。

LESSON 3 ▲ Dates and Time

Dialogue I: Taking Someone Out to Eat on His/Her Birthday

DIALOGUE I

(Little Gao is talking to Little Bai.)

小高：　小白，九月十二(1)(G1)号(G2.3)是星期
　　　　几(G2.1)？

小白：　是星期四。

小高：　那天是我的(G3)生日。

小白：　是吗？你今年多大(2)？

小高：　十八岁(3)。

小白：　星期四我请你吃晚饭(G4)，怎么样？

小高：　太好了。谢谢，谢谢(4)。

小白：　你喜欢吃中国饭还是(G5)美国饭？

小高: 我是中国人，可是我喜欢吃美国
饭。

小白: 好，我们吃美国饭。

小高: 星期四几点钟？

小白: 七点半(G2.6)怎么样？

小高: 好，星期四晚上见。

小白: 再见！

Dialogue II: Inviting Someone to Dinner

DIALOGUE II

(Wang Peng and Little Bai are talking to each other.)

王朋: 小白，现在几点钟？

小白: 五点三刻。

王朋: 我六点一刻有事。

小白: 王朋，你明天忙不忙(G6)？

王朋: 我今天很忙(1)，可是明天不忙。有事吗？

小白: 明天我请你吃晚饭，怎么样？

王朋: 为什么请我吃饭？

小白: 因为明天是小高的生日。

王朋: 是吗？好。还有(G7)谁？

小白：还有我的同学小李。

王朋：那太好了，我也认识小李。几点钟？

小白：明天晚上七点半。

王朋：好，明天七点半见。

LESSON 4 ▲ Hobbies

Dialogue I: Talking about Hobbies

DIALOGUE I

(Little Bai is talking to Little Gao.)

小白：小高，你周末(1)<u>喜欢做什么</u>(G1)？

小高：我喜欢打球、看电视(2)。你呢？

小白：我喜欢唱歌、跳舞，还喜欢听音乐。

小高：你也喜欢看书，对不对？

小白：对，有时候也喜欢看书。

小高：你<u>喜欢不喜欢</u>(G2)看电影？

小白：喜欢。我周末常常看电影。

小高：<u>那</u>(G3)我们今天晚上<u>去看</u>(G4)一个外国电影，怎么样？

小白：好。今天我请客。

小高：为什么你请客？

小白：因为昨天你请我吃饭，所以今天我
　　　请你看电影。

Dialogue II: Inviting Someone to Play Ball

DIALOGUE II

(Wang Peng is talking to Little Zhang.)

王朋：小张，好久不见⁽¹⁾，你好吗？

小张：我很好。你怎么样？

王朋：我也不错。这个周末你想(G5)做什
　　　么？想不想去打球？

小张：打球？我不喜欢打球。

王朋：那我们去看电影，好吗(G6)？

小张：看电影？我觉得看电影也没有意
　　　思⁽²⁾。

王朋：那你喜欢做什么？

小张：我只喜欢吃饭、睡觉。

王朋：那算了⁽ᶠ⁾。我去找别人。

LESSON 5 ▲ Visiting Friends

Dialogue: Visiting a Friend's Home

DIALOGUE

小高：　　谁呀？ (F)

王朋：　　是我，王朋，还有李友。

小高：　　请进，请进！李友，快进来！
　　　　　来，我介绍一下(G1)，这是我姐
　　　　　姐，高小音。

李友：　　小音，你好。认识你很高兴(1)。

高小音：　认识你们我也很高兴。

李友：　　你们家很大(G2)，也很漂亮。

小高：　　是吗(2)(F)？ 请坐，请坐。

王朋：　　小音，你在(G3)哪儿工作？

高小音：　我在学校工作。你们想喝点儿(G1)
　　　　　什么？有茶、咖啡，还有啤酒。

王朋：　　我喝啤酒吧(G4)。

李友：　　我不喝酒。我要一杯可乐，可以
　　　　　吗？

高小音：　对不起，我们没有可乐。

李友：　　那给我一杯水吧。

Narrative: At a Friend's House

Narrative

昨天晚上，王朋和李友去小高家玩儿。在小高家，他们认识了(G5)小高的姐姐。她叫高小音，在学校的图书馆工作。小高请王朋喝(1)啤酒，王朋喝了两瓶。李友不喝酒，只喝了一杯水。他们一起聊天儿、看电视。王朋和李友晚上十二点才(G6)回家。

LESSON 6 ▲ Making Appointments

Dialogue I: Calling One's Teacher

DIALOGUE I

(李友给(G1)老师打电话。)

李友：　　喂(F)，请问，王老师在吗？

王老师：我就是。您是哪位？

李友：　　老师，您好。我是李友。

王老师：李友，你好，有事吗？

李友：　　老师，今天下午您有时间吗？我

想问⑴您几个问题。

王老师：　对不起，今天下午我要(G2)开会。

李友：　　明天呢？

王老师：　明天上午我有两节⑵课，下午三
点钟要给二年级考试。

李友：　　您什么时候有空？

王老师：　明天四点以后⑶才有空。

李友：　　要是您方便，四点半我到您的办
公室去，行吗？

王老师：　四点半，没问题(F)。我在办公室
等你。

李友：　　谢谢(F)您。

王老师：　不客气。

Dialogue II: Calling a Friend for Help

DIALOGUE II

李友：喂，请问，王朋在吗？

王朋：我就是。你是李友吧⑴？有事吗？

李友：我想请你帮忙。

王朋：别(G3)客气，有什么事？

李友： 我下个星期(2)要考中文(3)，你帮我
　　　 练习说中文，好吗？

王朋： 好啊，但是你<u>得</u>(G4)请我喝咖啡。

李友： 喝咖啡，没问题。今天晚上你有空
　　　 儿吗？

王朋： 今天晚上有人请我吃饭，不知道(4)
　　　 什么时候<u>回来</u>(G5)。我回来以后给你
　　　 打电话吧。

李友： 好吧，我等你的电话。

LESSON 7 ▲ Studying Chinese

Dialogue I: Asking about an Examination

DIALOGUE I

(王朋跟李友说话。)

王朋： 李友，你上个星期考试考<u>得</u>(G1)怎么
　　　 样？

李友： 考得不错，因为你帮助(1)我复习，
　　　 所以考得不错。但是老师说我中国
　　　 字写得<u>太</u>(G2)慢！

王朋： 是吗？以后我跟你一起练习写字，
　　　 教你怎么写，好不好(2)？

李友：那太好了！我们现在<u>就</u>(G3)写。给你笔。

王朋：好，我教你写"难"字。

李友：你写字写得很好，也很快。

王朋：哪里，哪里(F)。你明天有中文课吗？

李友：有，明天我们学<u>第七</u>(G4)课。

王朋：你预习了吗？

李友：预习了。第七课的语法很容易，我都懂，可是生词太多，汉字也<u>有一点儿</u>(G5)难。

王朋：今天晚上我跟你一起练习吧。

李友：好，谢谢你。

王朋：不谢，晚上见。

Dialogue II: Preparing for a Chinese Class

DIALOGUE II

(李友跟小白说话。)

李友：小白，你平常来得很早，今天<u>怎么</u>(G6)来得这么晚？

小白：我昨天预习中文，半夜一点<u>才</u>(G3)睡觉，你也睡得很晚吗？

李友：我昨天十点<u>就</u>(G3)睡了。因为王朋
帮我练习中文，所以我功课做得很
快。

小白：有个中国朋友<u>真</u>(G2)好。

(上中文课。)

老师：大家早(1)，现在我们开始上课。<u>第
七</u>(G4)课你们都预习了吗？

学生：预习了。

老师：李友，请你念课文。...你念得很
好。你昨天晚上听录音了吧？

李友：我没听。

小白：但是她的朋友常常帮助她。

老师：你的朋友是中国人吗？

李友：是的。

小白：<u>他是一个男的</u>(2)，<u>很帅</u>(3)，<u>叫王
朋</u>(G7)。

LESSON 8 ▲ School Life

A Diary: A Typical School Day

AN ENTRY FROM LI YOU'S DIARY

李友的一篇日记

八月九日　星期一

我今天早上(1)七点半起床(G1)，洗了澡以后就(G2)吃早饭。我一边吃饭，一边(G3)听录音。九点钟到教室去上课(G4)。

第一节课是中文，老师教我们发音(G5)、生词和语法，也教我们写字，还给了(G6)我们一篇新课文(2)，这篇课文很有意思。第二节课是电脑(3)课，很难。中午我和同学们一起到餐厅去吃午饭。我们一边吃，一边练习说中文。下午我到图书馆去看报。四点钟王朋来找我去打球。五点三刻吃晚饭。七点半我去小白的宿舍跟他聊天(儿)。到那儿的时候，他正在(G7)做功课。我八点半回家。睡觉以前，给王朋打了一个电话，告诉他明天要考试。他说他已经知道了。

A Letter: Talking about Studying Chinese

一封信

张小姐：

你好！好久不见，最近怎么样？

这个学期我很忙，除了专业课以外，还(G8)得学中文。我们的中文课很有意思。因为我们的中文老师只会(G9)说中文，不会说英文，所以上课的时候我们只说中文，不说英文。开始我不习惯，后来，我有了一个中国朋友，他说话说得很清楚，常常跟我一起练习说中文，所以我的中文进步得很快。

你喜欢听音乐吗？下星期六，我们学校有一个音乐会，希望你能(G9)来。我用中文写信写得很不好，请别笑我。祝

好

你的朋友

意文

八月十日

LESSON 9 ▲ Shopping

Dialogue I: Buying Clothes

DIALOGUE I

(买东西)

售货员： 小姐(1)，您<u>要</u>(G1)买什么衣服？

李小姐： 我想买一<u>件</u>(G2)衬衫。

售货员： 您喜欢什么颜色<u>的</u>(G3)，黄的还是红的？

李小姐： 我喜欢穿(2)红的。我还想买一<u>条</u>(3) (G2)裤子。

售货员： <u>多</u>(G4)大的？大号、中号还是小号的？

李小姐： 中号的。不要太贵的，也不要太便宜(4)的。

售货员： 这条裤子和这件衬衫怎么样？

李小姐： 很好，在哪儿付钱？

售货员： 在这儿。

李小姐： 一共多少钱？

售货员： 衬衫二十<u>块</u>五，裤子三十二<u>块</u>九<u>毛</u>九，一共是五十三<u>块</u>四<u>毛</u>九<u>分</u>(G5)。

李小姐： 好，这是一百块钱。

售货员： 找您四十六块五毛一。谢谢。

Dialogue II: Exchanging Shoes

DIALOGUE II

李小姐： 对不起，这双鞋太小了。能不能
换一双？

售货员： 没问题。您看，这双怎么样？

李小姐： 也不行，这双<u>跟</u>那双<u>一样</u>(G6)大。

售货员： 那这双黑的呢？

李小姐： 这双鞋<u>虽然</u>大小合适，<u>可是</u>(G7)颜
色不好。有没有咖啡色的？

售货员： 对不起，只有黑的。

李小姐： 那好吧。我还要付钱吗？

售货员： 不用，这双的钱跟那双一样。

LESSON 10 ▲ Talking about the Weather

Dialogue I: The Weather Is Getting Better

DIALOGUE I

谢小姐： 今天天气<u>比</u>(G1)昨天好，不下雨
<u>了</u>(G2)。

高先生： 明天天气怎么样？希望明天也不
下雨。

谢小姐： 我看了报上的天气预报，明天天气比今天更好。不但不<u>会</u>(G3)下雨，而且会暖和一点儿。

高先生： 太好了！我约了李小姐明天去公园看红叶。

谢小姐： 是吗？可是李小姐今天早上跟王先生去上海了。

高先生： 真的啊？那我明天怎么办？

谢小姐： 你在家看录像吧！

Dialogue II: Complaining about the Weather

DIALOGUE II

小叶： 真糟糕，<u>又</u>(G4)下大雨了。

小夏： 刚才我看报了，报上说，这个星期天气都不好，下个星期天气才<u>会</u>(G3)好。

小叶： 真的啊？那这个周末不能出去玩了。最近天气太热，真不舒服。

小夏： 台北夏天的天气就是这样。两个月以后，天气就会比现在凉快一点儿了。

小叶： 两个月以后？下个月我就回美国去

了。

小夏： 台湾春天常常下雨，冬天很冷，夏
天<u>又</u>闷<u>又</u>热(G5)。你下次最好秋天
来。

LESSON 11 ▲ Transportation

Dialogue: Going Home for the Winter Vacation

DIALOGUE

王朋： 寒假你回家吗？

李友： 我要回家。

王朋： <u>飞机票你买了吗</u>(G1)？

李友： 已经买了。是二十一号的。

王朋： 飞机是几点的？

李友： 晚上八点的。

王朋： 你怎么去机场？

李友： 我想坐公共汽车<u>或者</u>(G2)坐地铁。你
知道怎么走吗？

王朋： 你先坐一号(1)汽车，坐三站下车，
然后换地铁。<u>先</u>坐红线，<u>再</u>(G3)换绿
线，最后换蓝线。

▼▼▼▼▼▼▼▼▼▼▼▼▼▼▼▼▼▼▼▼▼▼▼▼▼▼▼▼▼▼▼▼

李友：不行，不行，太麻烦了。我<u>还是</u>
(G4)坐出租汽车(2)吧。

王朋：坐出租汽车太贵，我可以开车送你
去。

李友：谢谢你。

王朋：不用客气。

A Letter: Thanking Someone for a Ride

A LETTER

王朋：

谢谢你那天开车送我到机场。不过，让
你花那么多时间，真不好意思。我这几天
<u>每</u>天<u>都</u>(G5)开车出去看老朋友。这儿的人开
车开得很快。我在高速公路上开车，真有
点儿紧张。可是这儿没有公共汽车，也没
有地铁，很不方便，只能自己开车。

新年快到了，祝(F)你新年快乐！

李友

十二月二十六日